PREFACE TO

AN AMERICAN
PHILOSOPHY *of* ART

$\diamond\!\!\!\!\diamond\!\!\!\!\diamond\!\!\!\!\diamond\!\!\!\!\diamond\!\!\!\!\diamond\!\!\!\!\diamond\!\!\!\!\diamond\!\!\!\!\diamond\!\!\!\!\diamond\!\!\!\!\diamond\!\!\!\!\diamond\!\!\!\!\diamond\!\!\!\!\diamond\!\!\!\!\diamond\!\!\!\!\diamond\!\!\!\!\diamond\!\!\!\!\diamond$

By

A. PHILIP McMAHON

UNIVERSITY OF CHICAGO PRESS · CHICAGO

University of Chicago Press · Chicago 37
Agent: Cambridge University Press · London

To

ALFRED C. BEROL
WALTER W. S. COOK
RICHARD P. McKEON
AUDREY F. McMAHON
LIONELLO VENTURI

For Aid and Encouragement

Table of Contents

I

Introduction

FOR those who sincerely love both art and America, the opinions and conclusions here presented may help to make a concern for art something honest as well as reasonable. This is intended to be a constructive contribution for Americans who find satisfaction in art and would welcome a reason for the faith that they practice. In order to do so they ought not to be compelled to adopt a position so illogical and immoral that those who profess it might claim the exemptions of mental defectives or hasten to the rigid seclusion usually imposed on convicted criminals.

The reader will find here an argument as to why the prevailing attitude of philosophical idealism with regard to art is inacceptable; but the conclusion of the discussion is not simply negative, for immediately afterward contributions toward a superior alternative are offered. This alternative is held to be superior because it does not demand subservience to an alien mode of thought and because it makes art worthy of the devotion of those who prefer a theory of art in accord with our normal habits of thinking and acting. Yet even if that expectation is fulfilled, it is not to be supposed that this is the last word. To think that would be to usurp the function of Gabriel, who will sound the trumpet of doom on the last day. He alone will be in a position to declare what is the final view, for he should be present to record it.

Admitting this reservation, is it proper to qualify "A Philosophy of Art" by the addition of the adjective "American"? Is a philosophy of art appropriate to Americans something different from what the Germans judge to be true for themselves? The direct answer to these questions is affirmative; for when the German theory, although manifestly congenial to their ways of thought and action, is something neither

1

logically coherent nor consistent with American traditions, it is well to stress what is a distinction rather than a limitation by adding the word "American."

Again, this book is published in the United States of America, and it is to be expected that most of those who read it will be Americans. The initial and principal audience is here. The viewpoint from which it is written and from which it will normally be read is American and cannot avoid being so. At the very least, to mention this fact is to recognize its existence, while at best the recognition of this obvious reality may lead to explicit realization of other things that are more often debated but ought to be equally plain.

This is far, however, from saying that native prejudice or innate bias are deliberately encouraged. The very opposite is more probably true, for it will shortly appear that the broad rationalization of art most frequently found even in America has two conspicuous but extraordinary traits. It is of alien origin and it is also fundamentally inconsistent with basic American patterns of thought and feeling. The explanation of the nature of art here put forward as a substitute is one that contradicts beliefs about it that have long been established among us, after their importation from European sources, mainly during the nineteenth century; but it is, on the whole, more in accord with the structure of the American mind.

The errors and mistakes we make with regard to art or to other matters cannot easily be accounted for by the plea that this is a new, undeveloped country and that our faulty thinking is due to our national inexperience. If the historical origins of our present culture had not occurred in Europe, the very language that we speak and the thoughts that we convey by means of it would be inconceivably different from what they now are. Doubtless there was a new birth of freedom in this land, but it is misleading to speak of it as a new country, for its constitution or comprehensive plan of political existence has persisted since the late eighteenth century, without substitution through internal revolution or external compulsion; and that is something that can be said of few other countries today.

But our present position in the world is a rather recent development. Until the United States came into conflict with Spain in 1898, this nation had not figured as a major power, and until 1917 it had not intervened actively in European affairs. Until 1939 responsibility for defending the democratic mode of living did not lie with us. The enlarged range of our existing obligations now requires that we rid ourselves of obstructive notions; and when we observe the attendant circumstances of a fallacious theory of art in Germany, we are bound to re-examine that view, abandoning a certain worse for a probable better.

Many factors in the American way of life still exhibit marks of their European origins, and most of these are sources of strength that constitute positive goods in our spiritual economy. They cannot be disdained because they were European—in particular, Greek, British, or French—before they became part of us. On the other hand, philosophical principles which may be found incompatible with our basic ideals are justly to be viewed with suspicion, whatever their source. And while it is inexpedient to survey the many benefits we have received from Europe as participants in the traditions of Western civilization, it is necessary now to consider one of the evils that has come to us from abroad.

While some museums, art dealers, and wealthy collectors here have usually shown preference for works produced abroad in centuries past, this trend has also been accompanied by a corresponding deference toward foreign critical opinion and a docile, unquestioning submission to a foreign philosophy of art. The collection of such objects serves to illustrate the cultural heritage that is ours at its best. But, since 1898, 1917, and 1939, we should not be expected to yield place to importations, either literary or artistic, as self-evidently and inherently superior to anything we can do.

We have little right to expect conspicuous success in creating or in understanding art so long as we are content to receive, like grateful provincials, what others are willing to dispose of at a profit to themselves. Among the fields in which America has definitely affected preference and practice abroad are architecture and motion pictures. In these we have been least dependent on European precedents, having realized a freedom to create and enjoy without awaiting foreign approval.

A philosophy of art worthy of Americans should not impugn the normal impulses of a rational human, and therefore social, being; nor should it assume to begin with that Americans are impotent to create or to analyze art. A theory that warrants their happiness by justifying interest in art as an activity proper to self-respecting adults may well be called American by those who live here while pursuing it.

The man who loves an alien land better than his own or who regrets that he lives in the time and place where he must abide is a pathetic but not an unfamiliar figure. But for those who now live in the very refuge of the persecuted—the longed-for hope of the oppressed—to promote a way of thinking hostile to our best interests, as is the case with the German theory of art, is a strange and perplexing activity.

It is well within the bounds of possibility that America will, however reluctantly on its own part and on that of those who until recently exercised it, be called upon to assume cultural leadership in the years that lie ahead. In that event it would be absurd that a principle which defends the motives of the very forces that have been arrayed against us should continue to be received here without analysis.

The customary theory of art entertained by cultivated, as well as by popular, opinion in America is not simply European, it is definitely German in origin. The great prestige of the German universities during the nineteenth century aided the diffusion of this theory of art, for its development and that of the centers of research were contemporaneous. But, with the abdication of the German universities and the collapse of the German state as it existed in that era, the defects of the German understanding of art become equally patent.

An honest and fair-minded American, who is conscientiously attempting to think honestly and act honorably in every other relation, need not accept a dubious theory because it is a theory of art. But it must be acknowledged that the consideration of data afforded by art as evidence in a search for philosophic truth may offend some. It is quite natural that those who adhere to the idealist view of art should resent the exposure of its fallacies and be disturbed by an exposition of its source. The popular belief that art is a mystery, a sublime paradox, does not, however, automatically exempt it from critical examination. Through such analysis it will even be found that a fundamental error in the structure of German speculative thought comes from its special theory of art, vitiating the whole fabric. It is often supposed that the German view is a product of the idealist philosophy, whereas it is a cause or necessary condition of that broad intellectual attitude.

Some may also be inconvenienced by the claim that moral values affect abstract issues. But here we may consider another archangel and note that a living human being who is a professional philosopher is in far different case from Michael. That archangel can lean out over the parapet of Heaven and gaze with admirable detachment at our incomplete, imperfect world, for he is able to judge our triumphs and our failures without himself being implicated. A man who concerns himself with basic intellectual, but still human, problems is no detached or disembodied spirit; he is still a man entangled in the difficulties of this present world; and when a false doctrine has an immediate connection with our troubles, then even the most complacent should not object to the exercise of moral judgment upon a philosophy of art.

Although those thinkers who call themselves idealists have until recently been proud to be numbered among the disciples of German intellectual leaders, we should have some acquaintance with the opinion of things American held by German philosophers.

As a sample, an extract from a book published in Leipzig in 1934 will suffice. This is a pocket dictionary of philosophical terms compiled by a professor at Jena—a popular and, on the whole, a useful manual. It has been so successful in Germany that the edition from which the following entry is taken is the ninth. By 1934 many of the terms had been revised to accord with the new official instructions, but this particular item did not require revision, for in this sense it had become part of the German vocabulary long before.

AMERICANISM. A common term, by which the nature of North American civilization and culture is characterized, in contrast with European and Asiatic. As true marks of Americanism, these should be given prominence: superficiality, hurried pace, excessive appreciation of material goods, unrestrained struggle for championship records, leanings towards the sensational, mechanization of work and life, ruthless exploitation of natural and human resources.

German books published in 1927 are given as sources for this estimate.[1]

From this condemnation the compiler of the dictionary would probably have rescued the few Americans who in philosophy other than that which deals with art still conform, with minor deviations, to idealist teachings. But the rapid material expansion of America is chiefly responsible for the envious contempt with which central European idealists habitually treat a country whose pattern of life is fundamentally realistic. To most German thinkers it would seem inconceivable that an American should have a different theory of art, when they deem it their own peculiar province.

It should also be said that not only is the present contribution toward an American philosophy of art provisional as well as American, but it is also democratic in a genuine sense. Not only those who have taught philosophy abroad or who now profess that subject in an

American college are to be regarded in such an undertaking. Philosophy ought not to be something restricted to those who are employed to teach it; for in principle it should relate to our common human experience, whether that of the man in the street or that of the man in the library working up a difficult article to be read only by those similarly engaged.

Nor is there any attempt made here to develop a complete history of philosophical idealism, even within Germany. The most notable constituents of the typical German view are shown in the chronological order in which they emerged; but the factors are usually subjected to critical analysis at once, rather than waiting for a final evaluation in a concluding section long after they have made their initial appearance. In general, important ideas follow one another in their historical sequence, but this is interrupted by a close scrutiny of each novel concept when it first looms large in European speculation. No pretense is made of indifference to the merits of ingredients in the German concept of art.

Experts in some of the special fields touched upon will doubtless feel that the situation has often been excessively simplified and that to characterize a thinker or a principle in such brief terms is to report only a partial truth. Students of Spinoza, Leibniz, or Locke, for example, may properly point out that many important views have been ignored, that qualifying statements on the part of these authors have been omitted, that wholeness has been sacrificed to directness. But this charge may be laid against any condensation or interpretation that fails to include the complete works of the original author in his own language, something superfluous, even if possible. A thorough treatment of the views of each thinker cited is also irrelevant here, since only those aspects which are connected with a theory of art are in order.

At the same time, it is well to remember that important ideas, affecting large masses of people, have had to be simplified in order to exert such influence. After all, when a philosophical position gains such broad and popular acceptance that it is a characteristic presupposition underlying national policy, it is no longer the monopoly of professional students but a common intellectual property of the people concerned. We ought to examine closely the bases of such a belief, rationalized and systematized in abstract form; but principles which first find lucid expression in the words of professed philosophers, and may be best scrutinized there, become mainsprings of national action only when they become part of the stock of ideas that the man in the street takes for granted.

The German idealist theory of art had acquired that status long before our time, so that an uneducated, unstable leader of the German people could rely on its universal acceptance by his countrymen. The subtleties of thought elaborated from the seventeenth through the nineteenth centuries had been simplified in the course of time to the point where that leader could assume it as a premise on which German policy could be justified. It was not the rounded, coherent product of the philosophers' pens that immediately counted in the tragic result but the simplified formulas to which it had been reduced by popular approval. The philosophers were responsible for presenting their views with authority; such expressions reflected broad currents of opinion in the first place, serving, in turn, to fortify and perpetuate them. But while professional utterances of the philosophers are at the level where logical analysis may best be employed, it was not until wider sympathies had eliminated the complexities and abolished the obscurities in their statements that they became eventual sources of popularly approved action.

Finally, it should be observed that it is probably more natural for a young child to draw or to paint than to spell and write. The processes by which works of art are produced hold few impenetrable mysteries, and a certain standard of performance is not beyond the reach of almost anybody who begins early and persists long enough. Optimism as to the eventual outcome and a ready belief in the capacities of the average human being are intrinsic articles of the democratic tradition; and the view that will be advanced in these pages, after the German theory has been examined, makes the democratic attitude toward art theoretically justifiable.

In general, logic has surrendered most of its idealistic presuppositions, while mathematics, biology, physics, and history have been largely purged of such elements; but when the hopeful and capable young American reaches the study of art and aesthetics, he is almost certain to encounter an alien doctrine. The mystery that surrounds art, the awe that invests museums, the unintelligibility that characterizes too much discourse of art and beauty,[2] come not from the nature of those things but from the initial assumptions by which they are customarily explained in Germany.

DISCORD BETWEEN PRACTICE AND THEORY IN ART

The discrepancy between the theory and the practice of art in America, occasioned by reliance upon a philosophy of art incongruous with our fundamental insights, becomes obvious when we examine both these aspects of art. Our explanations of that field and our related activities, instead of being consistent and mutually harmonious, are, more often than not, directly opposed.

Beginning with our educational activities, we are aware that public and private schools now usually include departments of art; colleges and universities frequently offer courses in the practice, as well as the history, of painting, sculpture, and architecture. Many imposing museums have been organized through the enthusiasm of able directors and the generosity of benefactors who desire to promote American interest in art and share with the public their enjoyment of fine and precious things.

In elementary and secondary education, art is one of the favorite subjects, for it is employed to develop the personality of normal children and it is also directed to alleviating mental disturbance among the abnormal. The remarkable growth of museums during the past half-century, the zeal of wealthy collectors, and the successful application of art to the problems of education all testify to its exceptional importance.

During the depression the American government engaged in the relief of artists, who, as a group, had never been economically secure, even in times of prosperity. In return, millions of Americans learned something of the practice and appreciation of art. Their public buildings were enriched with sculpture, with murals and decorative paintings; many to whom art had been an unattainable luxury or a mystery watched artists at work so that they now understand how the things that they possess were first made.

There are many reasons for an increased attention to art in recent years. To begin with, there are immediate, personal satisfactions to be derived from making or looking at works of art. They reward the eyes, the hands, and the mind. They are actual objects that can be seen and touched. Certificates in a safe-deposit vault may not yield direct or frequent pleasures; but pictures, prints, and sculpture afford inexhaustible dividends. A work of art says something to our senses, and it renews a vital situation whenever we turn to it, so that sensory reality is a great reason for the interest in art.

It has other intangible but indubitable benefits to offer those who cultivate it. Art is a vivid, as it is also a persistent, embodiment of human values. Through it the preferences of civilizations that have long since disappeared still survive. Written histories dwell largely on evils of the past, on crimes committed by those in high places, and on wholesale wrongs; but works of art preserve for the present the best that men have done in times past. When we delight in a Gothic Madonna or a Chinese statue of the Buddha, we have before us results of the beliefs by which their makers lived, and these objects are positive goods. Works of art present facts to our senses that stimulate the imagination and refresh the spirit.

There is no difficulty in pointing out values in art that justify taking an interest in it. But when we inquire what is the nature of the thing we call art and what is the function of the man who produces it, the case is very different.

We are often seriously embarrassed when we undertake to explain what art is, although we experience keen and unmistakable satisfaction in it. Some understanding of the nature of art might, for example, properly be expected of any book on its history. But it is not uncommon to find historians of art who preface their books by saying that art is indefinable, whereupon they classify the products and trace the development of this indefinable thing. As such histories are serious enterprises and the authors know what they are doing, their words lack meaning when they say that art is indefinable, unless they intend to express in that way their dissatisfaction with current explanations and their inability to offer a better one.[3]

Many current views display logical contradictions or suggest such irrational implications that we can readily sympathize with the irritation of those who reject popular theories, such as the claim that it is the nature of art to express ideas or to stimulate emotions. No doubt we do grasp ideas and we do feel emotions when we are keenly aware of works of art, but is that its distinctive aspect? Does nothing else convey ideas or stir emotions? If it is said that art communicates artistic ideas or stimulates artistic feelings, the question is not yet answered: What is the art that expresses and excites?

The term "art" is also often very vaguely used to mean anything that is beautiful. But if anything beautiful is art, everything whatever might have that name applied to it, for any conceivable thing could on occasion be found beautiful by somebody. If art includes everything, it refers to nothing in particular. We still lack an answer to the question: Granted that the object is beautiful, what is it?

It is also common to use "art" to indicate general approval for things that belong to such types of object as music, the drama, the dance, painting, sculpture, architecture, ceramics, metal-work, and textiles. When something is referred to as "art" in this way, is the object a poem or a vase, a melody or a woodcut?

Even when confusion is relieved by the context, we find it impossible to accept the implication that things belonging to all these privileged techniques are invariably beautiful. How can we suppose that certain groups of products alone possess this attribute? We do not have to go far to discover that, on the contrary, not all poems can be admired; nor are paintings invariably beautiful. Again, it is difficult to account for the fact, when beauty is believed to be the exclusive and distinctive quality of certain technical groups, that we still find charm, grandeur, and other aesthetic realities in birds, sunsets, and flowers, which are natural products and not things made by men. Honest observation soon indicates that some works of art are not beautiful and that beauty is to be found in things that are not works of art at all.

If the claim on behalf of art is modified to the extent of saying that art ought to be beautiful, this can hardly be a distinction belonging solely to art. It can properly be demanded that the world and everything in it should be beautiful, including art. Many experienced things fall short of desired perfection; they present defects and fail to satisfy our demands; but is art alone subject to this familiar lapse?

In daily contacts with art such difficulties do not exist. Those who attend art schools, who read books or articles about art, who attend art exhibitions or deal with artists, do not encounter obstacles corresponding to the intellectual problems raised by the popular theory of art.

But treatises on aesthetics, as a matter of custom, normally identify art and that particular field of philosophy.[4] By limiting the kind of thing they will consider to technical products assumed to embody the quality of beauty as an intrinsic property, the task of aesthetics may seem to be greatly facilitated. But the convenience of aestheticians can hardly control the structure of facts.

If art and aesthetics were one and the same, what advantage would be gained by arranging exhibits in a museum on a historical, rather than an aesthetic, basis? Since the nineteenth century it has been found that a cultural and chronological scheme of display is the most effective one, but this would not be so if art and aesthetics were identical. Objects would then be selected or rejected for exhibition solely on account of their beauty; historical function and cultural significance would be irrelevant. As a result, we could study catalogues of collections, but we could not read histories of art.

Again, little study is required to discover that in ages previous to very recent times, works of art were not made with the purpose of being beautiful and nothing else. In the main they have been instruments or objects with religious and other social functions.

For these and other reasons it is distressingly clear that, while art may be significant, valuable, and vividly delightful, current theories are, on the contrary, self-contradictory, confusing, and disturbing. But minds with any sense of responsibility are not to be satisfied with irrational explanations of valuable experience.

While it would be possible through speculative analysis alone to detect the errors in the customary view and escape from the contradictions it involves, there is a better, more reliable procedure. This is to distinguish the several components of the formula and then trace them from their separate origins. In that way we can understand how the dogma acquired its present form and at the same time test the logical validity of each distinct factor as it first emerges in the history of thought.

In studying the sources from which this theory of art springs, we are not compelled to rely on surmises, nor should we suppose that we can guess what it might have been, without examining the records. Thought about art in antiquity, but especially from the sixteenth through the nineteenth centuries, remains accessible to us in documents that still survive. The necessary postulates and the factual beginnings of the German view are both open to historical criticism.

The principal factors are five in number, and each one can be located in time with sufficient precision; for, although we may not be able to determine the date when these ideas first occurred to a human mind, we can fix the period when they gained strength enough to attract the attention of a number of minds through presentation in published documents.

The doctrine that combined these five factors in one view had great consequences for philosophy. It was the primary assumption, as clear-

ly appears in Schelling, on which has been founded the whole romantic idealist philosophy of Germany. The belief that art and aesthetics
are the same thing is not a result of the idealist philosophy; rather it
is the necessary hypothesis to which that speculative position must
appeal. Rationalist idealism appropriated the belief, and when romantic idealism appeared as its successor, a supposed proof of its contentions was provided ready-made.

The systems of the idealist philosophers can, in general, therefore
be more effectively tested by inquiring about their views on art than
by proceeding first with an analysis of their aesthetics. Their views
in aesthetics are likely to be contingent upon conclusions in other
fields of philosophy, but their preliminary assumptions imply a specific theory of art.

II

The Natural History of Art

IDEAS are, indeed, like other natural forms in that they also have a history or record of development. Thoughts that men think are most frequently conveyed or recorded by means of words, so that, by observing how they have used words, we can see how their ideas have evolved in the course of time. The popular notion of art is so recent that until 1880 no English dictionary had noted that meaning,[5] although in England and on the Continent this significance had been attached to it, outside the dictionary, for more than a century.

While some of the elements composing the prevailing concept have been studied, their function as the original sources of the modern concept of art has not been fully considered, and the share of this idea in determining the basic principle of romantic idealism has not been properly appreciated.

The first step, historically, was to change the status of Plato's Ideas to that of psychological ideas or concepts.[6] Then a basis had to be found for grouping together the several techniques of painting, sculpture, and architecture and their products, so that they could be collected into one classification. Next, those who practiced these skills aimed at a social position superior to that of artisans and mechanics, and their aspirations had to be satisfied. As a consequence, there was substituted for the traditional liberal arts something indicated by the term "fine arts." Justified by the improved social prestige of these techniques, that designation was rationalized by the altered theory of Ideas to indicate that beauty was their special distinction. The result of all this was that a new philosophical discipline—the realm of aesthetics—had to be founded to deal with the problems for abstract analysis provided by these accumulated notions.

The first line of development was that by which Plato's Idea could

13

be transferred from an inaccessible plane in metaphysics to the human psychological level; and apparent authority for this was to be found in Aristotle, the disciple and in some respects the opponent of Plato. When this had been done, it was then possible to make the Idea of beauty the essence of art.

THE IDEA TRANSFORMED

Like many other fundamental concepts in Western thought, the notions that we express by the words "idea" and "technique" had their sources in ancient Greek speculation. The difference between products of nature and those of human technique was a dominant consideration in Aristotle's philosophy, and he referred to this distinction when he said: "From technique come the things whose form is in the soul."[7] As illustrations he mentioned building and medicine, which are human skills that produce corresponding results. The Greeks of antiquity used a word from which our "technique" and "technology" derive, as did Aristotle in this instance; and when employed by them it had not the slightest suggestion of the significance that Kunst had later for the Germans. Yet it is typical of the frequent misunderstanding of the classical sources that a recent translator of Aristotle could render this very passage in the words: "But from art proceed the things of which the form is in the soul of the artist."[8] Aristotle had evidently intended to point out that before any technical product can be created, its plan or design must be present, as a formal cause, in the mind of the agent who makes it. This he held to be true of any technical product whatever; it was not relevant solely to such things as buildings, statues, and paintings, which the modern word "art" suggests. Yet his use of an illustration drawn from architecture afforded a pretext for subsequent thinkers to limit his observation, relating it almost exclusively to art.

Long afterward, the Romans assimilated Greek speculation as well as they could, and the term by which they translated the Greek word for "technique" was ars, from which English and the Romance languages derive "art" and parallel forms. Both the Greeks and the Romans often cited works of art in connection with philosophical analysis, since these objects were familiar and vivid; they provided convenient examples drawn from normal, everyday classical experience.

Cicero, for example, followed a reliable precedent when he was expounding his view of the perfect orator.[9] He compared his imagined idea of the public speaker with the mental image which appeared to

Phidias when he produced his Jupiter and Minerva. According to Cicero, it was that image which Phidias contemplated and imitated as he worked. Cicero here relied upon the view set forth by Aristotle, and he repeated a widely accepted explanation of how it was possible for Phidias to imitate the appearance of gods whom he had never seen.[10] Cicero concluded that it was in the way mentioned by Aristotle that forms and figures could possess a certain perfection and excellence. In addition, he drew some philosophical corollaries, for he asserted that these forms were what Plato called Ideas, and in this connection he briefly summarized Plato's doctrine as he understood it. But his view led him far from the position of Plato, who did not admire art and who conceived of the Ideas not as psychological phenomena or mental images but as metaphysical absolutes.

Seneca went still further astray when he found occasion to outline Aristotle's doctrine of the four causes, and to these he added the Platonic Idea as a fifth. To make his exposition plausible he cited sculpture and said that the Idea was an eternal model or exemplar, before, rather than outside, the actual object that imitated it.[11] This recourse to the Platonic theory of the Idea was even more seriously at fault than Cicero's had been, since Seneca merely added together two sets of incompatible principles.

In both cases the trouble resulted from acceptance of the traditional doctrine of imitation. Aristotle had used sculpture, also, to illustrate his theory of causation; but when Cicero and Seneca mentioned it in connection with the Idea, to explain imitation, they prepared the way for thinkers after the Renaissance to associate the Idea particularly with art.

In addition to difficulties due to the principle of imitation, there was another ancient belief which was responsible for the dilemma referred to by Cicero and many others. The problem was: How could Phidias imitate the appearance of the gods when he had never seen them? This question had pointed significance for antiquity because at that time the locus or place where ideas occur was judged to be just the opposite of the view popularly entertained today. In the early stages of Western civilization it was held that a man's mind must be where his thoughts are. When, during either waking hours or sleep, imagination brings before the mind places not present to the bodily eye, the mind must be absent from the body, it was then believed. Unless Phidias had ascended to the place where the gods dwell and seen Jupiter, how could he imitate the god's appearance?

The explanation invoking Plato's Ideas amounted to this: the mind of the artist left his body and viewed the Idea or eternal pattern of Jupiter. In modern times, popular opinion still respects imitation as a ground of excellence in art but holds that the mind does not wander away from the body. On the contrary, images of things external to the body visit the mind, and thus the locus of ideas is properly inside the skull where the mind is. The modern popular view was facilitated after the Romans transformed the eternal Idea into a transient idea; but, as Locke pointed out, "Our ideas are . . . . actually no-where."

During the Revival of Classical Learning in Italy, the ancient sources were first studied, not as opportunities for the exercise of philological ingenuity, but as authorities from whom truth could be gained. One of the most influential figures in the early Italian Renaissance was a scholar with this approach, who became a leader of the Accademia Platonica in Florence. Marsiglio Ficino translated both Plato and Plotinus, regarding the latter as an inspired expositor of unadulterated Platonism. His own views were, in the main, Neo-Platonic; but he adopted the version of the Ideas devised by the Church Fathers—that the Ideas were models existing in the divine mind.[12]

Alberti, like Leonardo da Vinci somewhat later, prized art as a means to knowledge. He pioneered in studying the theory of painting, architecture, and sculpture, writing important treatises on these matters and creating celebrated architectural designs. But Alberti also contributed to making the Idea of beauty the essence of art. In one place he condemned those who neglected nature, saying: "That idea of beauty escapes inexperienced minds which even the best trained can hardly discern."[13]

The full development of this trend occurred, however, during the Mannerist and Baroque periods. Between the end of the High Renaissance and the middle of the seventeenth century the transformation of the Idea into the idea was completely effected. The artists of Mannerism may find rather few admirers today; but the age had looked upon itself as called to maintain a great tradition rather than to surpass it, when the leaders—Leonardo, Raphael, and Michelangelo—had passed from the scene. Theirs was the task of conserving gains already made and preserving a rich heritage. To this end they closely analyzed the manner or style of those models whose merits they desired to continue; but it was soon found that these styles were not simply different, they were in some respects definitely opposed to one another.

In the first edition of his *Lives*, in 1550, Michelangelo was for Vasari the supreme model; but in the interval before the second edition of 1568 appeared, Vasari acquired greater appreciation of the excellence of Raphael. The obvious conflict between ideals in this instance led Vasari and other thinkers to more searching analysis and critical reflection. They looked for grounds where the differences could be harmonized and a solid basis secured for correct production, as well as sound understanding, of art. In this way it happened that, for all their sense of inferiority to the immediate past and their disappointing achievements in practice, the Mannerists were the first to elaborate comprehensive philosophical principles for the explanation of art.

Vasari is the most familiar source for knowledge of the artists of the Italian Renaissance, and his influence in the diffusion of Mannerist views was therefore considerable for several centuries, although the theoretical parts of his work are today often neglected. In the second edition there is an added passage in which he said:

Because design, the father of our three arts . . . . extracts from things a universal judgment, like a form or rather Idea of all the things in nature, which is most regular in its measures,—by which, not only in human bodies and those of animals, but also even in plants and buildings and sculptures and paintings, it knows the proportions which the whole has with the parts, and the parts with one another and with the whole taken together,—and because from this knowledge arises a certain judgment, so that in the mind there is formed a thing which, when expressed by the hands is called design, it may be concluded that design is nothing else than an apparent expression and declaration of the concept that is in the spirit and of that which is imagined in the mind and constructed in the Idea.[14]

In this statement Vasari introduces references to design and to proportion; but the main point is that he here treats the Idea as a principle to be observed in nature, grasped by judgment, and expressed in art. Owing to the effectiveness of Vasari's biographies, the theoretical views which they contained were widely accepted; his authority and that of other writers of the Mannerist period secured almost universal approval for the belief that the Idea was the essence of art.[15]

In his own day the contribution of Giovanni Paolo Lomazzo to the theory of art was even greater than Vasari's, for critical matters were not introduced by him as prefaces to biographies; he furnished a theoretical foundation for the systematic treatment of all topics directly connected with art. His first publication was a comprehensive *Treatise* which was Aristotelian and even scholastic in temper; but in his later book, *The Idea of the Temple of Painting*,[16] he presented a metaphysics of art which was rather Neo-Platonic.

It has been ingeniously shown that Lomazzo's theory of the Idea in art derives almost verbatim from Ficino's commentary on Plato's *Symposium*,[17] and this is only one instance of a practice almost habitual in Europe after Ficino's works appeared, until well into the nineteenth century. Ficino's Latin prose was customarily read rather than the Greek original and, together with the text, Ficino's Neo-Platonic interpretation was accepted as an authoritative explanation. The doctrine that had been presented in the Florentine Accademia Platonica was revived a century later by Lomazzo as something quite different from what it had been in either Plotinus or Ficino. It had been converted into a metaphysics of which art was the obvious proof and example.

This trend was carried still further in the next century, when Giovanni Pietro Bellori published a collection of artists' lives. To it he prefixed a theoretical introduction entitled: "The Idea of the Painter, of the Sculptor, and of the Architect, Chosen from Natural Beauties, Superior to Nature."[18]

He began in approved Neo-Platonic fashion by declaring: "The supreme and eternal intellect, author of nature in making his marvellous works, deeply contemplating within himself, constituted the primary forms called Ideas." The celestial bodies, he said, do not change but remain ordered and beautiful forever. Terrestrial things, on the contrary, because of the opposition of matter, are never perfect, even though nature always intends perfect results. He then applied inferences from this position to the facts of art:

Wherefore noble painters and sculptors, imitating that first maker, also form in their own minds an example of superior beauty and contemplate it, emending nature without fault of color and of line. This Idea, or rather Deity of painting and sculpture, opens the curtains of great minds such as those of Daedalus and Apelles, reveals itself to us, and descends on marble and canvas; having an origin in nature, it surpasses its origin and makes itself the original for art; measured by the compass of the intellect it becomes a measure in the hand, and animated by imagination it gives life to the image. . . . . Idea of the painter and of the sculptor is that perfect and excellent example in the mind, which things presented to the eyes resemble through imitating that imagined form.

It was Bellori's distinction to assert that nature imitates the Idea, which is more perfectly manifest in art, and to praise the Ideal in the sense of the typical or general. Bellori discovered in art something much superior to nature; the Idea, of divine origin, was revealed primarily in art. Ancient thinkers found in art convenient illustrations of philosophical truths, but for this seventeenth-century writer the Idea possessed importance as the essence of art. At the same time, the extraordinary attributes that Plato had claimed for the metaphysical Idea were still retained for the psychological phenomenon in the artist's mind.

Because of Bellori's influence on the thought of Winckelmann, the appreciation of ancient art is even now often rationalized on Bellori's grounds: it is admirable because it typifies or generalizes. In Winckelmann's *History of Ancient Art* there is a long theoretical chapter "On the Reality of Art,"[19] which largely repeats materials taken from Bellori; and in this way his critical principles have gained acceptance to justify admiration of other art as well.

Because of the exceptional popularity of Winckelmann's history, the Neo-Platonic interpretation, long applied to Plato, became generally admitted as the abstract explanation of art. In Germany, as a result, belief in the Idea of beauty as the substance of art has been practically universal in literate circles ever since Winckelmann.

According to this dogma, art is valuable above all other things, since it is the sole privilege of art to manifest the Idea. The artist's idea is the Idea, and, as such a permanent correlation of beauty and objects in human experience is nowhere else to be found, art enjoys a unique function.

German philosophy has been able to profit from this belief in several ways. In art conclusive proof is found, it often supposes, of its favorite conviction that the world consists of ideas and that our ideas are what we will them to be. It has also secured a name for the systematic development of the assumption that the Idea is the essence of art; "idealism" is the title of the philosophy characteristic of Germany from Leibniz to the present day. The powerful speculative interests that have distinguished Germany for over two centuries do not cultivate aesthetics simply because it is a field as difficult as it is attractive; the idealist philosophy has drawn a name and a demonstration of its convictions from what it supposed to be the nature of art.

THE ACADEMY

After the transformation of the Idea, the next logical step was to gain social position for art and artists corresponding to that enjoyed by learned professions, such as the law and medicine. It was only proper that the man whose privilege it was to manifest the Idea in his work should hold an elevated position acknowledged by the public. This object was attained by regulating the training and activity of the artist in the same fashion as that employed by men of letters, that is, through the establishment of the academy.

In classical antiquity the rank of the artist was little better than that of the artisan or mechanic. The demand of Isocrates that Phidias, Zeuxis, and Parrhasius should not be classed with vase-painters and doll-makers would indicate that in practice most artists were rated in just that way.[20] It was through literature that some distinguished Greek artists managed to acquire superior status; for, by writing on their occupation, Apelles, Lysippus, Protogenes, Polyclitus, and Pamphilus not only provided technical instruction but also raised general questions of intellectual interest through their study of proportion and similar topics.[21]

While these individuals advanced their own personal fortunes in this way, Greek opinion did not radically alter as a result. Plutarch declared that however much a young man might admire the works of Phidias and Polyclitus, he would never wish to be a sculptor.[22] Lucian also said that, although the works of Phidias and Polyclitus might be highly esteemed, nobody in his right senses would wish to find himself in the sculptor's place, for he would still be only an artisan, a manual laborer.[23]

During the Renaissance, those who read Pliny's compilation of data on the art and artists of antiquity gathered an impression that the social position of the artist had then been far better than it was in reality. When enthusiastic interest in the Greek and Roman world revived among Italians, that world was studied as a model for emulation, but the only surviving evidence of its vanished glory consisted of products of the techniques of writing and drawing. Fragments of sculpture, architecture, and the minor arts were examined as adequate equivalents of the inspiring thoughts discovered in ancient literature.

Ghiberti and many other artists of the period lamented that the theoretical treatises of those who had produced such noble works of art had entirely disappeared. For about a century studies in proportion and perspective were pursued in an effort to recover the principles by means of which the ancients had achieved their triumphs. The creators of the monuments that survived for the admiration of Renaissance Italians must have been equally successful thinkers, it was supposed.

It seemed inconceivable that the contemporaries of the ancient masters should not have shared the same enthusiasm for their abilities that the Renaissance Italians professed. To regain the rank which they assumed that their ancient predecessors had held was for the artists of the Renaissance a pressing and genuine problem. Their solution was that this advance could be accomplished through study of the liberal arts and the transformation of the practice of art from traditional routines of the handicrafts to a profession based upon abstract principles.

Although they differed somewhat in their judgments as to what the young artist should study, Ghiberti, Alberti, and Leonardo by precept and example all urged that the artist should be trained in a way superior to that of the artisan apprenticed to a master in a workshop. Ghiberti had argued that the artist should be accomplished in all the liberal arts and in some additional subjects.[24] Alberti, besides insisting on a good general education, particularly stressed geometry and optics.[25] Leonardo opposed uncritical reliance on traditional authority, but he stressed the importance of theoretical investigations, and to such work he devoted the greater part of his life.[26] The claim to professional standing had behind it a persistent interest in liberal studies of a literary and scientific character, advocated by leaders of Italian Renaissance art from the beginning.

The academic movement began with informal meetings of scholars and writers; and, their assemblies having gradually become formally organized, they took distinctive names. The most important group was one founded about 1442 by Cosimo de' Medici, to which the name Accademia Platonica was given in honor of Plato and the place where he had taught. Among its members were Marsiglio Ficino, Angelo Poliziano, Machiavelli, and Pico della Mirandola. This academy devoted its energies to the study of Plato in the light of Plotinus, but it was also concerned with the systematic exposition of Dante. It took upon itself the special task of purifying and regularizing the Italian language for the use of educated men, so that it set an example to later academies by its pedagogic, as well as its critical, pursuits. While this academy did not last very long, it afforded an influential model for similar institutions that grew up later.

The systematic *Treatise* of Lomazzo and other works, such as that of Armenini,[27] provided a philosophical doctrine and detailed instruction on all aspects of art which were of interest at that time. When the literary academy was imitated as a form of organization by the artists at the end of the sixteenth century, there was available for

academic use an adequate supply of manuals and methodical compila-
tions for systematic instruction.

In 1577 a breve issued by Gregory XIII announced his intention of
founding an academy of painting, because the decadent state of contemporary art in Rome was due to a lack of education and Christian
charity. By 1599, Romano Alberti, its secretary, could write on the
*Origin and Progress of the Academy of Design of the Painters, Sculptors, and
Architects of Rome.* This group had a fixed location, it followed a program that included discussion and teaching through classes directed
by members, and it undertook to achieve for artists what the literary
academies had tried to do for writers. Its foundation was a sign that
art was by now a profession and no longer a trade. The Roman example was eventually followed in most other Western countries, including the National Academy of Design, established in New York in
1826. Leading artists, by incorporating in the form adopted by literary
and scientific societies, professing a theoretical doctrine, and engaging
in educational activities, soon acquired great social influence. The
academies provided for the intellectual, as well as the technical, discipline of their own members, and they made art a matter of cultural
importance to the general public by the policy that they supported.

The prestige of belonging to an academy and the co-operative activities in which the members engaged gave extraordinary coherence to
the development of a theory of art, and the lectures and debates that
were fostered extended knowledge of the issues beyond small professional circles. In this way the earlier aspirations of Alberti and Leonardo approached fulfilment. But in Italy the atmosphere of the academies, as indicated by the attitude of those who compiled lives of artists on the plan of Vasari, was much more tolerant and generous than
was the case when the academic form of organization for artists was
transferred to France.

The ground was well prepared in France for the reception of the new
Italian importation. By the seventeenth century it had become a fixed
French prejudice that artistic virtue was to be found in Italy alone.
This led, in March, 1666, to the establishment of a French Academy in
Rome where promising students might expand in that inspiring environment. Eminent French artists of the seventeenth century, including Poussin, Claude Lorrain, Sebastian Bourdon, Pierre Mignard, and
others, were trained in Italy, and some of them spent a large part of
their lives in that country. Along with the artistic came intellectual
influence; the works of Lomazzo and other theorists, including Al-

berti and Leonardo, were translated for the benefit of those French-
men who had not learned Italian as students in Rome.

Some time before the appearance of a French Academy in Rome, a
French academy of art had been founded in Paris. The painter Charles
le Brun had appealed to Colbert,[28] who quickly saw in the suggestion
an opportunity to concentrate and unify an important cultural activity within the framework of the centralized state. On January 20,
1648, there was founded under Louis XIV the Académie royale de
Peinture et Sculpture, and on December 31, 1671, a similar institution
for architecture; but the academy for painters and sculptors did not
gain supremacy over its rivals until 1663. Government support, with
an official monopoly of instruction and state commissions, lent this
organization, constituted along bureaucratic lines, more power than
its Roman prototype ever possessed.

The periodical formal conferences of the Academy at the same time
served to clarify and systematize the doctrine of art. The spirit of Descartes, with sharply defined principles, was exhibited in the methods
and results of the Academicians' discussions.[29] Their conclusions were
imposed on students and on the public by a centralized control.

Having attained independence through an institution modeled on
that already employed by writers and scholars, artists still seemed to
think that the only way in which art could continue to maintain its
privileges was to strengthen the alliance and, in fact, subordinate art
to literature.

A well-known formula was devised from passages in classical authors to justify this subservience. Assumed as an unimpeachable truth
up to the time of Lessing, it provided a text for frequent exposition in
the academies. Passing reference had been made to it by Lomazzo,[30]
but it remained for French theorists to press its implications to an extreme.

Horace had written that poetry should be like painting, in that some
works have to be viewed close at hand and others from a distance.[31]
Plutarch had quoted the remark of Simonides that "painting is mute
poetry and poetry is a speaking picture."[32] The observation of Horace
was merely an analogy to point out that different types of poetry, like
different kinds of painting, require corresponding differences in approach, and the remark of Simonides was simply a witty rhetorical
antithesis without serious critical value.

But, wrenched from their context, these classical phrases were uti-
lized as infallible authorities for academic policy. Horace's words, *Ut*

pictura poesis ("as a picture, so a poem"), were taken to signify that it was the function of poetry to present vivid verbal descriptions and of painting to offer parallel visual reports. Two disciples of Poussin were responsible for stating this conclusion so concisely that it had binding force for several generations. A Latin poem on art by Du Fresnoy was published after the author's death by Roger de Piles, with a translation into French and a commentary.[33] The very first lines quoted Horace's words, changing the punctuation and adding a paraphrase to convey the meaning: "A poem will be like a picture; a picture should be like a poem."[34]

The foundation of the Academy was therefore the second logical step after the transformation of the Idea into the essence of art, and by that means the artists gained what they so greatly desired—a social position superior to that of the artisan.[35] Their object was to appropriate the professional privileges already gained for writers through academic associations; and artists emphasized their pride in achieving a status equal to that of men of letters by means of a neat formula drawn from classical literature. To stress still more emphatically the equal rights of art and literature, the term "fine arts" was devised to include both.

THE "BEAUX-ARTS"

Although the term was not generally adopted until the eighteenth century, *beaux-arts* was already current in the seventeenth when the Academies were founded by Colbert. At first the phrase seemed to indicate little more than fascination with imported excellence and an intention to compete with the Italians in a field where they were conceded to enjoy long-established domination. By 1690, Charles Perrault, a disciple of Le Brun, had used *beaux-arts* in the title of a book;[36] and, when expounded theoretically by Dubos and Batteux in the eighteenth century, it became exceptionally popular, with unforeseen and prejudicial consequences for German philosophy.

A volume that came out in Paris in 1719 represents the point of view prevailing in the eighteenth century. This was the *Critical Reflections on Poetry and Painting* by the Abbé J. B. Dubos, the secretary of the French Academy.[37] A book with a similar title, by Charles La Motte, came out in London, in 1730.[38] Dubos has been praised by some modern writers because he held that there existed no guide except feeling in matters of art. Although this doctrine was contrary to the official teaching of the Academy in the seventeenth century, he inherited from it his choice of a theme and his principal views.[39] His attitude toward the assumptions indicated by *beaux-arts* displayed not the slightest deviation from authoritative academic policy.

Dubos insisted that neither art nor literature should imitate things that would be regarded with indifference in nature. But the spectator should be moved by a painting just as he would be if he were reading a poem. After the Academicians had ceased to discuss the matter, because the issue had been decided in their favor, Dubos was still writing of the expression of feeling by both art and literature as his most frequent topic. The criterion that he actually employed in judging poems and paintings on this basis was that of propriety or decorum. Where the seventeenth century had developed a theory of the passions, the eighteenth was now content with sentiments. In both periods the principle of decorum—that which is socially appropriate and proper as judged by its rulers—was to control passions as well as sentiments. This conclusion had first been elaborated in connection with rhetoric but had been transferred to the theory of poetry in the seventeenth century. In effect, Dubos was in the main a popularizer of academic dogmas revealed in the previous century, and in this office he was very successful.

His *Critical Reflections on Poetry and Painting* was received with great favor, appearing in numerous editions. It was characteristic of the cosmopolitan culture of the age that this work was soon translated into German and English and that important books in English also came out in German.

The Academy through its periodical exhibitions and the publication of its discussions had stimulated wide public interest in art, but to maintain its position it had made a critical doctrine of a rhetorical commonplace. As a result, when the lay public finally took away exclusive control of art and literature from the Academies and when journalistic criticism was born to record judgment on pictures currently exhibited at the salons, the conviction still held sway that art was to be approached only by way of letters. Both art and literature were believed to improve on nature while they imitated it; and, although the expression of feeling was approved, feelings were to be expressed in accordance with official standards.

In 1747 there appeared in Paris a book by another abbé, Charles Batteux, which continued the doctrines of Dubos. The French title may be translated as *The Fine Arts Reduced to a Single Principle*,[40] since "fine arts" and *beaux-arts* are equivalents. By this time *beaux-arts* had attracted such favor that it was taken over by other European languages, which retained it as *schöne Kunst*, *belle arti*, *bellas artes*, and "fine arts."

The phrase met with general favor because it condensed into two words the whole body of views developed through several previous centuries. This formula carried with it the sixteenth-century conclusion that the Idea of beauty is the essence of art. It implied the theory of the relation between poetry and painting that had been advanced by the Academy to make good its claims in the seventeenth century, although the only common principle that philosophical critics could discover was this same Idea of beauty. By the eighteenth century the delightful vagueness of the term *beaux-arts* made it possible to apply the phrase not only to poetry and painting but also to such things as music, the drama, and the dance, which Aristotle had classified as imitative techniques.

Batteux disseminated a principle of basic confusion whose influence still persists and dominates popular opinion with regard to art. *Beaux-arts* by its brevity concealed internal contradictions, but a neat and convenient phrase could not dissolve the illogical nature of its assumptions. As a layman and a writer, obedient to the authority of the Academy, he ignored the essential differences between painting and poetry. When he failed to preserve their necessary distinctions, he did not gain insight into their natures; on the contrary, he lost the possibility of dealing with either in a rational way.

The only difference he could see between painting and poetry was that painting produced a visual illusion, and he unhesitatingly accepted the classicist view that art imitates but corrects nature. His definition of taste as "an habitual love of order" reflected the narrow rationalism of seventeenth-century France. He made an immediate appeal to an abstract principle and thereby reached an erroneous conclusion, because he disregarded the empirical differences in the patterns of sensation presented by painting and poetry and in the particular techniques by which they are produced. But it was on such differences that the field of architecture had been established, as well as all the human activities grouped together by Aristotle in the techniques of imitation.

There was some precedent for connecting the adjective "beautiful" with the noun "art," for Vasari had spoken of the arts of design as "most beautiful arts" and Baldinucci had used the phrase "beautiful arts where design is employed."[41] But the term then simply indicated admiration; it was not a stereotyped and hyphenated phrase, signifying a definite classification, as was afterward the intention in France. In Italy we find in 1591 such works as *The Beauties of the City of Florence*,[42] one of the first guidebooks to the artistic treasures of that city, followed by similar compositions to assist visitors to other Italian towns. But when French theorists had appropriated the teachings of Lomazzo, Bellori, and Zuccaro and when the Academy had exaggerated a literary parallel between poetry and painting, making it a critical doctrine that authorized indifference to the essential distinctions between them, then the dogma that such a group was alone distinguished by the Idea of beauty was concentrated in the formula *beaux-arts*.

One of the most effective means by which this term was made popular in Germany was an encyclopaedia compiled by Sulzer, called *The General Theory of the Fine Arts*.[43] First published in 1777, it went through numerous editions, each enlarged to include more material. Sulzer's work was, however, only the most popular of many similar German publications, each in three or four volumes.[44] By 1790 there had appeared in England a history of art written by Bromley, under the title *A Philosophical and Critical History of the Fine Arts*.[45] Shortly before, the work of Milizia had come out, combining the old and the new names in the phrase "fine arts of design."[46] A similar title was to be found in a German publication, issued in 1781, by Büsching.[47] The celebrated history of Italian art by Lanzi, first published in 1789, also announced that it was a history of the fine arts.[48] These and many other examples prove that the formula *beaux-arts* had been devised to unite art and literature under one designation and that the term had been extended to include other techniques which Aristotle had classified as those of imitation; but in practice the name was chiefly applied to what by this time had also come to be known as the "arts of design."

The ambiguities and irrational implications of the term *beaux-arts* attracted the attention of Lessing in Germany; and, as a consequence of his systematic attack on its German equivalent, *schöne Kunst*, particularly in his *Laokoon*, that phrase was replaced by *bildende Kunst* ("plastic" or "figurative" art). But his condemnation of an unintelligible formula that abolished the significant distinctions between poetry and painting did little more than modify the popular vocabulary.[49] Elsewhere critical terminology was not altered, and in German all the implications formerly included in *schöne Kunst* now adhered to its successor, *bildende Kunst*.

In France no change in terminology took place, and, owing to the efforts of the Academy from the middle of the seventeenth to the end of the eighteenth centuries, the place of art and the artist was firmly fixed in public esteem. During the French Revolution there was no popular proposal to abolish the Academy, only programs to reform it.[50] As a result of the popular attitude, not one artist perished on the scaffold during the Terror of 1793–94, and the royal collections of art were carefully protected.[51] The royal palace was converted into a museum open to the public, and there the original stock of works of art, acquired by commission, expropriation, and conquest, was enlarged through private donations and purchases with public funds.

In 1793, it is true, Quatremère de Quincy and David had secured the suppression of the Académie royale de Peinture et de Sculpture, as well as the Academy in Rome. Although the Academy of Architecture was also extinguished, the school attached to that institution was allowed to continue. But in 1803 something of the previous organizations was revived under the name of the Académie des Beaux-Arts, at the same time the school in Rome was re-established. However, the architectural instruction was continued as a section of the École des Beaux-Arts, and the Académie des Beaux-Arts was simply a part of the Institute and was no longer in direct control of teaching. Thus, ironically enough, the *beaux-arts* doctrine which had been sponsored by the Academy did not become the source of its official designation until that corporation had been dissolved and then resurrected after the Revolution!

In Germany, however, and in most other countries, philosophers have for the most part accepted the formula *beaux-arts* and its implications without critical question. Beginning with the latter part of the eighteenth century, they have devoted some attention to the problems occasioned by the formula. The real problem was: How is it possible for a classification originally based on technique to possess the quality of beauty as its essence? Usually the answer arrived at has been open to serious objections because many have supposed that by an analysis of art alone we can determine what beauty is or through logical analysis of the concept of beauty we can judge what is excellent in art. Both of these procedures display a somewhat naïve docility in accepting the initial assumption presented by *beaux-arts*.

Before professional philosophers could earnestly set to work on such problems, genuine or counterfeit, a distinct field had to be established, and thus, in the eighteenth century, we first encounter a term novel at that time, the word "aesthetics." The inventor of this name, basing his thought largely on the pre-Kantian tradition, did not himself approach his subject primarily with reference to the relation between art and beauty. But after he had marked out the field, his successors hastened to elaborate systems dealing especially with that question.

AESTHETICS

In 1750 there appeared the first volume of a work by A. G. Baumgarten, entitled *Aesthetica*, and a second followed in 1758.[52] The author was concerned primarily with filling a gap in the theory of knowledge as it had been developed by Leibniz and his successor Wolff rather than with discussing beauty in art.

In his *Meditations on Knowledge, Truth, and Ideas*, of 1684, Leibniz had given the artist as an instance of his basic classification of the types of knowledge. He wrote:

An obscure or vague idea is one that does not suffice for the recognition of its object. . . . . If I can recognize the thing I have a clear or vivid knowledge of it, but this again may be confused or distinct. It is confused if I cannot enumerate one by one the marks which suffice for distinguishing the thing from others. . . . . Thus we see painters and other artists well enough aware of what is right and what is faulty, but often unable to give any reason for their taste: if asked, they reply that the work they dislike lacks a *je ne sais quoi*.[53]

By "confused knowledge" Leibniz meant sensory experience, and by "distinct" he referred to truth manifest to the intellect. But, in agreement with the opinion of his age that knowledge is true only when it is expressed definitely and unambiguously in words, he declared that knowledge was confused if he could not "enumerate one by one the marks which suffice for distinguishing the thing from others."

According to Leibniz, imagination originated in the turbulence of animal spirits, and poetry was to be tolerated only when subject to the rule of reason. In practice this meant the moral principle of decorum or propriety, a position in which Dubos and Batteux agreed with him.

Leibniz had found an outstanding example of confused knowledge in artists, who know what they are doing and are confident of their judgments but are unable to state conclusively in words the criteria by which they act and judge. He solved the difficulty by means which, from his own point of view, must be considered an admission of defeat, a surrender to irrationality, when he resorted to *je ne sais quoi* in French or *nescio quid* more concisely in Latin. Leibniz and the professional thinkers of his age overlooked the fact that words, too, when they are actual objects always present patterns to the eye or ear, and they are produced by practiced skill or technique. But after he had identified reason with accurate verbal formulations, when he was confronted with evidence to the contrary drawn from the artist's activity, he took refuge in an unphilosophic, popular phrase.

The Leibnizian view was developed in a textbook that Baron Christian von Wolff put forth in 1732, presenting a theory of the beautiful.[54] He considered beauty and ugliness to be matters of pleasure and displeasure; true beauty, he said, arises from perfection, while apparent beauty derives from apparent perfection. That is, our judgments of beauty in things sensory are merely opinions, in contrast with the certainty that can be attained when we deal with concepts by means of words. Wolff's low esteem for the whole subject can be inferred from the title of his manual in which these views are stated. He called it *Empirical Psychology*, and "empirical" was for most of the thinkers of the Enlightenment a word that implied disdain. The only business worthy of a philosopher was the rational, not the empirical, and the rational was for them the verbally demonstrable.

Baumgarten, like many others, was impressed with the success of mathematics in attempting to organize deductive systems of clearly stated truth; and he felt that this model could be followed to advantage in dealing with confused, sensory knowledge. In his *Aesthetica* he intended to establish a field for sensuous experience parallel to that already worked out for abstract concepts. Aesthetics was to be the equivalent of logic. In his Doctor's dissertation, published in 1735 when he was but twenty-one years of age, he had introduced the new term.[55] As a product of his lectures at the University of Frankfort on the Oder he elaborated his theme into a more comprehensive work.

Baumgarten's conception was precisely stated in his first publication, in which he had said: "*Noeta*, as what can be known by the higher faculty of knowledge, are the objects of logic; *aistheta* belong to the aesthetical science or to aesthetics."[56] Aesthetics, as the scientific system of sensory ideas, was also to explain how poetry could be an imitation of nature. He concluded that poetry and nature both present us with confused, sensory ideas; but either may guide our attention to the clear, distinct ideas, which both nature and poetry imitate.[57] Accordingly, in the *Aesthetica* he declared: "The end of aesthetics is perfection of sensuous knowledge as such. This is beauty."

In the first paragraph of his treatise he had remarked that the science of sensuous knowledge or aesthetics dealt with such matters as the theory of the liberal arts,[58] the theory of the lower kinds of knowledge, the art of thinking beautifully, and the art of analogical reasoning. All these were concerned with the probable rather than the true, and the perfection of probable knowledge was beauty.[59] Yet Baumgarten did not view aesthetics as identical with the theory of the *beaux-arts:* he made it much more general in scope. For that reason, Baumgarten is usually honored in modern histories of aesthetics as the inventor of a name, but his failure to limit his topic to the theory of art is often counted against him. Carritt, for example, states: "Baumgarten's positive contribution to aesthetics was slight. It consisted chiefly in having, so far as is known, first used that word to designate the philosophy of beauty."[60]

Following the precedent set by Baumgarten, Kant also distinguished the two realms of transcendental aesthetics and transcendental logic, as the German idealists continued to do. But the latter tended to identify the field of aesthetics with the theory of art, a natural development when the transcendental philosophy adopted a conviction that had grown up for several centuries. When art was the same as *beaux-arts* or *schöne Kunst*, the ground for such a reduction was already prepared; and it was natural to conclude that, since certain techniques were intrinsically *beaux* and aesthetics was that part of philosophy which had beauty for its province, therefore the fine arts were the object of aesthetics.

As conceived by Baumgarten, aesthetics was founded to deal with the data of sensation in a scientific manner. But it should be remembered that, ever since Plato, the idealist tradition has held sensation in contempt as disorderly, contradictory, and irrational. The principal grounds for such an attitude were that the data of sensation could not be created at will or compelled to conform to one's desires simply by taking thought and that given sensory patterns could not be abolished or transformed solely through deduction from concepts. For the change or modification of such patterns technique was required. But, since techniques could be practiced as routines acquired by exercise, without clear, distinct analysis of the concepts implied, idealist philosophers despised techniques as well as sensation.

Some critics have reproved Baumgarten for supposing that aesthetics was a parallel to logic and have said that inductive reasoning is the proper correspondent to deductive logic. But it is more probable that organized technique is the genuine method for dealing with the data of sensation, just as logic and mathematics provide orderly treatment in relating, testing, and confirming abstract concepts.

Most of Baumgarten's successors failed to observe that mental images and concepts which are not immediate sensory patterns may also possess aesthetic value when they are objects for a mind. While the initial limitation of aesthetics to sensory knowledge tended to support the confusing identification of art and aesthetics, this restriction was responsible for most of the perplexities that afterward afflicted the subject, provoking philosophers to ingenious and subtle theories that have made it attractive because of its assumed right to explain art, but disappointing to many because of the incorrectness of its primary assumption.

DESIGN

Plato's metaphysical Idea had been converted into a psychological image in the artist's mind, and this was identified with beauty. The social position of the artist was improved through incorporation in academies, taking advantage of this belief. To strengthen the alliance with letters, *beaux-arts* was devised to include both art and letters, but in the course of time it was used to designate art as a rule. Then the philosophical discipline founded to deal scientifically with sensory knowledge was directed to solving the problems that resulted from the implications of the term *beaux-arts*. In this group of developments there was also included a fifth principle which, alone of the lot, stands up under critical examination, and this was the classification "arts of design."

In the passage already quoted from Vasari, to give his conception of the Idea, we observe that there was a close connection in his mind between the Idea and design. Of these two notions, design has been the more influential, for it is one that has persisted in practice, whatever the philosophy adopted to explain the relation of art and aesthetics. The classification of architecture, painting, and sculpture in the group of arts or techniques of design was effected also in the Mannerist period by Vasari, Lomazzo, and other thinkers who discussed the topic. Consequently, the things which we identify as museums of art, art schools, histories of art, and art exhibitions still conform to the term then devised for the objects with which they are concerned.

The group did not include technique in general, for that would be impracticable and would coincide with the whole range of orderly human activities. Museums of art could not even undertake to preserve and display all the numerous techniques and their products—such as the drama, poetry, the dance, instrumental and vocal music, landscape gardening, and gymnastics, all of which have at one time or another been included in the *beaux-arts*.

Plato's Idea was misinterpreted to make it the idea present in the artist's mind and secure for art the glories that Plato had ascribed to the Ideas, but the classification "arts of design" was Aristotelian in principle. Among the techniques of imitation Aristotle had counted the drama, painting, sculpture, the dance, and music, but he did not include architecture. By the sixteenth century it was no longer generally believed that music is primarily an imitation of human character or that excellent music is that which stimulates sound conduct. At the same time, it was felt that architecture was a technique on a par with sculpture and painting, and it was often practiced by the same men. Imitation was not a principle available to justify placing these three techniques in one group, but design was a factor which they all possessed in common.

Design had two meanings, and both were applicable to these three techniques. Design indicated a plan, preconceived in imagination, the formal cause of a work of art; and it also signified drawing, the particular technique by which the conception and execution of these three kinds of technical product was facilitated. The separate skills and their results, to which the names "architecture," "sculpture," and "painting" were given, were, to begin with, distinctions based on technique, and design was itself a ground of further technical discrimination by which these three could be put together and, at the same time, set apart from such things as music and poetry. The objective and rational nature of this designation was what commended it to artists, critics, and the public in the sixteenth century and has maintained it in practice ever since.

Among the earlier works to employ design as a unifying concept was a clever and amusing little book on *Disegno* by Doni, published at Venice in 1549.[61] Another small volume on proportion as exhibited in the arts of design was written by Danti and appeared in 1567.[62]

But it was probably Vasari's *Lives* that was most influential in gaining favor for the term, which is to be found in the dedication of the first edition, of 1550; and in the second, of 1568, there is a theoretica chapter devoted to the academicians of design. In the third sentence of the Preface to the *Lives*, he wrote of design as the foundation of painting and sculpture, illustrating his view by a pious reference to God's creation of Adam. A little later he mentioned

the Divine Architect of time and of nature, being all perfection, wished to demonstrate, in the imperfection of His materials, what could be done to improve them, just as good sculptors and painters are in the habit of doing, when, by adding further touches and removing blemishes, they bring their imperfect sketches to such a state of completion and of perfection as they desire.[63]

Borghini, an immediate follower of Vasari, explained design in almost the same phrases;[64] but a much more important book—one which has been called the "real Bible" of mannerism[65]—was the systematic treatise of Lomazzo, in which design in its twofold significance was assumed as the basis of treatment. Although the title of the first edition, of 1584, mentioned painting only, in the following year a new title-page was inserted, without reprinting the whole volume, and both sculpture and architecture were then included in the name of the book.[66]

In his Preface, Lomazzo again raised the familiar Renaissance problem, treated at length by Leonardo da Vinci, as to the relative ranks of painting and sculpture. This question he resolved by showing that both achieve results through design, understood as a prior idea in the mind and as drawing on paper.[67] He also stressed the helpful function of drawing in stimulating the imagination, saying of artists: "When they do not know how to show it in drawing, they cannot conceive in their minds the variety and beauty of things that can be imagined, because they lack that faculty of drawing which, as Vitruvius preaches at length in the beginning of his book on architecture, ought to be known perfectly."[68]

Vitruvius has, indeed, asserted that the architect should be "skillful with the pencil."[69] When the Roman writer outlined the proper training of the architect he had said: "An architect ought to be an educated man so as to leave a more lasting remembrance in his treatises. Secondly, he must have a knowledge of drawing so that he can readily make sketches to show the appearance of the work he proposes."[70] The necessary priority of the imagined design and the essential services of drawing in carrying through this planned structure to tangible completion were probably more familiar in architecture than elsewhere, and this passage doubtless had great weight with Vasari and his contemporaries.

Vitruvius had been known to the learned even in the Middle Ages; and the first great Renaissance author, even before Vasari, to write systematically on architecture, followed the scheme of his ancient predecessor. But Leon Battista Alberti approached the theme from a new point of view, and his book had long circulated in manuscript before its publication in print in 1485.[71] The first printed version of Vitruvius followed shortly afterward. In the first chapter of the first book, Alberti had discussed design, saying, among other things, that building consisted wholly of design and construction. The later treatises of Filarete[72] and of most of Alberti's successors, such as Scamozzi's edition of the works of Serlio, also paraphrased Vitruvius and expounded the relation of design to art. Aristotle, in the *Politics*, had stressed the utility and educational value of drawing, so that the theory of design could cite his authority. Lorenzo Ghiberti, in his *Commentaries*, had even said that drawing was the foundation of painting and sculpture.[73]

After Vasari, at the beginning of the seventeenth century, Romano Alberti published his work on *The Origin and Progress of the Academy of Design of the Painters, Sculptors, and Architects of Rome* in 1604.[74] He was then secretary of the institution whose foundation was mentioned on page 22 dealing with the Academy. But the most characteristic and elaborate book of the kind was one by Federigo Zuccaro,[75] also published in 1607; its author was president of the same Academy in Rome of which Alberti was secretary. The treatise was divided into two parts, one of which dealt with internal design or the mental image, and the other with external design or the drawing. This work so clearly and sharply presented the theory of design that it was one from which later writers could borrow freely.

Toward the end of the seventeenth century the learned labors of Filippo Baldinucci, intended to carry on the program of Vasari, produced his *Notices of the Professors of Design, from Cimabue to the Present*.[76] He also composed a dictionary of art, issued under the auspices of the Accademia della Crusca, in 1681, in which all the theoretical terms were explained in accordance with the theory of design.[77]

In France, where the principles evolved by Italian thought had by now been assimilated, there developed during the same century several important controversies in which the Academy supported the losing side. One was the quarrel over the ancients in comparison with the moderns, while another was the struggle between the partisans of

Poussin and the admirers of Rubens. The ground on which the issue was joined was drawing versus color.[78]

We can now see that the whole dispute depended on misunderstandings shared by both sides, and the debate simply made the fundamental error in the common assumption more obvious. In any case, design, as an imagined pattern, precedes the execution of both monochrome drawings and oil paintings that compose a pattern of many hues. Drawings may, it is true, be executed for their own sake; but they are also required stages in the achievement of a work of architecture, painting, or sculpture; in the process by which such a work is created, drawings are indispensable tools or instruments. There can be a legitimate difference in actual preference when the works of Poussin are compared with those of Rubens, but a painting by either master is bound to be the result of a pattern created in imagination, achieved with the aid of drawing, and presenting a pattern of color.

It was through a misunderstanding that drawing could be restricted to the representation of outlines or contours, and color could be referred exclusively to the colored pigments applied to surfaces by the brush, but it was only through such a mistake that the controversy had any meaning.[79] As a matter of fact, drawing is the means whereby imagination is guided and facilitated in the creation of any work of art, and that not alone in depicting contours; pigments have color but so has anything seen by the eyes, for color is the distinctive quality of all visible things. The prejudices of the followers of Poussin in conflict with those of Rubens had not been entertained by writers, from Alberti through Baldinucci, who established the theory of design as the bond of union among certain techniques.

After Vasari, historians of art outside of Italy also adopted the term "arts of design" to designate the same field that he had written about in his book. From the history by Monier in French, published in 1699, down to the lengthy work by Fiorillo in German, first appearing in 1788, as well as in many other examples, the phrase "arts of design" is to be found in the very titles.[80]

Winckelmann's *History of Ancient Art* was the first composition that deserved to be called a history of art in the scholarly sense. In 1777 Herder wrote a memorial to that great archaeologist, historian, and man of letters, which he concluded by saying that as a man, not as a poet, when he heard of that writer's death he wept youthful tears, full of gratitude and love for the beautiful hours, the sweet dreams, and the pictures which Winckelmann's works had given him.[81] Goethe, in 1805, published a long appreciation in which he declared that from Winckelmann's tomb he derived inspiration to carry on with proud love what his predecessor had begun.[82] Wilhelm Waetzoldt, writing in 1921, declared that Winckelmann was the first to elevate German prose to the rank of European literature, that he once and for all made art a part of German national culture, and that he was the first German writer to treat art in what the eighteenth century called a philosophical manner.[83]

But the first sentence of the first chapter of the first modern history of art begins with the words: "The arts which depend on design."[84] The phrase "arts of design" was then condensed to the one word "art," but the same distinction which had been publicized through the efforts of sixteenth-century Vasari was maintained in practice, even after the full name had been abbreviated. The shortening of arts of design to art was, indeed, largely due to Winckelmann himself, for at the end of the eighteenth century he gave his epoch-making work the name *History of Ancient Art;* and the precedent that he established has proved decisive.

This point, of exceptional importance to the theory of art and to the development of aesthetics, has rarely been noticed, although Winckelman's contributions to the history of art, to classical archaeology, to German prose style and German literature, as well as the establishment of art among the subjects to be cultivated by the well-educated, have often been extolled. By incorporating the understanding of art as beauty in his work, he was largely responsible for providing a name and a supposed proof of the German romantic-idealist position. This conviction he acquired from Bellori, whom he practically translated verbatim in places, without acknowledgment. At the same time, when he reduced the longer phrase "arts of design" to the single term "art," he made it afterward possible to retain that classification in the practice and in the treatment of art, particularly in the history of art, from his day down to the present.

Strange as the popular conception of art and the artist may appear when the evolution of its components has been marked out, it is even more remarkable to see how it has affected German philosophy. The course of idealism in Europe was such that by the end of the eighteenth century, Kant had incorporated all these principles into his system. Then, when rationalist idealism was replaced by romantic idealism, this view of art became the cornerstone on which was founded the intricate and confusing structure of abstract speculative thought in Germany. It was not as a consequence of romantic idealism that the popular interpretation of art grew up; rather, the misunderstanding of "art" as *beaux-arts* that has just been outlined underlies that systematic solution of ultimate intellectual problems.

If beauty is an idea and if the idea of beauty is the essence of art, then it is clear that this unique instance affords a proof of idealism. An ultimate positive quality is always to be discovered in technical products of a particular type. When the idea of such a quality is ever accessible through these means, we may conclude that as the artist makes the work of art he also creates the idea. In the development of the implications of this principle, it was also claimed that the artist or Absolute makes himself as well as his ideas.

III

Rationalist Idealism

ROMANTICISM and idealism are both much abused words, and any attempted clarification of the accumulated confusions may be held valid only for the context in which it is found. In what is to follow, romanticism is to be understood as a recurring mood of certain personalities in every age, but acquiring such intensity at the end of the eighteenth century that it became the distinctive mark of a period. Idealism, on the other hand, is a method of approach to the problems of philosophy which also had precedents in previous ages; but it gained a permanent residence in Germany, and its effects have persisted in various quarters down to the present.

The dominant ambition of German speculation during the nineteenth century was to systematize the emotional impulses of romanticism, and this was accomplished by means of idealism. It was not idealism in the moral and popular sense, but an intellectual conviction founded upon the misinterpretation of the Platonic Idea, which has already been discussed.

In metaphysics, idealism is based on the belief that the idea is the ultimately real, that even matter is a manifestation of spirit or mind. According to it, all objects of knowledge are concepts or ideas, so that existence and consciousness are identical.

Plato's lifelong endeavor was to emphasize the reality of his Ideas as universal ideals by every resource at his command; thus he attributed substantial existence to these impalpable essences and often spoke of them in terms proper to tangible objects. Modern European idealists, on the other hand, finding reality only in mental notions and faced with sensory patterns that are inconvenient obstacles to the instant

39

fulfilment of their desires, reduce the world to a dream, fancying that thereby they become able to do with it whatever they wish.

Although idealist philosophers are often willing to profit by the popular error which takes them to be identical, idealism for ordinary speech and idealism for metaphysics are far from being the same thing. However much adherents of that school may employ the facile equivocation, to take advantage of customary ignorance in this regard for ulterior purposes is unworthy of responsible leaders or of those from whom we expect disciplined thinking. But a lack of scruples in this case accounts for the frequent claim on the part of German philosophers who teach the idealist doctrine that the school to which they belong possesses exclusive rights to idealism as a trait of human conduct. The justice of this position can easily be examined to see whether, in fact, idealist philosophy is more consistent with virtue than any other; and the history of Germany since the eighteenth century would indicate that the opposite is more probably true.

A belief in the ultimate and sole reality of ideas is, to repeat, the common assumption of metaphysical idealism. On the other hand, idealism for the ordinary man refers to the motivation of one who pursues in his present conduct what he calls "ideals," that is, objects and situations not now present as things he can see and touch. This idealist strives after objects that now exist only in imagination or memory, and he does so in spite of the stubborn resistance of the environment and often at grave risk to his immediate welfare.

What the ordinary man means by "idealism" is what had better be distinguished as "ethical idealism," while what the philosopher intends is more properly termed "metaphysical idealism." For common speech, "idealism" derives from "ideal," to which -*ism* is added. But in the vocabulary of the speculative thinker, "idealism" derives from "idea," with -*ism* added and the letter *l* inserted for euphony, otherwise it would more accurately, though less pleasantly, be termed "ideaism."

Idealism of the metaphysical type has been popular in the Occident only since the seventeenth century. Ethical idealism, however, far from being the prerogative of a group of philosophers or even of a whole culture, is an essential human trait. Every living creature with its way to win in order to remain alive might conceivably be called an ethical idealist within the limits of its nature. But to follow ideals, to be an ethical idealist, is certainly the inalienable privilege of any man.

Without mentioning names and citing pages in books and articles written by Americans as well as by Germans, it is easy enough to observe how often their arguments are based on this very ambiguity. One does not have to read far in them to find that they often meet criticism of their metaphysical views by an appeal to their unique virtue and vice versa. When the idealist theory of knowledge is attacked, the idealist philosopher knows that escape is near at hand, for he can often expect his opponent also to admit the identity of idealism for ethics and for metaphysics. On the other hand, German statesmen have on occasion given out that evil deeds are sanctioned if their doers are idealists in philosophy.

But all anticipated goods, at least, must be ideal and they cannot be otherwise; purposeful beings direct their actions toward valuable future ends. Many philosophers who had no share in metaphysical idealism have been notable idealists in their conduct.

To understand idealism better as a serious system and the romantic phase in which the *beaux-arts* doctrine flourished as its very foundation, we should recall the intellectual atmosphere against which romanticism reacted and emerged as a distinct movement, although the idealist assumptions were held in common by both the rationalists and the romantics. That period is called the Enlightenment in Germany, the Age of Reason in England. It aimed to liberate ideas from the accumulated prejudices of tradition, and it originally adopted an objective, critical attitude toward beliefs that had inherited custom as their only warrant.

Free inquiry, again, has not been restricted to one period only, but it was vigorously revived in Europe from the middle of the seventeenth century on. A resolute attempt was made to reassert the independence of the self-reliant mind and to release it from external compulsion. At the same time, it was held that the light of reason reveals to every honest and fair-minded man basic principles that enjoy universal validity. As this view neglected historical development, it tended to replace the dogmatism of one authoritative tradition by a new one which, because it appealed to the evidences of reason rather than revelation, supposed that freedom was amply protected.

The effective beginnings of revived rationalism are to be found in Descartes, who sought final clarity of expression and rigid logical coherence in his views. With Leibniz and his successor, Wolff, the course of abstract speculative thought returned to a closed system. In many respects Kant was himself the culmination of the German Enlightenment, but he submitted its codified dogmas to his own methods of critical analysis.

The Age of Reason emancipated Europe from outgrown modes of thought and social organization, but certain elements in this particular type of rationalism finally defeated its original intentions. As we have already seen in the case of Leibniz, it was prone to identify reason with the capacity to present thought in unequivocal verbal statements. It felt that whatever is clearly and precisely stated must be true.

Through its neglect of historical evolution and its failure to appreciate the value of those differences that distinguish the unique and the individual, it also frequently reached other erroneous conclusions. It held that because reason is one and identical and all rational minds are universal in their reasonableness, the results achieved by the thinking of honest men must therefore be uniform. Those who did not assent to the self-evident truths announced by intellectual authority were guilty of wilful blindness and sin against the light of reason.

An insurrection against this narrow type of rationalism at the end of the eighteenth century was motivated by a profound resentment against a mentality that had hardened and become so inflexible that only through its destruction could freedom of thought and action be regained.

As a historical moment, therefore, romanticism had emotion as its chief characteristic. For the light of reason it substituted the warm glow of inner feeling. Intuition, unfettered imagination, and instinct were the tribunals to which it appealed for approval of its contentions. Instead of a normal or typical human nature, it esteemed individual differences, even those carried to the point of morbid or criminal eccentricity.

It despised the present, as the time when things are as they are, whatever our dreams may suggest; it preferred to prophesy and depict the future as a day when all hopes shall be fulfilled, while praising only the remote in time or space and admiring chosen epochs of the past that afforded models, it believed, for that future.

These moods are familiar as phases of adolescence in the individual, but such were the dominant traits of romanticism. It became the temper of an age rather than a temporary phase of youthful adjustment and succeeded in radically transforming European life. Through waste and devastation it prepared the way for that swift expansion of Western culture which took place during the nineteenth century.

Modern idealism prospered after Descartes until thought turned the solvent of critical analysis upon itself with Kant. The way was then thrown open for a thorough revision of philosophical attitudes, to justify the romantic temper. The idealist assumptions were common to both the Age of Reason and the Romantic Era; only the views to be admired, explained, and defended were different. German idealism was successfully reorganized to perpetuate adolescent postures, the rationalist principles of the Enlightenment were placed in the service of methodical irrationalism by romanticism, and idealism was directed to a rationalist defense of unreason. But before we can appreciate idealism in its romantic phase, we must first examine the rationalist idealism by which it was preceded.

DESCARTES

René Descartes, initiator of the modern movement in philosophy, was a French mathematician who extended his interest to metaphysical problems and who indulgently tolerated art.[85] His method was applied to art and poetry by other writers, such as Boileau and Du Fresnoy.[86]

But, like almost all philosophers, Descartes cited works of art to illustrate his views, when he compared things seen in dreams with the products of artistic imagination. They were unreal and untrue, although they resembled real things. He said:

At the same time we must at least confess that the things which are represented to us in sleep are like painted representations which can only have been formed as the counterparts of something real and true, and that in this way those general things at least, i.e., eyes, a head, hands, and a whole body, are not imaginary things, but things really existent. For, as a matter of fact, painters, even when they study with the greatest care to represent sirens and satyrs by forms the most strange and extraordinary, cannot give them natures which are entirely new, but merely make a certain medley of the members of different animals; or if their imagination is extravagant enough to invent something so novel that nothing similar has ever before been seen, and that then their work represents a thing purely fictitious and absolutely false, it is certain all the same that the colors of which this is composed are necessarily real.[87]

But Descartes did not rest with suspense of judgment, as did the ancient sceptics and some sophists when they mentioned works of art to show the unreliability of evidence provided by the senses.[88] The seventeenth-century thinker began with a methodical doubt by way of approach to what was for him an ultimate certainty and axiom,

rather than an inference. It already possessed in an invulnerable principle the self-evidence, the complete obviousness, demanded by this
type of rationalism.

The arguments by which he supported his basic conviction have
had great influence. He reasoned that, although belief in our sensations is open to doubt,

I am, I exist, that is certain. . . . . I am, however, a real thing and really
exist; but what thing? I have answered: a thing which thinks. . . . . What is
a thing which thinks? It is a thing which doubts, understands, affirms, denies,
wills, refuses, and which also imagines and feels. . . . .[89] As to the clear and
distinct ideas which I have of corporeal things, some of them seem as though
I might have derived them from the idea which I possess of myself, as those
which I have of substance, duration, number, and such like. For when I think
that a stone is a substance, or at least a thing capable of existing of itself,
and that I am a substance also, although I conceive that I am a thing that
thinks and not one that is extended, and that the stone on the other hand is an
extended thing which does not think, and that thus there is a notable difference between the two conceptions—they seem nevertheless, to agree in this,
that both represent substances.[90]

The leading principle of Descartes was in another work reduced to
the famous formula *ego cogito, ergo sum*.[91] It is often reproduced without the *ego*, but this word was essential. It gave a rhetorical balance to
ergo, and it made conspicuous the introspective, self-centered bias of
modern idealism when it started out by declaring "I myself am thinking, therefore I am."

St. Augustine had long before stated that if anything doubts, it is
and it thinks.[92] Descartes adopted this suggestion, however, to establish a new rationalism and to develop a proof of God's existence.
Among the ideas that he had, there was the idea of God, an infinite,
eternal being. As it was inconceivable to him that such an idea should
derive from the thinker who had that idea, he held that its source
must be God Himself. Further, to be perfect, that of which an idea
exists must itself exist; and, since truth is a necessary attribute of God,
it followed that any idea which is clear and evident must be true, for
it is impossible that God should deceive us, because He is the source of
existence and of ideas. In this fashion he could prove the existence of
God, of the soul, and of matter.

Descartes combined psychological idealism and metaphysical realism. He assumed that his mind perceived only ideas, but he did not
draw the conclusion later derived from this proposition: that, since

our ideas of sensory objects are mental, the objects are themselves also mental. Descartes inferred from his axiom *ego cogito, ergo sum* that I am a soul and a soul perceives only its own ideas, which was psychological idealism. But he then went on to deduce from the existence of such ideas, the existence of extended substance and of the soul or thinking substance, which is metaphysical realism. This created the persistent problem of the relation of the body and the soul. The solution reached by Descartes was soon found unsatisfactory and stimulated other theories, also in their turn discovered to be inadequate.[93]

In appealing to his awareness of himself, Descartes set an example followed by subsequent idealists, for here they found an ultimate fact that they could not doubt. Yet the celebrated formula, *ego cogito, ergo sum*, was at best an analytical judgment disclosing by way of conclusion one of its initial premises. At worst it confused two senses of the verb "to be," a sense in which it connects subject and predicate and one in which it asserts existence. "John is fighting" and "John is in camp" both employ the same word "is," but in one case it connects the action of "fighting" with "John" as the object of our attention, and in the other it asserts that "John exists in a camp." "I am" (myself exists) and "I am thinking" (my thinking occurs) use the same word "am" in two different senses also, but to infer the accuracy of one observation from the truth of the other is not rigid deduction. Because John is in camp, he need not be fighting; and if he is fighting, he can do it elsewhere.

The division of the world into two substances with relations that could not be satisfactorily defined was a bold but arbitrarily simple reduction. By "substance" Aristotle had meant something that exists independently as a distinct individual, but by his methodical doubt Descartes could not establish either that there are only two substances or that a thinking substance exists. The criterion of clarity, advanced by Leibniz and adopted by Baumgarten when establishing the field of aesthetics, has already been discussed. Vividness or distinctness and clarity, apart from adequacy and the satisfaction of tests for coherence and correspondence, are likely to be aesthetic, rather than logical, criteria.

The difficulties resulting from the thoroughgoing dualism of Descartes, with only two substances but with their relations left obscure, has been one of the main sources of perplexity in philosophical speculation ever since. On the whole, science and history have remained loyally realistic, but abstract thought has often been impeded by this

idealistic bias. To escape from the theory of the two substances, idealists have often preferred to believe that nothing but self-consciousness
exists, while other modern thinkers, as, for example, William James,
have reached the opposite conclusion—that a distinct thinking substance, a conscious thing, does not exist. A radical decision, reducing
the world to a single substance, in an effort to eliminate insuperable
objections to the dualism of Descartes, was taken by Spinoza.

SPINOZA

Declaring that there are not two distinct substances but only attributes of one, unique substance, Spinoza held extension and thinking
to be properties of an all-inclusive substance, which was at the same
time numerically one. The relation between the two attributes, extension and thinking, was for him that of two distinct expressions of
the same thing, so that the order of things was the order of thoughts.[94]
Spinoza used the concept of substance, not as signifying an individual
distinct from anything else, in Aristotle's sense, but with the meaning
that substance exists alone, from which he argued that there can be
only one substance and that finite things, being unable to exist alone,
are modes of the attributes of that unique substance.

In his own age, Spinoza's system was condemned as atheistic; but
it was enthusiastically revived by Herder, Goethe, and Schleiermacher, while it influenced Fichte, Schelling, Schopenhauer, and Fech-
ner in certain of their views.[95]

The dogma that there is an independent, self-sufficient, and self-con-
ceived substance, existing alone, was thought to give assured knowledge of ultimate, unique, and total reality. But the concept of totality,
when it occurs to a mind, is possibly one, and that is all that must be
conceded. That there is a totality, completely accessible as such to the
mind, remains to be proved, as well as the theory that reality is numerically one.

The belief that there is a unique, or sole, object, including all the
rest, perhaps satisfies an impatient or intolerant mind. Numerical unity is, nevertheless, a concept attended by innumerable others, and to
assert that it is an adequate representative of all the others is to identify the initial member of the series of numbers with the quality of
totality.

Ordinary experience testifies to the failure of things and thoughts
precisely to correspond. The central principle of rationalism is properly based on the confident expectation that the mind is not incapable

of understanding any reality; but this does not mean to take the extreme position that the tactile and mental orders are identical, differing only as distinct attributes. To suit their own purposes, later German philosophers, however, regarded with special favor Spinoza's numerical monism and identification of the order of thoughts with that of things. His one substance was made to support their esteem of the unique self, and his parallel order was given a dynamic interpretation, to the effect that to think a thing was for it to exist.

LOCKE

The major contributions of Locke to philosophical investigation were destructive to long-established theories and offended many rationalists on the Continent; but the idealists, including Leibniz, borrowed from him elements which seemed to strengthen the dominant role of self-consciousness in their metaphysical constructions.

Like Descartes, Locke had no special interest in art, yet several of his most important claims were supported by references to art that have made his views vivid ever since. His understanding of the mind as an empty receptacle, a blank tablet, or *tabula rasa*, was persuasively illustrated by that phrase. In accounting for the origin of our ideas, he raised the question: "Let us then suppose the mind to be, as we say, white paper, void of all characters, without any ideas; how comes it to be thus furnished?"[96]

A phrase of Aristotle's,[97] taken apart from its context, but misinterpreted by many, including the scholastics,[98] was the original source of the phrase *tabula rasa*.[99] The analogy was to the drawing or writing produced on a blank surface through technique, and its purpose was to show that the mind is not equipped with innate ideas, any more than an empty surface begins with the picture it afterward presents. Ideas are like words or pictures; as drawings are acquired by the paper, so ideas are acquired by the mind.

In another passage he commented upon the fruits of imagination, which he called "wit," in contrast with those of judgment, stressing that what we should now call their "aesthetic" quality was the chief characteristic of things produced by imagination. He wrote of judgment:

This is a way of proceeding quite contrary to metaphor and allusion, wherein for the most part lies that entertainment and pleasantry of wit, which strikes so lively on the fancy, and therefore is so acceptable to all people; because its beauty appears at first sight, and there is required no labor of thought to examine what truth or reason there is in it. The mind, without looking any farther, rests satisfied with the agreeableness of the picture, and the gaiety of the fancy; and it is a kind of an affront to go about to examine it by the severe rules of truth and good reason; whereby it appears, that it consists in something that is not perfectly conformable to them.[100]

To his own question regarding the origin of our ideas, Locke replied:

To all this I answer, in one word, from experience; in all that our knowledge is founded, and from that it ultimately derives itself. Our observation employed either about external sensible objects, or about the internal operations of our minds, perceived and reflected on by ourselves, is that which supplies our understandings with all the materials of thinking.[101]

Guided by such considerations, he reduced all our ideas to two sorts: those of sensation and those of reflection.

He explained the capacity of the mind to remember in a way which also appealed to an analogy drawn from art when he said: "Our ideas are said to be in our memories, when indeed they are actually nowhere, but only there is an ability of the mind when it will to revive them again, and as it were to paint them a-new on itself, though some with more, some with less difficulty; some more lively, and others more obscurely."[102] His rejection of the common belief that ideas are somehow contained by the mind was, however, even more important than his theory of memory.

While defining an idea in the customary fashion, he made another very influential contribution when he introduced his radically original view of ranks in qualities, saying: "Whatever the mind perceives in itself, or is the immediate object of perception, thought, or understanding, that I call idea." He then distinguished three kinds of quality in bodies of which the primary were such things as bulk, figure, number, situation, motion, and rest, for "those are in them, whether we perceive them or no," while the secondary qualities were colors, smells, sounds, tastes, and such as were then usually called "sensible"; the tertiary included the powers that were in any body to operate on the primary qualities of another body so that it affected our senses differently from the way it had before.[103]

This discrimination of rank in the hierarchy of ideas was soon to be condemned by idealists, and in the introduction to that part of the *Essay* in which he had laid down the doctrine of the three grades of quality, he himself had opened the way to abolishing these differences, when he declared of our ideas:

We may not think (as perhaps usually is done) that they are exactly in the images and resemblances of something inherent in the subject; most of those of sensation being in the mind no more the likeness of something exist- ing without us, than the names that stand for them are the likeness of our ideas, which yet upon hearing they are apt to excite in us.

He also declared that the idea of corporeal substance or matter is as re- mote from our conceptions as that of spiritual substance or spirit.[104]

These keen observations were directed against the theory, long popular, that our knowledge of things consists of mental images which are adequate representations of the things to which they corre- spond, but they were appropriated by critical rationalists later to show that we can have no direct knowledge of things in themselves.

Again like Leibniz, Locke distinguished between clear and obscure ideas. Another division of Ideas was "in reference to things from whence they are taken, or which they may be supposed to represent," classifying them as real, adequate, and true or fantastical, inadequate, and false. He concluded this section of his treatise by saying: "Our complex ideas of substances, being all referred to patterns in things themselves, may be false. That they are all false, when looked upon as the representations of the unknown essences of things, is so evident that there needs nothing to be said of it."[105] These considerations un- dermined the theory of substances put forward by Descartes and en- couraged the rationalist idealists in the tendency to fix the mind's at- tention upon the idea of itself as the only certain object of knowledge.

While accepting, with Descartes, some of the standard hypotheses of idealism, Locke still provided convincing arguments which may be turned against it. As an empiricist, the English thinker analyzed the proof for the existence of God given by Descartes and felt obliged to reject it on the ground that the argument of the French philosopher on behalf of "a knowing, immaterial substance" could just as readily be urged to establish the eternity of "senseless matter."[106]

Locke's position against Descartes on this point might be extended to disclose a tendency latent in the idealist position and one which enables us better to understand, while we disapprove, the actions of some who today are heirs of its convictions. In spite of their desire to identify moral idealism and the idealist philosophy, nothing more clearly suggests that they are at bottom inconsistent than the facility with which adherents of the idealist philosophy can pursue a course contrary to ethical idealism. They are easily indifferent to the good opinion of others; they insist on executing their will regardless of grave injury to others, treating their fellow-men as if they were inferior animals and not men like themselves. In their practical relations to others, it would seem, German idealists in philosophy can find it peculiarly satisfying to be immoralists in action.

In theory, also, systematic immorality is much more congenial to the reasoning by which metaphysical idealism is defended. The arguments advanced on its behalf can more successfully be employed to sustain materialism. Ordinarily by materialism is meant the belief that only sensations truly exist; that the final, substantial realities are the data of the senses, although this might more properly be called "sensationalism." The materialist attitude can be interpreted ascetically or hedonistically; but, since nothing except the passing excitement of the senses has any meaning, ethics is often reduced to self-indulgence, tempered by shrewdness.

Materialism is at least as plausible a conclusion from the idealist arguments as those which are usually drawn. If all I can know are my ideas and if my ideas are all eventually derived from sensation, then ideas are sound so far as they are instruments to the experience of satisfying sensations. The aim in scrutinizing the self is to confirm ideas of one's sensations, pleasant or otherwise. The data of touch or pressure are usually given a pre-eminent position by materialists, and the data of other senses are somehow made dependent upon or derived from it. Tactile experience becomes ultimate, and ideas become guides to the satisfaction of this sense.

The idealist reasoning, if we pursue Locke's argument, would appear to lead as easily to materialism as to ethical idealism. In the life of action, as well as in the career of thought, the implications of philosophical idealism then would not differ significantly from those of sensational materialism, which becomes, in popular practice, the gratification of vulgar, wilful impulse.

When two precisely opposite conclusions are possible from the same premises, there are usually several possible explanations. There may be errors in the sequence of deductions in one case or in the other; sometimes there are such mistakes in both arguments; but the most frequent situation is that the assumption common to both trains of thought is itself defective, and that is so in the present instance.

We do know ideas, but we also know other things. We are immediately acquainted with sensory patterns, for example; we are also aware of memory images and of things presented through imagination, but neither is an immediate sensory object in any case. Ideas are not necessarily equivalents of actual or potential sensory patterns. Ideas or concepts are necessities for discourse and verbal communication, but no autobiographer could possibly describe in detail the range and variety of even his sensory experiences as fast as they occur. Ideas are facts in experience, but our experience does not consist wholly of ideas; and as living creatures we are not condemned to deal solely with ideas which may or may not correspond to the things for which they stand. Apart from these difficulties, when the world is made to consist of ideas derived from sensations, there is the one, which Aristotle pointed out centuries ago, that this assumption does not lessen the problems with which philosophy must deal; it at least doubles them, for we are faced with the fact that the orders of thoughts and of sensory patterns do not precisely coincide. When we reduce the world to ideas but consider these ideas as derived from sensations, we still have the relation of each idea to its original to deal with, even if we suppose ourselves incapable of knowing the source itself.

LEIBNIZ

Leibniz, the hostile critic of Locke, has already been mentioned as supplying the classification of ideas which led to Baumgarten's invention of the term "aesthetics." But the arguments by which he accelerated the growth of German idealism were also of great importance, for he was the first great modern German philosopher, and in him are to be found traits which have characterized German speculation ever since.

In spite of their controversy, Locke and Leibniz were not so far apart as the latter supposed in their estimate of ideas. Locke denied innate ideas, but he conceded the capacity of the mind to elaborate them; Leibniz, while insisting on innate ideas, admitted that they existed in the mind, not actually, but virtually.

In several works, one of which was an explicit parallel to the four books of Locke's *Essay*,[107] as well as in one of the letters in which he set forth his views more concisely,[108] Leibniz asserted that necessary truths can be proved by means of principles implicit in the spirit, but the senses tell us only what occurs, not what necessarily occurs. He claimed that Locke had failed to observe that the ideas of being, substance, identity, truth, and good are innate in our spirit, since it is native to the spirit to conceive all of these. It was in this connection that he formulated a theory which afterward aided some thinkers to escape from the idealists' self-centered delusion. He changed the sensationalists' standard formula to read: "Certainly there is nothing in intellect which has not been in sensation, except the intellect itself."[109] To put it in a modern version, whenever there is experience, there is present, in addition to things experienced, the activity of experiencing, so that when sensory objects are experienced there is a factor at work which is not itself sensory.

The most celebrated contribution of Leibniz to philosophy was his doctrine of the monad, for which, as for Descartes and Locke, his starting-point was the self. He wrote: "Substantial unity calls for a thoroughly indivisible being, naturally indestructible. . . . . It can be found, however, in a soul or a substantial form, such as is the one called I. These latter are the only thoroughly real beings."[110]

Through introspection and analysis of his self, Leibniz discovered the nature of the monad, a soul, a spiritual reality, such as the I, since, "in order to determine the concept of an individual substance, it is good to consult the concept which I have of myself."[111] Reasoning on this basis, Leibniz reached a number of interesting conclusions with regard to the monad. It depends on God;[112] it is active;[113] it is independent and apart from every other one, having no windows by which anything can enter or pass out;[114] it is a unity of its own states;[115] and every monad at the same time mirrors or expresses all reality.[116] To reconcile the two conflicting claims that every monad is absolutely apart from every other and that it also expresses the universe, Leibniz evolved his ingenious theory that God had predestined each monad to exist in harmony with the others. As an instance of such preestablished harmony he gave two clocks which keep exactly the same time.[117]

Leibniz also accepted the proof of the existence of God devised by Descartes, believing with him that, from the idea of a perfect being, His existence must necessarily follow; but to this argument he added another. Observing that we are aware of both concrete objects and of abstract truths, Leibniz claimed that God must exist as the perfect being from whom they derive, for otherwise they would lack a sufficient reason for their existence,[118] introducing in this way the celebrated principle of sufficient reason.

But, as Santayana has pointed out, the doctrine of sufficient reason —the demand that all effects must be the necessary results of efficient causes—instead of proving God's existence, usurps His place, making Him unnecessary.[119] By Plotinus the relation between the One and the world could be explained as a matter of eternal procession and attraction, but the solitary self-sufficiency of the monads rendered God superfluous.[120] It eventually culminated in the deification of the self, the truly active monad; for, in a system founded upon introspection of the self, the principle of sufficient reason indicated that it, rather than God, was the source of the self's experiences.

Aside from this consequence of the principle of sufficient reason, it can be shown that since Leibniz made his system depend on his proof for the existence of God, if that collapsed, his structure had no foundations. Since he reconciled the absolute solitude of the monad and its complete expressiveness through pre-established harmony, and this saving coincidence operated through God's intervention, the proof of His existence had to be persuasive before an appeal could be made to His aid.

But harmony is not the most singular attribute of events, so that, whether pre-established or not, we properly entertain doubts as to the existence of a state of things which this doctrine is invoked to explain. The monad bears witness to ugliness, error, and evil as inevitably as it does to beauty, truth, and goodness; discord is as familiar as harmony. It required a fantastic degree of smug self-satisfaction to suppose that any such fallible, ignorant, and feeble creature as a human being could reflect or represent the totality of the real. As for the unmitigated isolation of the monad, it knows other things, including other persons, no less truly and perhaps more accurately than it knows itself.

Leibniz, on the whole, developed the implications of egocentric idealism through collecting a variety of the divine attributes and giving them to the monad, which was a new name for the self. To hold these contradictions in suspense he introduced a God whom he had already rendered unnecessary. His construction had a high degree of clarity and precision, but it was the expression of intellectual pride in that omniscience which the eighteenth century supposed that it finally possessed.

BERKELEY

Berkeley's direct influence on German speculation was slight, but the sceptical side of this British idealist's thought was exploited by Hume, and Hume was closely studied by Kant. His views were in some respects parallel to those of Leibniz; but as he did not find it necessary to burden his philosophy with the concept of a pre-established harmony, it was, at least on the surface, simpler. As a plausible statement of the position of rationalist idealism, it later provided an easy introduction to German speculation in Great Britain and America.

The views of both Leibniz and Berkeley were believed by their inventors to be intellectual supports for orthodoxy. Nowhere is this attitude more apparent than in Berkeley's views on art. Here the radical initiative for which he is praised in metaphysics is absent; he simply reflects conservative doctrine and authorized preference.

In his *Alciphron*, Berkeley arrived at the conclusion that, "as there is no beauty without proportion, so proportions are to be esteemed just and true, only as they are relative to some certain use or end, their aptitude and subordination to which end is, at bottom, that which makes them please and charm."[121] He cited architecture as evidence, saying: "It seems, above all other arts, peculiarly conversant about order, proportions, and symmetry." He hoped that it would afford a way out of the difficulty which Leibniz found the artists to be facing: "May it not therefore be supposed, on all accounts, most likely to help us to some rational notion of the *je ne sais quoi* of beauty?" But in this connection he was able to introduce an argument for his general philosophical attitude, stating: "Beauty . . . . is an object, not of the eye, but of the mind. . . . . It is, therefore, one thing to see an object, and another to discern its beauty."[122]

In this discussion Berkeley cited with approval the drapery to be seen in prints after Raphael and Guido Reni; at the same time he condemned the costumes of English magistrates and ladies of fashion, to which he applied the opprobrious epithet "Gothic." The criterion of proportion and utility led him to censure mediaeval architecture, as it supplied "the grand distinction between Grecian and Gothic architecture; the latter being fantastical, and for the most part founded neither in nature nor in reason, in necessity nor use, the appearance of which accounts for all the beauty, grace, and ornament of the other."[123]

He founded his speculative enterprise, as did Descartes, Locke, and Leibniz, on what he believed to be obvious inferences from the nature of the self known to introspection. He practically repeated Locke in saying:

It is evident to any one who takes a survey of the objects of human knowledge, that they are either ideas imprinted on the senses; or else such as are perceived by attending to the passions and operations of the mind. . . . . But besides all that endless variety of ideas or objects of knowledge, there is likewise Something which knows or perceives them; and exercises divers operations, as willing, imagining, remembering, about them. This perceiving, active being is what I call mind, spirit, soul, or myself. By which words I do not denote any one of my ideas, but a thing entirely distinct from them, wherein they exist, or, which is the same thing, whereby they are perceived; for the existence of an idea consists in being perceived.[124]

This claim he then developed into the formula ever since attached to his name, asserting:

That neither our thoughts, nor passions, nor ideas formed by the imagination, exist without the mind is what everybody will allow. And to me it seems no less evident that the various sensations or ideas imprinted on the Sense, however blended or combined together (that is, whatever objects they compose), cannot exist otherwise than in a mind perceiving them. . . . . Of the absolute existence of unthinking things, without any relation to their being perceived, that is to me perfectly unintelligible. Their *esse* is *percipi;* nor is it possible they should have any existence out of the minds of thinking things which perceive them.[125]

Locke had already cleared the ground for Berkeley's conclusions when he demolished the accepted interpretation of substance as the substratum of reality and defined it as a complex of qualities. To transform Locke's philosophy, all that Berkeley had to do was to point out that matter, according to Locke's analysis, does not really exist, for the distinction between primary and secondary qualities, made by Locke, could not be maintained. Reality, Berkeley therefore believed, was wholly mental or spiritual, so that the existence of objects depended on their being perceived.[126]

But there are grave defects in the formula, *esse est percipi*, "to be perceived is to exist." The situation of creative thinkers and artists while they are at work provides evidence that to imagine or to wish is not enough. The concepts on which the attention of a philosopher or mathematician is fixed while he is in action may be the clearest and most vivid objects within his immediate experience, and the images before the mind of the artist while he designs a work of art may be for him more intensely real than the tools in his hands. Philosophers, mathematicians, and artists at those moments have lively knowledge of their objects; and when they have finished their work, they then view with the pride of achievement what they have done. Yet while their minds are concentrated on the solution of an abstract problem or the designing of a specific sensory pattern, the ends toward which their efforts are directed do not then exist. Because a man is engaged in relating concepts or in imagining a work of art, it cannot be claimed that the final result must simultaneously exist. A satisfactory pattern of concepts or of sensory data need not immediately be projected into the world of other persons' experience or be available on the morrow for the creator's own enjoyment. It is true that no mathematical formula can be studied unless some mathematician has devised it, and no work of art can be seen or touched unless some artist has designed it. But not every hour devoted to abstract analysis or to the planning of sensory images necessarily leads to a successful result; and even when it does, the product is the culmination of an orderly sequence of acts, not a sudden, miraculous apparition.

In one of his earlier books, Santayana had refuted the assumptions condensed into the formula *esse est percipi*, urging:

Such idealism at one fell swoop, through a collapse of assertive intellect with a withdrawal of reason into self-consciousness, has the puzzling character of any clever pun, that suspends the fancy between two incompatible but irresistible meanings. The art of such sophistry is to choose for an axiom some ambiguous phrase which taken in one sense is a truism and taken in another is an absurdity; and then, by showing the truth of that truism, to give out that the absurdity has also been proved. It is a truism to say that I am the only seat or locus of my ideas, and to say that whatever I know is known by me; but it is an absurdity to say that I am the only object of my thought and perception.[127]

It is also worth noting that, as in the case of the famous formula of Descartes, *ego cogito, ergo sum*, in Berkeley's *esse est percipi* we also have the ambiguity of the verb "to be" employed to afford a demonstration. But where Descartes had used only two of the meanings of the verb—those of predication and existence—Berkeley added a third in his celebrated proposition. That third use is the one that indicates equality. In his proposition, *esse* means "to be" in the sense of "to exist." *Percipi* means "to be perceived," the passive infinitive of the transitive verb. The equivocation so far parallels the Cartesian unjustified identification of the verb "to be" as meaning the same thing in "to be thinking" and "to be existing." To these Berkeley added further confusion by also introducing *est* as the equivalent of "equals." In the multiplication table we say three times four is twelve, the product equals twelve, so that twelve also equals three times four. In this way Berkeley could achieve a superficial plausibility for his view that "to be" is "to be perceived," but the whole claim rested upon three distinct, and by no means identical, meanings of a familiar word. Because the word employed or implied is the same, the concepts are not thereby also guaranteed to be identical.

There are other equally grave errors of observation or analysis inferred from this doctrine; but, as they become more conspicuous in the later progress of German idealism, they had best be left for discussion when the romantic idealists are reached.

KANT

Wolff,[128] who inherited the system of Leibniz, produced a systematic exposition of his predecessor's theories, something which Leibniz himself had never done. But, without realizing the effect of his revision, Wolff revived the Cartesian notions of extended and unextended substance, which was quite inconsistent with the doctrine of monads. By giving his work the appearance of rational integration and expressing himself in clear language, Wolff became the leading philosopher of the German Enlightenment.

Hume,[129] on the other hand, had been attracted by the sceptical elements in Berkeley's approach to philosophical problems; and he applied these methods of reasoning to certain popular views with deadly effect, creating a sort of intellectual panic.

Eventually repelled by the dogmatism of Wolff and unable wholly to evade the corrosive arguments of Hume, for he felt obliged to admit their cogency, Kant spent a patient, laborious, and uninspired lifetime in erecting a vast, interlocking structure. In spite of its impressiveness, it did not include many original discoveries, unknown to those who had gone before; nor did it provide a permanent mansion in which speculative thought could feel at home. For several generations afterward, German thinkers were prone to select some particular doctrine from Kant and then develop it separately, alleging that in this way they were expounding Kant's own convictions. Since this philosopher's thought on the topics that have already been discussed was so extensive and at the same time so influential, it is well to consider the several related doctrines at somewhat greater length than has been necessary in dealing with the rational idealists who went before him.

ART

Following the British writers, Hutcheson, Home, and Alison, Kant made a distinction between free beauty (*pulchritudo vaga*) and dependent beauty (*pulchritudo adhaerens*).[130] As examples of the first class, he mentioned "Greek decorative designs, foliation for margins or on wallpapers, and so on," for they "mean nothing in themselves; they represent nothing of which we have any definite conception and are free beauties." Of dependent beauty, Kant said: "But the beauty of mankind, whether man, or child, of a horse or a building, whether church, palace, arsenal, or summer-house, presupposes a purpose which settled what the thing ought to be (that is, a conception of its ideal) and is consequently only dependent beauty."[131] This statement was in line with a previous remark: "Flowers, arabesques, decorative intertwining of lines in what is called foliation, mean nothing and depend on no definite conception, and yet please us."[132]

But this distinction between free and dependent beauty, like the parallel classifications of the sublime and the beautiful,[133] was derived by Kant from previous thinkers. He shared that preference for the sublime and the free, as against the beautiful and the dependent, which gained strength in the course of the eighteenth century; and this was itself a symptom of deep discontent with the prevalent rationalism, which finally resulted in the romantic movement. When they placed meaningless beautiful things above those which had clear significance, their preference indicated chiefly that they objected to the monotonous meanings of certain accepted forms and that the men of this age desired, instead, to look upon objects that were not boring and dull because too familiar and too easily understood.

To expect, however, that the mind could deal with genuinely meaningless objects was to wish for the impossible; and even Kant, in writing to convey his preference to readers, had to give them names, calling them "Greek decorative designs, foliation for margins or on wall-papers." It is true that such patterns need not be accurate representations of other objects, but the necessity of giving them names in discourse and of connecting them with others of the same kind, already known, rests on the ineradicable demand of the mind that it shall somehow know things, including works of art, when it has to deal with them.

In his sustained task of defining and relating concepts, Kant was very little concerned with specific works of art, but his rare remarks are indicative of his general attitude. His main preoccupation was to take the set of prejudices and the accumulated vocabulary which was available to him as a result of his predecessors' labors and adjust these materials so that they would constitute parts of a coherent, symmetrical system.

Because of the way in which he approached this problem, Kant himself called his philosophy "critical" and "transcendental." He held that before it could produce a finished structure, reason must first investigate the concepts that could be employed for that purpose. By the term "transcendental" Kant expressed his belief that he had successfully applied a method that enabled his thought to rise superior to the dogmas of sensationalism and the limitations of his idealist forerunners. He held it to be superior because it did not begin with things but with our knowledge of things, so far as this was possible in advance of acquaintaince with particular objects. But before concepts were to be fitted into his system, they must be able to survive sceptical criticism. He also called his conclusions "critical" because his method enabled him to discriminate between the theoretical, the practical, and the aesthetic realms.[134] Owing to his initiative, indicated by the terms "transcendental" and "critical," the problem of knowledge has replaced ethical and physical speculation as the favorite topic of modern German philosophers, and by thinkers elsewhere it has, since Kant's time, been accepted as an unavoidable preliminary to the cultivation of other interests.

THE SELF

Since Hume had already made a critical analysis of the prevailing notion of the self and had concluded that such a knowing thing does not exist, Kant felt obliged to justify belief in its existence. This he did by means of three arguments. First he appealed to the witness of introspection; then he pointed out the unity in experience which he thought could be due only to the unity in knowing of one self; and, finally, he cited the relations obtaining between ideas as requiring a self to relate them, for "the consciousness of relation can be created only by the subject."[135] Kant, while elaborating these views, did not, however, repeat the terms "soul," "self," and "spirit" which had been established by tradition but preferred such phrases as "the subject" and "the unity of apperception," to avoid earlier implications and to advance his own conclusions regarding the existence of the self.

Kant next distinguished between the empirical self, which is momentary, a series of separate ideas, and the transcendental self, which is persistent and identical. The latter he also referred to by the phrase "synthetic unity of apperception," for he considered it to be active in abstract thought and in assigning ideas to categories rather than passively aware of sensations. He declared that it was one, universal, and self-conscious. According to Kant, objects which are things located in space belong to this transcendental self, while the ideas of these things pertain to the empirical self.[136] Berkeley had a neat solution for the resulting difficulty occasioned by the need to reconcile temporary impressions and permanent realities; he said that things in space are real and at the same time ideas, because they are God's ideas.

But Kant could not base his conclusions on God's existence and activity; as a critical and transcendental idealist he began with himself.

One way to analyze the perplexing relations between Kant's empirical and transcendental selves and their corresponding objects is to follow a suggestion found in grammar. The first person singular of the pronoun has two cases represented by "I" and "me." These indicate my active consciousness of something and awareness of being the object of activity, respectively. But Kant treated both his transcendental and his empirical I as objects, whereas, properly speaking, I is not an object, it is having objects.[137] This is well illustrated by the activity of vision in living creatures, where I see things, which is the same as having visual objects. But I do not see my own eyes while I see, nor do I see my own seeing. My seeing—the familiar experience of objects which can be directly related to the eyes as organs—occurs, and this act can be intelligibly connected with a unique series of events which I call "mine." The unified series of experienced objects is identified as mine; the continuity present in my active experiencing is indicated by I.

Kant retained his peculiar, unique, remembered object—his me—and called it the empirical self. But when he wished to eliminate the differences in separate trains of experience, he called it the transcendental self, a ME written large. In fixing the relations of both the empirical and the transcendental me, Kant dealt with objects. A subject was inferred from that unique, historical series of experiences which Kant called "me" and which we call "Kant." The tenacious teacher of Königsberg attended to his memories and concepts; while he could treat his me with some confidence, he could not reduce his I to an object, for his I was the unity present in his thinking and remembering activity, whether he contemplated himself or some other object.

"I" and "me" are words that we understand; they can be effectively employed in analysis, communication, and record because they are not limited to one instance only and are therefore universals. They signify coherence in one's own unique series of experiences, but each speaker who employs them is aware of himself as one among a great many other things. It is in this way that the empirical self is universal, one, and self-conscious. But if, according to the idealist approach, the self was the only certain object of knowledge and this knowledge was to be reliable, it must, Kant supposed, in effect replace the deity. There had to be a transcendental subject which was all-inclusive, not simply an attribute possessed by many. This subject should also be numerically one. Thus it could fulfil the idealists' program; its knowledge would be wholly knowledge of itself.

Consequently, Kant took away the limitations which made his me a definite and determinate individual and called by the name "transcendental unity of apperception" what was after all only Kant's me, now raised to solitary, self-satisfied omniscience and omnipotence.

Such a solution of the problem naturally raised numerous additional difficulties. Kant had to admit that although the transcendental self was real, it was unknown; his me could be his object but his I could never be. He declared: "We have no knowledge of the subject in itself. . . . . Of that subject . . . . we have not and cannot have the slightest knowledge."[138] This was so on the empirical level; and on the transcendental, which Kant believed to exist, he could not conceive how the case could be different. But to employ a term to indicate something whose existence could not be proved, although such extraordinary claims were made for it, always troubled Kant.

He retained it, in spite of misgivings, in his *Critique of Practical Reason*, since he felt that moral obligation demands the existence of the transcendental self. In the other divisions of philosophy Kant also rescued his traditional sympathies from his professorial scepticism by introducing something which, on principle, he had to admit was unknown.[139]

Kant's doctrine of the self thus amounted to the conclusion that the transcendental self cannot be known and the empirical self is hardly worth knowing; but he felt compelled to preserve these concepts, since the ground of certainty was, for idealists, knowledge of the self. He reconciled this doctrine and his inherited Calvinist sense of guilt, which he called "conscience," by making an unknown transcendental unity of apperception the final ground of ethical value. His Pietist conscience he hypostatized and called it the "categorical imperative," but he should have inserted an adjective which would have described his own sense of ethical responsibility more accurately, had he termed it the "negative categorical imperative." He found himself accepting beliefs he could not prove, admiring things for which he could not discover any purpose, and performing actions whose utility he could not establish. Under such circumstances his own negative categorical imperative urged him to condemn these as untrue, ugly, and wrong.

Philosophical and rationalist idealism was an uncomfortable mate for a Calvinist conscience. If ideas rather than things are all we can ever know and if "the consciousness of relations can be created only by the subject," then the world is a futile and laborious illusion, of whose futility and laboriousness the very self is guilty.

Escape, to some extent, was, however, possible. Aesthetics was for Kant the one realm where rational justification is not required and where ethical responsibility is not imposed. The name *beaux-arts* he accepted as indicating that certain techniques possessed aesthetic value as a vested right; and when the idea of beauty was claimed to be the essence of the arts of design, aesthetics was the same as the theoretical analysis of art. Minds emptied of hope, when convinced by the study of Kant that genuine knowledge was impossible, found salvation in aesthetics. Art was a playground of speculative thought, where the mind could roam, untroubled by considerations of right and wrong or of true and false. The disciples of Kant and his successors turned to aesthetics with enthusiasm and relief.

AESTHETICS

Hume had contended that causality and universality cannot be rationalized on the ground of experience and that they have no objective validity. To this Kant replied by admitting that they were subjective but necessary mental categories.[140] He asserted that they were a priori because required by the mind, and the mind's activity he considered to be chiefly synthetic or formative. For him the initial problem of philosophy was: "How are synthetical judgments a priori possible?"[141]

In answering this question he made use of a distinction developed by Leibniz, Wolff, and Baumgarten: "The science of all the principles of sensibility *a priori* I call Transcendental Aesthetic . . . . as opposed to that which treats of the principles of pure thought, and which should be called Transcendental Logic."[142] He declared that time and space were pure forms of sensuous intuition, and therefore they were discussed as topics in aesthetics.[143] Kant thus kept the name that Baumgarten had invented to deal with sensory experience but treated it as the science of mental categories imposed by the mind on that type of experience. His conclusion with regard to time and space was, accordingly, that "nothing remains but to accept them as subjective forms of our external as well as internal intuition."[144]

As did Baumgarten, Kant also designed aesthetics to fill a gap in his system rather than because he had any very keen interest either in things beautiful or in art. Baumgarten had intended aesthetics to be a parallel to logic, but Kant also felt the need of a third theoretical realm to mediate between pure and practical reason. His definition of aesthetics was determined by characteristics that could not be classified as logical or ethical and were, in fact, opposed to the constituent realities of those fields. The practical judgment was, for Kant, interested, and the rational derived its conclusions from concepts. Therefore, from the practical point of view the judgment of taste was disinterested and unconcerned with the object as a means to an end. From the logical approach, the beautiful was taken to be the object of a universal satisfaction, without reference to concepts; but this universality was only subjective.

In other words, aesthetic judgments had to do with neither logical truth nor moral good.[145] The judgment of taste had nothing as its basis but the appearance of purposiveness, and it was also independent of the concept of perfection.[146] He was in this way able to conclude that "beauty is the form of purposiveness of an object, so far as this is perceived in it without any representation of a purpose."[147]

Kant mentioned such men as Lessing and Batteux very rarely, but on many occasions he accepted their views and those of the other writers already discussed under the "Natural History of Art." The relation of art and nature, the origin of the beauty found in art, and the essence of beautiful art were all problems for Kant because they presented contradictions that attracted his critical mind. The Idea of beauty as the essence of certain techniques, the *beaux-arts;* the ancient principle of imitation to explain the representation of nature by art—these and other inherited ideas were problems for Kant because he could not overlook the unprovable assumptions on which they relied.

It was proper for Kant to challenge traditional dogma by asking such a direct and significant question as this: How can art be beautiful? But he answered this demand, occasioned by the arbitrary nature of the claim implied in the very designation *beaux-arts*, by invoking another, equally erroneous, concept; for he replied: "Nature is beautiful because it looks like art; and art can only be called beautiful if we are conscious of it as art while yet it looks like nature." In that case, when does art look like nature? "A product of art appears like nature when, although its agreement with the rules . . . . is punctiliously observed, yet this is not painfully apparent; the form of the schools does not obtrude itself—it shows no trace of the rule having been before the eyes of the artist and having fettered his mental powers."[148]

This academic doctrine amounted to saying that art is beautiful when its technical origin is so well concealed that it appears to be a natural product, in other words, a charming deception. Nature appears to be beautiful when it seems to be designed as works of art are, but without human intervention—again, a pleasing deception. But it is hardly an answer to the question, How can either art or nature be beautiful? to say: When they successfully imitate each other.

Kant supposed that he had progressed beyond this unilluminating explanation when he defined the judgment of taste as presenting a universal satisfaction without reference to concepts. But in antiquity when imitation was a popular explanation, the question that Greek thinkers asked themselves was: How can that be beautiful which pretends to be something that it is not? How can a work of art which represents some model, but is not that thing itself, be admired? How can a lie be beautiful? Kant had claimed that beauty has nothing to do with truth, but the principle of imitation demands reference to concepts, as Aristotle saw and for that reason attributed intellectual value to representative art. It was entirely inconsistent for Kant to adopt imitation to explain the relation between nature and art, while he declared that the judgment of taste involves no reference to concepts; but he was not alone among philosophers who have found themselves in difficulties because they accepted the implications of the term *beaux-arts*.

TASTE

Kant's usual method was illustrated also by his treatment of the concepts of taste and genius. He asserted that "taste is the faculty of judging of an object or a method of representing it by an entirely disinterested satisfaction or dissatisfaction."[149] Then he raised the typical question of a critical philosophy: How is it possible for judgments to be made which do not involve the satisfaction of interest? To judge without a clear conception of the good desired was something that a rationalist moralist was reluctant to recognize, but he claimed that that was just what taste does.

According to Kant, "Beautiful art is the art of genius. . . . . Genius is the innate mental disposition through which nature gives the rule to art. . . . . Nature by the medium of genius does not prescribe rules to science, but to art; and to it only in so far as it is to be beautiful art."[150] This explanation has met with wider popular favor than his view that art and nature are beautiful when they successfully imitate each other; a conclusion that was abandoned by later idealists.

He decided that the relation of taste to genius was that between active creation and passive appreciation: "For judging of beautiful objects as such, taste is requisite; but for beautiful art, i.e., for the production of such objects, genius is requisite."[151] He then engaged in a long discussion, the forerunner of innumerable but equally inconclusive investigations, when he treated the topic "Of the faculties of the mind that constitute genius."[152]

Taste and genius,[153] the distinction between pure beauty and the beauty of representations, the limitation of aesthetics to sensory patterns, and the principle of imitation were all familiar before Kant wrote and were not original with him. The notion of taste was, indeed, an easy but illegitimate escape from intrinsic defects of the Cartesian philosophy. Although Descartes had divided reality into two substances—extended or unthinking and unextended or thinking—substance was for him the substratum of experience, and its model was a pattern of the data of touch or pressure.[154] This interpretation of reality ignored the data of other senses; it justified reducing causes to one kind only, the efficient; and it would have restricted science to physics, as change of movement of tactile bodies. The solid data of touch provided an example of ultimate substance which could exist independently, and thinking substance was a sort of ghostly replica of extended substance. It seemed that tangible bodies could exist without thinking, but thought could function only if it had tangible things to think about.

Descartes daringly simplified the elements to be analyzed and afforded welcome opportunities for rigid demonstration; but, in addition to an unwarranted omission of data furnished by sensations other than tactile, his system had no room for some of the qualities that Locke termed primary and none at all for those he called secondary or tertiary.

What, then, was to be done about acts of preference and the judgments of other than the simple attributes of extended substance? How could satisfaction in the visual data presented by a painting or in the sounds of a melody be explained? Taste was the answer,[155] a formula that could bring an end to verbal discussion but which meant nothing more or less than the whole collection of difficulties raised by the Cartesian view and was therefore no genuine reply.

The sense of taste has certain traits which made it the basis of an accepted metaphor. Its data are vivid, immediate, normally pleasant, and definitely internal, although very limited in range. The tongue touches what it tastes, so that tasting seems to be a result of touching and dependent upon it, a relation demanded by Cartesian prejudices. Taste rejects anything unpleasant, and the action of this sense occurs inside the mouth; tasting is internal to the body, so that thinking substance is somehow dependent upon and even contained within extended substance. For these reasons, all kinds of sensation and qualities of objects not directly incorporated into the Cartesian system could be explained away as merely matters of taste.

Artists and their audiences were then usually influenced, however indirectly, by idealist philosophies stemming finally from Descartes; but when they had occasion to defend their judgments on art, they were unable to do so by recourse to that philosophy. They could not establish their conclusions as necessary inferences from its elements, and they could not demonstrate that a painting was necessarily beautiful, as an inescapable consequence, clear to all candid minds, from axioms universally acknowledged. What they could do was to say that judgment of such things was the affair of taste.

Le grand goût was the taste which prevailed during the reign of Louis XIV, when the Academy was founded. The preference of patrons and artists at that time constituted a definite artistic style which it was proper, even advisable, to admire. Court circles and their adherents determined what was in the splendid manner. Good taste, *le bon goût*, has persisted through successive regimes as an innate capacity to judge excellence in art; and, although it has now become democratic, it claims the same sovereign authority that it once enjoyed as the decision of an absolute monarch. A man's honor, integrity, and other precious attributes may today on occasion be questioned without grave results, but to doubt his good taste is likely to be a final affront.

The concept of taste was, in the first place, developed to cover notable defects in the Cartesian system, and it was appropriated by Kant as a sound principle. But the void was not to be filled by a metaphor; and a word that merely represented all the problems to which it was supposed to provide an answer was little better than removing the question mark and substituting a full stop in its place. Kant's employment of the term involved critical examination of its implications, but his conclusion, characteristically, did not lead to discarding the concept. On the contrary, his work contributed to perpetuating a dogma.

Genius, the reciprocal of taste, was part of the stock of ideas that Kant inherited. He also supposed that, as the genius is a human being with specific anatomical, physiological, and mental equipment, careful study of these traits in men responsible for conspicuous achievements would lead to scientific generalizations. It should, he thought, be possible to prove a definite correlation between certain types of human organization and inevitable success.

The assumption made in the case of *beaux-arts* was paralleled here. According to that formula, we may analyze works of art to discover the nature of beauty, for they are always beautiful. Similarly, to understand how eminent accomplishments are possible, we can examine the traits of famous men, believing that certain specific types are invariably successful. Investigations that proceeded on this assumption have ranged all the way from phrenology to psychoanalysis. One group of students studied the anatomical and physiological properties of great men and concluded that it was entirely a matter of heredity, that blue blood was predestined to fame. Another school decided that mental aberration or abnormality, sometimes connected with particular diseases, was a requirement of genius.[156]

But the hypothesis on which such work has been done is plainly open to doubt. It is clear that genius is a title awarded for distinguished service by a contemporary society or its heirs and that no individual can, by virtue of his own wishes or his possession of the same traits that belonged to other great men, bestow the prize upon himself.

The needs of human societies are not at all times uniform or unchanging; what will greatly serve one social organization in its own time may be a crime, a despised and destructive course of conduct by one of its members, in the esteem of another group with quite different requirements under altered circumstances. There cannot be a special human pattern for which recognition can be guaranteed, and similarity in an individual structure to that of certain great men in the past is no basis for prediction that such a person will likewise become famous. The commonplace conclusion that may be drawn from the work of Kant and his successors in the analysis of genius is that either everybody is a genius or nobody is, and that means that the whole approach is unfruitful.

Although the concepts of both taste and genius were inadequate and resulted from attempts to compensate for defects in the Cartesian system rather than to reform that philosophy itself, they pointed to realities which men could not deny, although they could find no room for them in that closed, narrow pattern of concepts. The concept of taste was based on two unavoidable observations. One was that in human actions judgments can be and usually are made without express and immediate reference to concepts. The other was the sound observation that objects possess their qualities, not as additions or arbitrary accessions, but as immediate aspects when they are directly experienced. The concept of genius also derived from the familiar fact that men make and achieve things, some of which are notable contributions to the sum of potential experience, and the memory of those who have done so is regarded with admiration. But for a system in which nothing could be true except as deduced from a few initial axioms, the continuous increment of new forms to those already available was something that could not be denied, and yet room could be found for it only by invoking almost mythological concepts.

THE ANTINOMY OF TASTE

Inspired by the logical devices of scepticism, Kant was proud of his critical method and elaborated antinomies, or schemes of plausible but contradictory propositions, for concepts that he considered fundamental in organizing his system. Thus he drew up an antinomy for taste, employing deliberate and sustained equivocation as the proper procedure in analysis. The contradictory terms of his antinomy he termed the thesis and the antithesis, and of taste he said that the two following opposed propositions seemed true:

Thesis. The judgment of taste is not based upon concepts; for otherwise it would admit of controversy (would be determinable by proofs). *Antithesis.* The judgment of taste is based on concepts; for otherwise, despite its diversity, we could not quarrel about it (we could not claim for our judgment the necessary assent of others).[157]

Kant had admitted that "the solution of an antinomy only depends on the possibility of showing that two apparently contradictory propositions do not contradict one another in fact, but that they may be consistent."[158] That is, he sought to find a conclusion which would permit the interpretation of the thesis and antithesis as both true. His solution usually consisted of a formula which preserved the ambiguities of both initial propositions. While he did not supply a proof that the claim of either the thesis or the antithesis was exclusively true, or go behind both propositions to discover the root of error common to each, his method did have the merit that it exposed inevitable contradictions in many fields when they were based on the Cartesian point of view.

Kant's solution of the antinomy of taste was: "But all contradictions disappear if I say: the judgment of taste is based on a concept (viz., the concept of the general ground of the subjective purposiveness of nature for the judgment").[159] That is, the judgment of taste is based on concepts, but these concepts are of a kind from which conclusions cannot be deduced. Because the one word "concepts" was used in both the thesis and the antithesis, he supposed that the same thing was indicated; but in the first proposition he meant rather the perception of form, while in the second he has reference to the denotations of words. Nevertheless, he retained the Cartesian conviction that uniformity in the word implied stability in the object of thought and that true propositions regarding it should be deduced from the necessary implications of the word. Uniformity in the word "concept" should lead to universality in the communication of aesthetic experience, demonstrable by rigid proofs. Kant was distressed by the fact that this was not so in aesthetic experience; his conclusion amounts to little more than an admission of this lamentable situation. His construction of a special class of concepts was a record of observation which should have led him to re-examine the Cartesian hypothesis; but he supposed that he had disposed of this evidence when he called it the judgment of taste and explicitly gave it attributes which were irrational from the Cartesian point of view. In Kant's case the reward for attempting to believe the impossible was disillusion; he fancied that he had solved an irritating intellectual difficulty when he had condensed his perplexity into a formula.

The synthesis or conclusion of the judgment of taste preserved the contradictions with which it began. He finally asserted that the judgment of taste was based on a concept of the general ground of purposiveness in nature for the judgment. That is, the concept from which we infer aesthetic judgments is evil for the practical reason, because its assumption of purposiveness in nature would have to be true if such a conclusion were to be good. Similarly, Kant felt that the concept on which aesthetic judgment was based was false, since we cannot deduce from it conclusions which are universal and therefore self-evident to all honest and reasonable men. In this way the judgment of taste was founded on a false and evil concept; its objects consisted of matters that were undeniable but inconvenient for his theories of ethics and logic.

Like Plato, Kant rescued a frustrated hope by placing it in a transcendental region, beyond even the heaven where the gods dwell. He claimed that "the antinomies force us against our will to look beyond the sensible and to seek in the supersensible the point of union for all *a priori* faculties; because no other expedient is left to make our reason harmonize with itself."[160] But Plato's was the nobler purpose; for he wished to maintain without reservation the absolute reality of ethical values, while Kant simply longed to escape the consequences of his own individuality by making his self transcendent and universal, so that he could preserve any traditional patterns of thought that he liked without suffering the pangs of professorial scepticism.

He believed that the only way of establishing truth was by means of strict deduction from uniform concepts, and in effect he desired to exist on a plane where he could make this so by virtue of an unimpeded, universal will. The existence of his transcendental self he could not prove, and from his hypothesis of such a self, he was aware, he could prove nothing. He concluded that the judgment of taste must imply a supersensible self, beyond human experience, for the paradoxical reason that the only kinds of evidence and of proof that he admitted contradicted such an assumption.

DENIAL OF THE INDIVIDUAL

Behind this confession of disillusion, glorified as the ultimate achievement of the critical philosophy, lay a radical error of the rationalist movement in Europe from Descartes through Kant. Constructively, it was the view that identity, uniformity, and universality are the criteria of truth, goodness, and beauty. Destructively, it was a rejection of the individual as the ultimate object to which qualities pertain.

If the individual is, however, the object in which qualities are directly experienced, the only requirement is that it be possible to discover qualities of various types in such an object. Uniformity need not be the sole ground of sound ethical judgments, identity of correct logical conclusions, or universality of aesthetic experience.

The difficulties that troubled Kant could all have been alleviated had he recognized that the major and controlling principle is the individuality of objects in actual experience. Qualities are vividly and directly known as the qualifications of such objects. Individuality is logically prior to identity, uniformity, and universality. These are but special kinds of a more inclusive term which may be designated "similarity." Similarity and difference are, however, simultaneously the distinguishing characteristics of the individual object. It is unlike and distinct from some things to which it is related, and it is at the same time similar to others. Variety in the judgment of experienced qualities should be no more surprising or objectionable than diversity in the objects judged. As the individual objects known by any individual experiencer are more than one in number, so the experiencers of one object can also be plural. Similarity and difference are the fundamental traits of individuality in the activity of knowing and in the objects known, and this necessarily implies plurality in both.

Positions in space and time, for example, are determinations which can be discovered in terms of similarity and difference, but these do not derive from identical, uniform, and universal concepts, assumed to have been imposed as an arbitrary pattern on objects by a supersensible but unknowable self. Location in either of these extensive continuities requires that they be comprehensive, including a number of ascertainable positions, and that they be continuous, with the positions they include arrayed in an ascertainable order. Either if the positions were identical with one another or if the positions were not intelligibly related to one another, there would be no pattern of reference to which individual positions could be assigned and no positions for individuals.

This requirement is illustrated by the phenomena of vision, one of whose dimensions is value, that characteristic of all data of vision or color, which consists in the relative lightness and darkness of any actual object seen. The dimension of value includes a great number of different degrees of lightness and darkness, and these stages are parts of a gradual, progressive series from one extreme to the other. There is a range from extreme darkness to extreme lightness as limits, with a set of intermediate grays in between, each imperceptibly merging into its neighbors. Any actual colored object can be effectively related to this scale and its position determined, because it will be lighter than the next position on one side and darker than that on the other side. All colored objects are alike in being members of this series, but at the same time they occupy different positions within it. Without both similarity and difference in value, we should not be aware that things seen always possess the attribute of lightness and darkness or that an actual object seen can always be intelligibly related to a coherent series of differences in this respect. Some concepts are always relevant to the individual as indicating qualities which it shares with other things, but at the same time it must be perceptibly different from them, to exist as an individual and to be an object in experience.

From this example we can also derive several other important conclusions. Any given datum of color can be analyzed in terms of hue and intensity, as well as of value. But the concept of color is not visible and need not be. The word "color" signifies this concept in English; the sign brings the thing signified to attention, the sign and what it signifies are not identical.

It is the word "color" that may be written or read; and to be perceived as an object it must present differences from, as well as similarities to, other words that are seen. Black ink on white paper is the means whereby all the words on this page are visible, but at the same time the words have different shapes, consisting of distinct sets of letters. As similarity and difference are the traits of the individual object in actual experience and as perception is of individuals, so uniformity, identity, and universality are not the sole grounds of true knowledge. These are extreme cases of similarity, but differences are equally necessary for genuine knowledge of objects.

The rationalist idealists, as a result of their prejudices in favor of a world structure consisting of spatial relations ultimately confined to the data of touch, were also indifferent to temporal factors in experience. Uniformity, identity, and universality were considered to be the grounds of true knowledge of their world, and the romanticists corrected this error so far as they were vividly conscious of the past and future, however much they might ignore the present.

Time, indeed, is a set of relations that connects all actual differences, diversities, and varieties. Without awareness of development, of advance and recession, of appearance and disappearance as temporal relations, there would be no genuine field for the exertion of human energy and no effort to attain imagined ends; no ground for regretting failures and mistakes; and no justifiable hope of improvement. Any dream of progress is contingent upon the expectation that things change in time and that, where change is inevitable, something better is possible.

Lacking an adequate awareness of the temporal factor in human experience, for all their noble ambition to rid the world of obstructive institutions and outmoded patterns of thought, the rationalist idealists intended to impose a rigid, absolute form upon the human spirit. Louis XIV and Descartes, Frederick the Great and Leibniz, all looked forward to a massive, unalterable good which, once achieved, should and could not be modified. But time itself defeated this aim to impose permanent bonds; the careers of Louis and Frederick, of Descartes and Leibniz, came to an end, and their works also eventually perished. The scepticism of the ancients was revived, from Berkeley it passed to Hume and thence to Kant, and the pretensions of rationalist idealism were partially defeated.

The romantic idealists advanced beyond the limitations that their rationalist predecessors had set themselves, by discovering the pervasive reality of time in all human experience, and they effected a revolution whose effects have not yet ceased to be felt. But the romantic idealists did not go far enough in their reform. For the expansion of the self they looked back to the past as a time when they would have fared better, and they saw the future as the day when all hopes would be fulfilled. In their eagerness they neglected that temporal region of which they were in actual and exclusive possession—their present.

The romantic idealists did not abandon idealism, although they were profoundly impressed by temporal relations and by the individuality of their own precious selves. They undertook to preserve the rationalist-idealist attitude and to reconcile it with the principle of the self's individuality. This was accomplished by deciding that there could be only one true individual—an absolute I who creates all things by his own thinking, who makes the world to, by, and for himself. It was a bold reduction, and, if it had been true, there would have been only one experiencer of one world. But each romantic idealist made this absolute I, as did Kant, an inflated image of his own self. As the romantic philosophers were ascertainably different individuals, the result was a plurality of sovereign absolutes.

The empirical self was derived from an observed similarity in experiences as all forming parts of one continued series. A transcendental I was then postulated as a consequence of the fact that I is a universal concept. I is a word that can be properly used by innumerable men; at the same time each me is a unique, individual object. Kant could use these expressions intelligibly because they could similarly be employed by any number of other men. But the fact that the same word was used was no proof that the user was always the same. The existence of the transcendental I was not guaranteed by its conception. After the transcendental I had been created by imagination, the individual and multitudinous instances that gave it meaning still remained and could not be sacrificed to this abstraction. Because Kant was, his contemporaries and successors did not cease to exist in their own rights. Herder and Hegel were not merely imagined by him. They had ascertainable relations to Kant; but when they spoke, it was not his I that was speaking. The transcendental I was a flattering device to justify extreme intellectual arrogance, and to this end it was directed by the romanticists.

Kant himself was extraordinarily sensitive to the contradictions involved in the dogmas that he accepted at the hands of tradition. But his solutions were naïve rather than hypercritical, for he compounded those initial inconsistencies in his synthetic conclusions. He maintained still in suspense the dilemmas of which he was aware in the realm of speculation, and therefore his philosophy was exceptionally stimulating, for nearly every thinker could find in his work an inspiration to some more penetrating, if less comprehensive, system. Kant simply schematized the Cartesian view while exhibiting all its internal incoherence. He hoped that he had achieved a critical, transcendental philosophy when he had systematically recorded his disillusion in it; and then he undertook to maintain it by making the whole rest on an unknown, undemonstrable, and hypothetical I. If, to solve the riddle of the Cartesian universe, the self was the only thing he could not doubt, it should be magnified to the rank of an ultimate absolute.

When Kant accepted the traditional view that art provides the proper object of aesthetics, indicated by the term *beaux-arts*, he examined this dogma critically. But to solve it he concluded that recourse must be had to transcendental unity of apperception, the observed temporal coherence of his own experiences or self exalted to the order of the universe. Thus the transcendental was the answer to the critical.

Kant's authority, his patient ingenuity in analysis, and his care to retain the whole stock of irrational prejudices that he had inherited encouraged his successors to develop consequences of this doctrine. In a world in which certainty was not to be achieved when the Cartesian postulates were entertained and where a Calvinist conscience pronounced nearly everything evil, there still remained one thing that was invariably beautiful, and that was art. In his laborious exposition of disillusion, Kant was consoled by his negative categorical imperative; but his followers, lacking the stern religious discipline of his youth, turned to the only field where they could be sure of a value in experience. In art they were led to believe that they would always encounter beauty, and the only imperative they had to recognize was to develop philosophy on a foundation of aesthetics, with ethics justified by what they thought to be the nature of an artist.

IV

Romantic Idealism

HERDER

THE romantic reaction against the Enlightenment did not lead to surrendering idealism, since it resulted in substituting another kind for that which was given up. When the time came to work out reformed metaphysical systems congenial to the new emotional attitude, the romantic philosophers found a rich quarry of materials in Kant. His doctrines became dominant in the German universities; although there were few who carried on his teaching without modification, there were fewer still who questioned its broader assumptions and implications. One of the latter was Herder; but his protests were phrased in such unphilosophical language and his constructive ideas were so poorly related to one another that Kantians found it easy to discredit him.

Herder objected to the a priori mental categories of Kant; a study of the development of language, he said, shows that reason and speech advanced together and depended on each other. Time and space, instead of being imposed on things by the mind, were concepts derived from experience. According to Herder, both human history and nature evolved from certain natural necessities and followed fixed laws. The rule of progress in history corresponded to a parallel law in nature, apparent in the advance from the inorganic to the organic, as well as in the spiritual struggles of mankind. History was progressive development toward humanity. But this principle was not understood by Herder in the current sense; things did not evolve from one another, but rather, he thought, they all emerged from God, the eternal and infinite being, so that the orderly development of the world resulted from divine power and reason.[161]

Herder was, however, a principal source for one of the distinctive beliefs of scholarship and science in the nineteenth century—the conviction that history is a continuous process, an unfolding progress, in time.

His treatment of art and aesthetics was, on the whole, less influential, but it was at least voluminous. He published a critical analysis of Lessing's *Laokoon*[162] and also a work on the theory of sculpture;[163] but his chief production of this type was his *Kalligone*,[164] a systematic attack on Kant's *Critique of Judgment*. Before this he had written a hostile analysis of Kant's *Critique of Pure Reason*, of which one Hegelian seemed to think he had fully disposed when he said: "It would have been better for Herder's reputation if he had left it unwritten."[165] Herder felt keenly the lack of ethical seriousness, as distinguished from the categorial imperative of a censorious conscience, in the Kantian attitude; but it was hardly a persuasive refutation to call it "infinite phantasmagorias, blind guesses, fantasies, schematisms, empty printed words, so-called transcendental ideas and speculations . . . . a public market-place for extreme impudence."[166]

In his constructive theory of art and aesthetics Herder was himself unable to achieve superiority to Kant because he also accepted such principles as taste, the *beaux-arts*, the sublime, and others that Kant had assumed as self-evidently true. He was, at the same time, partially responsible for a popular inference from the term *bildende Kunst*, with which Lessing had replaced the older *schöne Kunst;* for he declared that art was therefore plastic or formative and cultural or educational, but it was the same as *beaux-arts*.[167]

Herder's hostility to Kant has been explained as an unwillingness to follow his teacher in leaving dogmatism behind and advancing to critical transcendentalism; it has also been connected with an unfavorable review written by Kant on his book dealing with the philosophy of history. Although in some respects he anticipated by a few years the extreme nationalism of Fichte and although his early attacks on Kant were unsuccessful at the time, his importance in developing a modern, romantic type of history is recognized.

SCHILLER

A profound dissatisfaction with the ethical views of Kant was also felt by Schiller; a harsh, negative conscience seemed to him an unpromising guide to moral perfection. In its place he put the concept of freedom; for, while in nature, he thought, all things act by necessity, man alone is free to do what he will. The transition from the passivity of sensation to the activity of thinking and willing occurs, he believed, through the mediation of aesthetic freedom. Before carnal man can become rational, he must first become aesthetic. Souls that are aesthetically refined possess a faculty which functions where virtue is lacking and aids it when present. This faculty is taste, Schiller asserted, and it is the duty of the civilized state to foster the aesthetic development of man, because only through it can man progress ethically.[168]

By placing Kant's *Critique of Judgment* at the basis of his speculative thought, instead of the treatises on ethics and logic, and by stressing aesthetic freedom rather than a forbidding imperative he worked out a positive program for romantic expansion. He rejected fear as the ruling human motive and set love in its stead. Ethical perfection was to be the characteristic of the "beautiful soul," in which impulse and duty were no longer opposed but in complete harmony.

Schiller was himself a potent source of inspiration to poets and philosophers of the Romantic Era in Germany, although his views were expressed with greater vagueness than the later, more systematic, and less admirable interpretations of his opinions. If ethics was to be based on aesthetics, it was an easy step to assert that the beautiful, loving soul is free to do what it wills and that what it wills is right because it is beautiful.

Fully as important in the history of thought as Schiller's concept of the beautiful soul was his theory of the play-impulse as the ground and origin of art.[169] The term "beautiful soul" has almost vanished as a result of the ridicule with which it eventually met, but play as an explanation of art has long met with a favorable reception, and this view, again, was based on a suggestion to be found in Kant. According to Schiller, the play-impulse springs from superfluous energy, it is a preparation for mature responsibilities, and it manifests itself early in life through pleasure in imitations. But, he claimed, "in man's every situation it is play and only play that makes him complete and develops his twofold nature in unity. . . . . Through the ideal of beauty which reason presents, an ideal of the play-impulse is also offered, which man in all his playing should keep in view."[170]

But Schiller's notion of taste, as in Kant's *Critique of Judgment* from which he derived it, is a traditional metaphor and not a solid, philosophical principle. His assimilation of aesthetic value and art to play assumed the *beaux-arts* doctrine; and, even if art and beauty were the same, the differences between them and play are more significant than the similarities. Such examples of play as Schiller cited—the gymnastic games of the Greeks, Roman gladiatorial combats, English horse races, Spanish bull-fights, and Venetian gondola races—may have conspicuous aesthetic value, it is true; but it is no more necessary a quality to such designated activities than it is to products of the techniques of design. Art, games and sports, and play all seemed to Schiller the diversions of idleness; they were wasteful but almost innocent in principle. The bond that these things had in common was freedom from ethical and serious responsibility, in Schiller's opinion, but this negative moral criterion was hardly an adequate way to distinguish the aesthetic field. It reduced art and aesthetic value to the rank that they might hold in a stern Calvinist school of virtue; they were, like recesses on the playground, mild evils, easily tolerated in brief intervals between grim, predestined tasks.

Thus, in spite of Schiller's stirring and hopeful appeal to freedom rather than to natural necessity or a negative human conscience as the mainspring of conduct, he still retained concepts that continued to oppress German speculative thought—principles such as taste and *schöne Kunst*, to which he added the reduction of art and beauty to incidental aspects of play.

FRIEDRICH SCHLEGEL

Like Schiller, Friedrich Schlegel was both a poet and a philosopher, and he has properly been called the spiritual leader of the earlier romantics in Germany.[171] His father was the man who had made the work of Batteux known to the German public. With his brother August Wilhelm, Friedrich Schlegel was the source of many controlling ideas in the movement, since he fostered an enthusiasm for the Middle Ages, and his opinions on such matters as the forms of literature appropriate to the new spirit were decisive. He was also one of the chief founders of oriental studies in modern Europe, and in Indian philosophy he discovered many precedents for rationalizing the romantic temper.[172]

During his residence in Paris he studied the paintings in the Louvre, becoming especially interested in the art of the Netherlands. This led him to investigate the special characteristics of Christian art and to ask: "Is it to be expected that again in our present time a true painter will arise and develop? It is not to be expected, but who could decide that it is absolutely impossible?" Apparently even the leaders of the romantic movement were aware of the sterility of early romanticism as a source of inspiration to painting. At the same time, August Wilhelm Schlegel and his wife Caroline wrote conversations on paintings in the Dresden gallery, and soon afterward Tieck published his novel, *Franz Sternbalds Wanderungen*, the imaginary account of a journey to Rome made by a pupil of Dürer.[173]

Friedrich Schlegel's view that love is the basis of philosophy—a view which became an intrinsic part of the movement that he guided —is set forth in a book that contained the substance of his lectures on philosophy. He approached his theme in a way typical of idealism, through introspection of the self: "The philosophy of life, as it sets forth with only one simple position—life, viz., man's inner life, is restricted to no particular sphere, but embraces them all in their fit seasons and occasions. . . . . Philosophy, I said, takes nothing for granted but life—an internal life, that is."[174]

The essence of the soul as disclosed to Schlegel through introspection is love: "The soul is nothing less than the faculty of love in man."[175] But he condemned the transcendental philosophy, the culmination of rationalist idealism, because, "without proper end or aim, it goes on continually revolving around itself as a centre, and within its own charmed circle. . . . . It places perfection in an abstraction carried continually higher and higher in its emptiness."[176] Against the futility of such philosophizing, he reported: "There is, moreover, another state, or rather quality of the soul, wherein the else divided reason and fancy are intimately associated and entirely reunited. This is a natural, pure affection and the very faculty of love, which is itself the soul and the peculiar essence of man's spiritual soul."[177]

This was romanticism at its best, a generous and humane attitude which won for it admiration and sympathy. But it rested on the idealist foundation of introspection, on the me as the sole, uniquely true object. When Schlegel's loving soul was merged with Schiller's beautiful soul, the consequences were not altogether happy, for to be in love with one's own beautiful soul was not a promising way to construct a theory of ethics, and in practice it could conveniently ignore the social aspect of moral obligations.

WACKENRODER AND TIECK

Wackenroder, whose work was edited, with additions, by Tieck, was more effective than the philosophers in relaxing the control of letters over art that had prevailed in Europe since the late sixteenth century. Instead, he urged a direct and enthusiastic approach to the works of art themselves. Wackenroder died when only twenty-five, but his influence was largely responsible for transforming the popular German attitude toward art. His *Heart-Throbs of a Cloistered Art-Lover* combined with the prestige of Winckelmann's *History of Ancient Art* to stimulate an emotional, romantic ardor—an almost religious cult of art.[178]

The notes prepared by Wackenroder were not made with a view primarily to publication, but when Tieck saw them he realized at once that this approach to art would appeal deeply to the new generation; and, given a title that referred to Lessing's *Nathan*, it was a potent force in shaping the opinions of such writers as the Schlegel brothers. Wackenroder had a fairly limited acquaintance with art, except for his visits to certain German galleries, but he stirred up a vigorous admiration for mediaeval art as an expression of the national German character.[179]

He had to rely on the popular sources current in his day,[180] so that modern scholarship has superseded a great deal of what he accepted as historical facts. But a special veneration for art that finally springs from Wackenroder has sustained the efforts of archaeologists, connoisseurs, and historians ever since.

A religious, mediaeval atmosphere was created by the very title of Wackenroder's principal book, and the lives of artists were explicitly treated as those of the "blessed saints of art."[181] He longed to visit Italy, he wrote, "in order that I may kneel down before the immortal works of the great artists, and confess all my wonder and love to them."[182] He concluded his life of Francia by saying: "The genius of art, in the eyes of the initiated, has at length also called him holy, and surrounded his head with the halo which is his due as a true martyr of enthusiasm for art."[183]

Although he accepted the identification of beauty and art, he did not do so without reservations, for he insisted that each work arouses a new feeling for which the vague word "beauty" does not suffice.[184] His attitude toward works of art led him to say: "I compare the enjoyment of noble works of art to prayer."[185] But he deliberately rejected the theory of the Idea as the essence of art, because of his belief that the immediate sensory object should be that to which enthusiasm is directed: "just as poets, in whom an unquenchable lyric fire burns, are not content with great and astonishing ideas but strive to discharge their keen, wild strength above all in the visible, sensory instruments of their art, in expressive words."[186]

This recognition that the work of art is concretely always an immediate sensory pattern and not a mental form or abstract idea was one which would have been offensive to the rationalist idealists, and it was practically ignored by the professional thinkers of romanticism. It had been a distinctive trait of idealism, and a view of which it was proud, to hold the data of sensation essentially unreal compared with the abstract ideas treated by reason. The empirical was an inferior realm from which philosophers should fly to the transcendental. A deep-seated prejudice against the data of the senses as unreliable, transient, uncontrollable by reason, and tempting to evil prevented an effective and sound theory of art. Leibniz and other teachers of the Enlightenment clearly failed to realize that words themselves, spoken or heard and written or read, are also sensory objects, and hence in their opinion words alone were innocent of the original sins of sensation.

Prizing concepts only and believing that word and thought are identical, idealists also turned the mind inward and found in contemplation of the self a unique source of intellectual security. Schlegel's doctrine of love, acutely appreciating value in an object, and Wackenroder's realization that a work of art, when it is actually an object, is necessarily a sensory pattern were both illuminating insights, but they could not prevail against the fixed convictions of idealism.

By other romantic idealists Wackenroder's religious zeal for art, substituting works of art for relics of the saints, was appropriated for the benefit of the Idea of art, instead of leaving it where he had placed it and where it definitely belonged.

It is true that philosophers, like other writers and speakers, must fix their attention on things intangible while they consider what they will say; but in that particular their case is not radically different from that of artists, who must also design their works before producing them. The cost of an artist's materials and the technical difficulties in producing a work of art are greater than when dealing with words. The medium of the philosopher is so flexible and efficient production of words is so familiar an activity that to make words is easy and cheap compared with the cost and labor involved in creating a work of art. The gap between conception and sensory realization in speech and writing is so brief that most philosophers, however, often mistakenly infer that words and thought are identical.

In the case of art it is obviously false to say that all we can know is our ideas. We do know ideas which are not sensory, but we also know statues which are objects for our senses as well. To call all things in experience ideas, as did Descartes, Berkeley, and the idealists in general, because philosophers attend only to ideas while they are writing, ignoring the sensory aspects of their own actions and exiling large tracts of ordinary fact from reality, was an unjustified procedure.

Only idealists sworn to uphold the dogma of their sect could claim that all we can know are ideas. When they examined the self as a uniquely reliable object, it is true they did not attend to a sensory object, but the official thinkers could feel the pens with which they wrote and see the hands that held those pens. If by the term "ideas" they meant objects in general, the name is in error, for objects include more than ideas. If they insisted that objects consist wholly of mental forms and there are no distinctly sensory objects, then the witness of works of art should have freed them from their solitude.

It was not a vague transcendental idea that stirred Wackenroder's enthusiasm. He knew what he was doing when he awarded his devotion to the tangible and visible objects produced by artists. He found precious values and exceptional significance in those sensory patterns, but he did not suppose that he was dealing with purely mental forms. He was not limited to shadows projected inside the walls of a mind where he was forever imprisoned; he opened his eyes, and he was enraptured by things that other men had made. It was not a mental sign or an imaginary image that he had before him, and no such objects intervened between his attention and the work of art. With confident happiness he possessed the work of art itself.

FICHTE

The romantic mood achieved powerful expression in the works of Fichte and Schelling. Fichte, indeed, carried out the implications of previous idealist speculation to their natural conclusions; he enunciated principles by which German political programs have been rationalized ever since. He was not much concerned with art; but, as Schelling was later to discover, the romantic theory of art and the artist was pre-eminently congenial to Fichte's philosophy, in which the ideal ruler was called an artist. Fichte's most influential book appeared shortly before those of other leading romanticists;[187] but, since he initiated the particular development known as "absolute idealism" and since it was this point of view which persisted even when the original emotional impulses of romanticism had declined, it is better to consider him after discussing the poet-philosophers. It is significant that

Fichte, Schelling, and Hegel, who led absolute idealism, began their careers as students of theology, and perhaps major aspects of their thought can be traced to certain less admirable aspects of primitive tribal beliefs.

Fichte's first publication was issued anonymously at Königsberg, with the aid of Kant; and when its true authorship was revealed, the young man's reputation was immediately established, for the learned had believed it to be Kant's own composition.[188] Fichte felt that he alone truly grasped the critical philosophy and was loyal to its teachings, but the older thinker declared later that Fichte's system, as represented by the *Science of Knowledge*, was untenable; he particularly resented appeals to the *Critique of Pure Reason*, in which Fichte supposed that he was simply expanding the Kantian philosophy and freeing it from misinterpretations.

Fichte held that philosophy has nothing to do with independently given facts, since our experience is composed exclusively of our ideas, behind which there is nothing that transcends them; speculation should concern itself, instead, with the investigation of how our ideas necessarily develop. The method by which he deduced the necessities governing the development of ideas was afterward glorified as the distinctive contribution of the absolute idealists and held to be superior to the orthodox logic of Aristotle. He held that reality consisted of a threefold act; thesis, antithesis, and synthesis; but any equilibrium attained in the synthesis was only temporary, for it again functioned as a thesis, opposed by a new antithesis and followed by another synthesis.

Fichte also based his views on his doctrine of the self; it did not appear in empirical manifestations of consciousness but was necessary for their existence and made them possible. The individual I had a world external to it which limited the individual's thoughts and actions. This ordinary I was human, individual, and finite, as distinguished from the divine, universal, and absolute I. The absolute I, he said, was not a precise something but a self-sufficient force creating itself in action.

Fichte established three stages of the self: thesis, the I posits or creates itself; antithesis, the I posits or creates that which is not itself; and synthesis, the I and that which is not I limit each other. The foundation of theoretical science, he held, is the I limited or defined by that which is not I. The practical sciences are based on that which is not I but is limited or defined by the I. According to Fichte, the not-I is an object which the I gives itself rather than an object independently presenting itself. The objective world exists only as a determination which the I sets itself; therefore, the world is dependent upon the I, and without this I there would be no world.

In creation, Fichte believed, the I limits itself and by an act of will determines itself. The dualism of subject and object is an illusion of the pure reason, but from this dualism the I is free in action. The conflict between the ideal and the practical is the motive power of historical development. Freedom is superior to theoretical truth; it is not an abstraction but the essentially real. Freedom is indeed the capacity of the I to create itself and to assert itself through limitations of time and space. To realize itself, the I must struggle; the necessary liberty of the will to assert itself demands that it create something against which it can be exerted.

But Fichte also said that the absolute I, if separated from individuals, is an empty abstraction and that God is not a person, for in that case He would be limited by His object. The freedom of the absolute I, he declared, progressively to manifest itself through the moral order in history is itself God.

The purpose of the state, according to Fichte, is to direct individuals toward the achievement of culture by all mankind. The relation of the state of which he was a member to the rest of humanity was that of a special mission. A zealous and prophetic nationalism had stirred him after the collapse of the Prussian state in 1808.[189] He proclaimed that everything good is German, everything evil is foreign. The development of national culture depends on national independence. The inner revival of Germany is necessary to mankind in general. The renovation of the species begins with the German as the highest type; and if Germany should perish, humanity itself will be lost, without hope of resurrection.

In his teaching on the philosophy of history,[190] Fichte had already announced his doctrine of the "normal folk"—the race which sets a standard for the rest of mankind. From the very beginning, without either science or technique, this people was in a condition of perfect, rational culture, for the rational could never have developed from the irrational. Along with the "normal folk" there existed entirely primitive peoples—a teaching consistent with his philosophic idealism and absolute self-assurance. According to him, the masses of the people, even those of the "normal folk," were only instruments in the hands of the *political artist* and were tolerable only so far as they surrendered themselves to the will of the creative individual. To serve humanity, it was their first duty to place their wills at the disposition of the state.

Fichte's program was a natural result of the romantic view of the artist's nature, as this had been developed in the manner described in chapter ii, the "Natural History of Art." Fichte described his absolute I in terms based on what he understood to be the activity of the artist. The artist selects and transforms his materials; the world exists only for that purpose. The transcendental artist creates his materials, besides giving them new shapes; to exercise his genius he gives himself materials to work with. Whatever he makes is both good and beautiful because his actions make it so.

When Fichte gave up Kant's doctrine of the unknown thing by itself, he supposed he had rid himself of an embarrassing difficulty; but he could not so easily dispose of it. Kant had said that there was a synthetic unity in all ideas which is the self, but Fichte had reduced the multiplicity of individual selves to one, in which all were merged— an absolute I. He concluded that there could be only one true I; for if there were to be more than one absolute I, there would be as many different worlds. To avoid a plurality of worlds, Fichte denied a plurality of selves. But the relation between the numerous empirical selves and the one absolute I still constituted a difficulty fully as serious as Kant's unknown thing by itself. Fichte condemned Kant's thing by itself, but he pretended that he had adequately dealt with the great gap in his own system when he simply declared it to be a mystery.[191]

When Fichte asserted that the moral order of the universe was itself God, he was obliged to resign his professorship at Jena on charges of atheism. Later, however, he returned to this principle, phrasing it in a fashion more satisfactory to introspection. The I alone is now real, and the world is something I create to exercise my will. The revised version he supported by appeals to local pride, and this made him not an outcast but a national hero. He had told the chosen people something of which they had been aware all along but had never dared to say. Santayana paraphrased this doctrine, so delightful to Fichte's audience, with the words: "the German mind is the self-consciousness of God."[192]

Fichte was in this way responsible for the view, so acceptable to an ambitious, centralized government, that it is man's first duty to serve the German state. The government-controlled universities of Germany, by fostering idealist philosophies of one type and another, were indoctrinating the leaders of the German people with the conviction that they were members of the "normal folk," whose conscious will must subdue what it created unconsciously.

In practice the consequences of combining the rationalist demand for uniformity with the romantic dogma of absolute will were destructive. When the ruler became the self-sufficient source of the state's untrammeled will, his followers were ready to ignore the truth that the responsibilities and capacities of mankind are really to be found only in human individuals. To survive, human individuals must co-operate in societies, but they are numerous and must be so. Any particular specimen who asserts the contrary as to himself is bound to be brought to account in the course of time. To make other men passive instruments in the hands of the state reduces them to means for executing the ruler's ambitions or wreaking his vengeance; and, although they may willingly consent to such self-abasement, it will still remain true that they attempt in vain to sacrifice themselves to a deified abstraction, for they cannot abolish the fact that the living, multitudinous human individuals are the sole possessors of human intellects, wills, and feelings.

But in a culture conducting itself on principles justified by romantic idealism, the wills of inferiors should be only wills that conform and obey. Where there is any doubt or hesitation on this score, the absolute I, residing in the state's administration, is quick to exercise the compulsion of force. Arbitrary force and violence are not the final resort of a decent society, as in other types of civilization, but the initial ground of reality for romantic idealists.

The beliefs with which Fichte indoctrinated Germany seemed to be confirmed by events in 1813, in 1870, and again for a few years after 1914. The verdict of 1918 was really a self-made obstacle for the absolute I, which could in 1939 reassure itself by declaring that it was by nature an artist. It could proceed to grasp the materials that it needed, clearing neighboring lands of inferior, more primitive, peoples, to accomplish its beautiful design and increase the goods of the superior, normal, and obedient folk.

When national policy rests frankly upon an appeal to violence, one might expect the decision reached through force to be accepted. Consistently with their beliefs, the German idealists invoked force in 1914. But after 1918 they did not acquiesce in the result of their assaults; they carried on an uninterrupted campaign to mitigate and suspend the sentence. Liberal opinion was persuaded to view sympathetically the German plea to dismiss the charge that Germany was guilty of responsibility for the war and to respond generously when Germany aspired to economic reconstruction and rehabilitation in the eyes of the rest of the world.

But the grounds of German demands after that war were misunderstood or ignored. The absolute I can do no wrong, it can admit no mistakes or errors; it can see in obstruction of its ends only a temporary defeat of its beautiful aims, a stimulus to persist, using any means whatever. For the romantic idealist, when he encounters temporary defeat, the proper mood is self-pity. The only sense of wrong he can feel is the injustice of resistance by the inferior races who resent the attempt to exterminate them. Moral conversion or regeneration of the absolute I is unthinkable. It can be wounded, but only in its pride; it can beg for mercy to heal its wounds while it prepares to renew the attack, but it will show none.

SCHELLING

The dependence of romantic idealism on a particular theory of art was at last clearly brought to the surface by Schelling. The implications of the belief condensed into the formula *beaux-arts* were fully accepted; a conviction that art is always beautiful and beauty is always to be found in art gave the romantic idealists what seemed to them an undeniable example of the creative will. So long as this relation of a set of techniques to aesthetic value was admitted as a matter of course, the idealists had what appeared to be obvious proof of their position, for the simple reason that romantic idealism was itself a system of inferences founded upon the assumption, without parallel elsewhere in human experience, that only certain human products possess aesthetic value as an intrinsic property. Schelling's contribution, then, was to make explicit and definite the place of art and the artist in the ordered conclusions of the school to which he belonged.

His intimate connection with other intellectual leaders of that period in Germany helps us to see that his views were not those of a solitary eccentric but were natural results of the German spirit in its most characteristic and fruitful phase. At Tübingen he was friendly with Hölderlin and Hegel, who were both five years older than he but were his fellow-students. Later he became acquainted with Schiller at Weimar, and on the recommendation of Goethe he was called to a professorship at Jena in 1798, when Fichte was also teaching there. The chief source of romantic zeal in Jena was Caroline, the wife of A. W.

Schlegel, whom Schelling married in 1803 after her divorce. He was for a number of years, following 1806, secretary of the Academy of Sciences in Munich, and in 1841 he was called to Berlin, at the invitation of King Friedrich Wilhelm IV, to oppose Hegelian pantheism. Schelling was a celebrated and popular teacher before Hegel became known, but in his old age he was neglected, since the theosophical character of his later speculation had little interest for a newer generation already tending toward a materialist interpretation of idealism. It is only recently that Schelling's theory of mythology has been revived as a justification for views officially authorized in contemporary Germany.[193]

Although some historians have distinguished as many as five distinct stages in the thought of Schelling, other critics have found but two. In the first, from 1797 to 1806, his emphasis was on the principle of identity, while from 1806 to 1854 he developed a mystical theosophy and monotheism. The first stage he afterward called his "negative" philosophy in contrast with his later thought, which he called "positive." But the differences between these had to do with the topics discussed and his method of treating them rather than changes in his fundamental point of view, for throughout he adhered to a monism based on the will.

His attitude is concisely presented in a discussion of freedom: "There is, in the last and ultimate instance, no other real being at all than will. Will is original being and to it pertain all the predicates: self-founded, eternal, independent of time, self-affirming. The whole of philosophy strives only to find the highest expression for it."[194] While the absolute I is genuinely free, since it follows no law but of its own making, the empirical I is limited by its objects.[195] To affirm the primacy of will was recognized by Schelling as Fichte's greatest achievement; Kant had reached it as the culmination of his practical philosophy, but Fichte had made the autonomous will the very first and ultimate concept of philosophy.[196]

The famous principle of identity originated with Schelling and was explained by him in this way:

How can ideas be conceived as shaping themselves according to objects, and at the same time as shaping themselves to ideas? . . . . How at once the objective world conforms itself to ideas in us, and ideas in us conform themselves to the objective world, it is impossible to conceive, unless there exists between the two worlds—the real and the ideal—a preëstablished harmony. But this preëstablished harmony is not itself conceivable, unless the activity, whereby the objective world is produced, is originally identical with that which displays itself in volition, and *vice versa*. Now it is undoubtedly a productive activity that displays itself in volition; all free action is productive and productive only with consciousness. If, then, we suppose, since the two activities are one only in their principle, that the same activity which is productive with consciousness in free action, is productive without consciousness in the production of the world, this preëstablished harmony is a reality and the contradiction is solved.[197]

Spinoza's view that the order of things and of thoughts is parallel, because both are aspects of one substance, was in this fashion revived to explain away a recurrent problem of idealism. If orderly but independent sensory patterns could not be instantaneously transformed through the magic spells of volition, it seemed hard to believe that will was the very essence of the world. But will, whether conscious or unconscious, was still the same identical will, and the principle of identity should preserve desire as the only genuine cause and essential reality.

History was interpreted by Schelling as a never ending revelation of the absolute I, which divided itself into the conscious and the unconscious solely to make itself manifest, while remaining the eternal ground of both and their identity.

He confessed that the absolute was not conceivable by the empirical I, but it could be experienced in the beautiful. Art and religion—manifestations of God—were therefore superior to philosophy; for, although reason could conceive no more than the idea of God, art gave us His presence. Art afforded experience of the absolute through intuition of beauty.[198] With this claim the return of romantic idealism to its origin was complete; art became proof of that absolute I which is will.

Such statements might lead us to suppose that Schelling shared Wackenroder's enthusiasm for art, but Schelling corrected any such expectation by stating that the importance of art for philosophy was not the beauty to be found in sensory things, because philosophy was concerned solely with truth. It was not satisfaction in works of art that delighted the thinker but the logical conclusion that if beauty is always to be found in art, then art always manifests the absolute. Schelling declared of the philosopher:

Art is to him a reflection of the divine, a necessary and immediate image of the absolute. . . . . . Philosophy, in spite of its essential identity with art, is always and necessarily science, that is, idea, while art is always and necessarily art, that is, real. . . . . Genius is its own law; it rejects foreign authority, but acknowledges its own, for it is only genius in so far as it is the highest law. Philosophy recognizes the fact that genius is an absolute law unto itself, because it is itself not only self-government, but aspires to the principle of all self-government. It has been seen in all ages that true artists are calm, simple, great, and necessary, like Nature herself. . . . .

We say that the philosophy of art is a presentation of the absolute world in the form of art. . . . . That which the philosopher sees in it, and which it is his duty to demonstrate, is truth of a higher kind, is identical with absolute beauty, the truth of ideas. . . . .

And, finally, let me say that it is a disgrace for those who have a direct or indirect part in the government of the state to lack either a real love or a real knowledge of art. For nothing honors princes and those in authority more than to prize the arts, to admire their products, and to encourage their production; and there is no sadder or more disgraceful sight than when those, who have the money to promote the highest perfection of art, spend their money to encourage bad taste, barbarity, and insinuating vulgarity.[199]

The field named by Baumgarten, organized by Kant, and prized by Fichte was elevated to a new position by Schelling. For him aesthetics was merely another term for the philosophy of art, but he made it the culmination of speculative thought.

When he cited specific examples, his conclusions were less persuasive, since, for example, he called Guido Reni the genuine painter of the soul.[200] His evaluation of the function of art has, however, had more durable success. He declared: "The objective world is only the primitive and still unconscious poetry of the mind; the universal organon of philosophy, and the keystone of its entire arch, is the philosophy of art."[201]

The romantic idealists saw in art and the artist an obvious proof of human freedom, and in the beauty of art they supposed they had discovered final proof of the absolute I as will. But it was as much an error to suppose that art was always and alone beautiful, as it was to fancy that only the artist enjoyed a measure of freedom. In their enthusiasm the romantics went too far and gave an example a monopoly of the truth which it merely illustrated. The truth was that any technical product whatever was a proof, although perhaps not so obvious, of this aspect of human experience. The capacities of human minds and hands to imagine and to create are such that they can never be wholly obedient, as inert tools. Anything that a man makes he must first have imagined; anything made is a genuinely new addition to the sum, although perhaps inconspicuous and unimportant. The techniques of design and the *beaux-arts* do not alone exhibit human freedom; any technique at all displays it. Human freedom to create is established by technique in general, not by a group of special techniques. The techniques of design enjoy a monopoly of aesthetic value no more than they do of freedom.

Schelling's energetic, wilful philosophizing cared little for internal consistency; and, although it flattered the artist, it still failed to solve a problem that had confronted Kant and his idealist successors.

That problem was: How is it possible for a technical classification of sensory patterns to possess positive and conspicuous aesthetic value as an invariable attribute? He had assumed a pre-established harmony between the transcendental I and the empirical objects of sensation, calling this harmony the principle of identity. Since his transcendendental I was a wayward, irresponsible, lawless sublimation of the irrational concept "genius," it was even more difficult than in the system of Leibniz to accept pre-established harmony as a satisfactory solution.

For Leibniz, as for Spinoza, both the self and its objects were orderly, and there was a clear relation between the two types of order. Since Schelling's infinitely expansive and self-creating will was no such predictable being, his hypothesis left the problem in an aggravated form. Spinoza's belief that the order of the two modes of substance was parallel and the view of Leibniz that there was a foreordained harmony between monads expressed speculative ideals which were unsustained by evidence and no more justified in abstract analysis than were their opposites. But Schelling's theory demanded harmony between things which were by definition irreconcilable.

THE PERSISTENCE OF IDEALISM IN THE THEORY OF ART AND AESTHETICS

The persistence of idealism in the explanation of art and aesthetics is a remarkable thing.[202] Many thinkers who are professed opponents of idealism have retained typical idealist attitudes in their understanding of art, although they have not, like the idealists, been left with little but art to cite by way of evidence. Even realists are often overawed and hesitate to investigage a field which the idealists succeed in reserving to themselves by surrounding it with a mystery, romantic in its capacity to excite curiosity but uninviting to inquiring minds because of its incredible assumptions. In America, where for some years idealist philosophies have ceased to occupy their once dominant position, aesthetics often is a preserve cultivated chiefly by thinkers of that type. But when art is identified with aesthetics and aesthetics is expounded in compliance with the teachings of German romantic idealism, it is not surprising that aesthetics is often regarded with suspicion and that art is a mysterious luxury when its function is to afford proof of idealist views.

The general distinction of idealist theories has been their reliance on self-contemplation as an irrefutable basis, an indubitable certainty in speculation, while discounting the evidence of the senses and the testimony of technique. An absolute I, unknown or else identified with the will, is set up against the empirical self.

The rationalist idealists held that ideas should exhibit traits which they admired. They demanded identity, uniformity, and universality; but when these expectations were defeated, they despaired of the efficacy of reason itself.

The romantic idealists entertained the notion of a self with precisely the contrary attributes, since the self-created and self-affirming will produced objects only to exercise its courage, vindicating in this way the claims of diversity, irregularity, and eccentricity. The inherited concept of genius and the recognized classification of the *beaux-arts* were accepted as conclusive proof of the romantic idealists' revised philosophy.

Their protest against rationalist idealism served to rid the world of a static and sterile monotony. But, prolonged as unceasing, desperate conflict waged only for the sake of exercise, it was something that the world could not bring itself to tolerate until a century later.[203]

Romantic idealism had been banished from many spheres of human interest, although it lingered still in the shallows of aesthetic theory and in the obscure depths of national policy and political theory. In these latter fields it was often convenient to disguise philosophical idealism as moral idealism, and it was not until recent years that political theory generally abandoned principles that had developed during the Age of Reason in favor of others that were implicit in romantic idealism.[204]

V

The Absolute Artist of Romantic Idealism

HITLER BY NATURE AN ARTIST

THE subsequent development of German idealism after Schelling need not be pursued further, for its essential presuppositions have by now been examined and the claim that metaphysical idealism and ethical idealism are identical can be tested by the career of its most powerful exponent. The views of Hitler on art implied acceptance of romantic idealism if they were to be rationalized at all, but his own thought was not much affected by any of the professional philosophers, such as Hegel or Nietzsche, who came after Fichte and Schelling.

The German Chancellor's esteem for himself as an artist was dramatically recorded in the crucial days just before his armies crossed the frontier into Poland. He gave an audience to Ambassador Sir Nevile Henderson in Berlin, and his statements were reported to Lord Halifax in dispatches which were soon afterward published in a Blue Book by the British government.[205]

In his telegram of August 25, 1939, the Ambassador related that during his conversation with the Chancellor on that day, Hitler was "absolutely calm and normal and spoke with great earnestness and apparent sincerity."[206] He then continued with a most significant statement: "Among the points mentioned by Herr Hitler . . . . were that he was *by nature an artist*, not a politician, and once the Polish question had been settled he would end his life as an artist, not as a warmonger."[207]

Public reaction to the statement was immediate and significant. Hitler's words were analyzed with reference to sanity and sincerity, but the underlying romantic doctrine was not attacked. The question raised was: How could the leader of a powerful people, speaking with earnestness and apparent sincerity, claim that he was by nature an artist, under such circumstances, if he was absolutely calm and normal?[208]

Those who looked upon his statement as irrational or insincere pointed to his frustrated ambitions to enrol as an art student, and his mediocre works were reproduced in the press because they seemed to prove the logical incapacity of the Chancellor who, at the very moment he launched a campaign of conquest, could think of himself as an artist.[209]

Most distressed by Hitler's statements were, of course, those who held similar romantic views, although they had to concede that he was an artist, even if a mediocre one. They sometimes sought to preserve their precious doctrine by attempting to minimize the importance of this particular assertion of the Chancellor or by interpreting it in a sense which would permit them still to retain confidence in it. In this way there were three main types of response. First was the claim that Hitler meant he was a man who paints pictures and preferred the occupation of artist to the task of dictatorship. Second was the plea that the Chancellor accepted the role of the artist, with the implications attached to it by romantic idealism, simply for the purposes of effective propaganda. Finally, it was suggested that, even if Hitler did adopt the same conclusions entertained by Fichte and Schelling regarding the artist and art, his conduct did not depend on views expressed by sophisticated philosophers who lived over a century ago and whose names Hitler had perhaps heard but whose works he had probably never read.

In reply to the claim that by the term "artist" Hitler simply meant a man who paints pictures, it should be said that, except for a very few critics and scholars, Germans do not normally mean that by the word *Künstler*. But philosophic idealism is the all-pervasive background of most German thinking and conspicuously so when it comes to art. Hitler never displayed the remarkable originality of thought which he would have to possess in order to differ so thoroughly from other German minds; and, by comparing what has been said earlier under the head of the "Natural History of Art" with the passages to be cited from *Mein Kampf*, it will readily be seen that while it is possible to entertain such an artificial hypothesis, evidence for it is completely lacking.

As for the suggestion that Hitler was not sincere in appealing to the romantic-idealist view of the artist and his function, if he was merely trying to produce a desired impression, his efforts were unsuccessful, for his audience on this occasion was primarily the British Ambassador and those to whom he reported. Hitler had no definite expectation, it may be supposed, that his words on the occasion of this interview would be published to the world; and if he did, his words aroused only perplexity and contempt rather than the sympathy to which he might have felt he was entitled when he made such an appeal.

It is, of course, true that Hitler was one of the world's most expert manipulators of language to achieve ulterior aims without any regard whatever for truth or honor in what he said. His greatest triumphs as an agitator came not, however, so much from Machiavellian calculation in advance as from an instinctive sympathy with the inarticulate longings and inner convictions of millions of his countrymen and an ability under conditions of hysterical exaltation, stimulated by the excited attention of large audiences, spontaneously to voice what his hearers already believed. But if his statement to Henderson were to be explained away as propaganda, it was a failure; and again there is no persuasive reason to suppose that he was otherwise than sincere when he expressed an opinion that it was natural for him to entertain.

In any case this particular plea is painfully reminiscent of many reactions to Hitler's writings and speeches earlier in his career. Those parts of Hitler's statements which were offensive or threatening were dismissed as sheer propaganda, mere talk to win favor with the German masses and not to be taken seriously. If he once gained power he would never think of carrying out his absurd program but would conduct himself reasonably.

With regard to the argument that Hitler was acting of his own volition and was not directed in his assertions and actions by futile professors who have long since been in their graves, this is to deal with a straw man. Few philosophers today would pretend for themselves or for others that dictation by speculative thinkers is accepted by masterful politicians. The fact remains, however, that in Germany the prevailing winds of doctrine are those of philosophical idealism; that this general attitude in modern times depends on a theory of art as its principal proof; and that while such ideas have by now percolated down to the rambling discussions in German beer-halls, they are first recorded in the published writings of the long-deceased Fichte, Schelling, Schiller, Schlegel, and others of that romantic band, where they can still be most profitably examined, for there they are best expressed.

As we have already seen, the title of artist which Hitler awarded himself on the occasion of his audience granted to the British Ambassador had meanings which were far from exclusively personal or eccentric. Instead of being an isolated and casual remark, he used what was a well-known word for a familiar idea in Germany to express his intense feelings at a fateful moment. The term "artist" carried all the implications of *beaux-arts* and relied on the equivocal significance of idealism, as that attitude was conceived almost universally in Germany.

Since Hitler cannot be considered a creative thinker in the realm of philosophy, his belief in this respect has evidently ceased to be the harmless conceit of obscure aestheticians. Nor was it an impotent mystic's way of escape from intolerable difficulties. Elsewhere, it is now evident, such a doctrine led chiefly to misunderstanding the nature of art; but when Hitler entertained it, the results affected vital interests of all mankind.

THE ROMANTIC IDEALISM OF *Mein Kampf*

When the German Chancellor in August, 1939, called himself by nature an artist, he indicated that his convictions had not altered since 1924, when he wrote *Mein Kampf* in prison after the uprising of the previous year. These volumes, expounding his views and policies, also announced the program that he proposed to carry out in accordance with them.[210] Events have shown that his actions were the natural and consistent consequences of German romantic idealism, the philosophy that rationalized all his ideas and his conduct.

In his book the Chancellor did not pause to base his opinions on the self, as was customary with idealist thinkers, but appropriated as obvious truths, without further discussion, the conclusions that Fichte and Schelling had reached. There is nothing of the sustained intellectual development of Hegel in Hitler's thought, and the poetic fantasy of Nietzsche is lacking in his utterances. The underlying envy and resentment that animated his spirit found sustenance in the principles of the absolute I as will, manifested in the activity of the artist.

With all its prolixity and repetition, *Mein Kampf* presents evidence on this point. Thus, inspired by the man who taught history when he was a boy in school, he declared himself to be a revolutionary.[211] This claim has often been repeated; but, specifically, his revolutionary attitude was nothing more than a persistent hatred of the Hapsburgs because they had not made the German-speaking group complete masters of the various minorities in the Austrian Empire. For similar reasons he resisted the governments of the German Republic, since they had made concessions to other European powers, who, he thought, had no more right to consideration in comparison with the Germans than had the Slavs in the Austrian Empire.

He advocated training of the will as the chief concern of education, beginning with the children's earliest schooling, to make them ready to sacrifice themselves without hesitation in the service of the state. He carried further the romantic doctrine when he urged that history should not be taught objectively but be made a vehicle to instil the youth with convictions like those of Fichte concerning the character and mission of Germany.[212] The method of reading by students should be that which he had followed during his own unhappy youth. Only those statements were to be remembered that could serve as persuasive illustrations of initial prejudice.[213] Such doctrines fell on receptive soil, for the whole German nation, after 1918, followed without question the view expressed by Spinoza, Fichte, and Schelling, that the order of thought and of thing is identical. Since the German army had been perfectly trained and equipped and since its beautiful aims were justified by the will to accomplish them, therefore it was contrary to reason to admit that such an army could ever have been defeated. Peace must have come about through a stab in the back administered by traitors in the government, and the only problem that concerned Germany was how to renew its war of conquest.[214]

To this end he argued against associations and representative government, asserting that the great deeds of the world had not been accomplished through mere co-operation of groups but had always been achieved by an individual conqueror with a will as hard as steel. The chapter in which this theory is set forth bears the title "The Strong Man Is Mightiest Alone."[215]

According to Hitler, the strong man is a creative force, and a substitute cannot be found for him any more than an artist can be discovered who is capable of completing the unfinished painting of a master. Admiration for the leader is only grateful acknowledgment of his creative force, and his leadership is a matter of art, a gift freely and arbitrarily given by God.[216]

His whole rationalization of dictatorship rests upon the concept of genius, handed on to Kant by his predecessors and employed by him to explain the production of beautiful art, *schöne Kunst*. Fichte had then transformed the will, the creative impulse, into the basic principle of philosophy, accounting for objects as the creatures of a unique, inclusive I. Schelling had next seen that art, interpreted in the paradoxical manner authorized by Kant, was the most illuminating example of creative will, for art was always beautiful. Irresponsible will was the essence of reality; the absolute I was an artist, and what it made was good because it was beautiful.

THE LEADER AS ARTIST

As a child, instead of being sent to the Gymnasium, where the humanities were taught, Adolf Hitler was enrolled in a Realschule, partly because he had already shown an interest in drawing. His father had decided to have the boy trained so that he, too, could enjoy a secure career as a government employee; but such routine discipline and so tame a prospect aroused his disobedient temperament, and at the age of twelve he announced that he was going to be an artist.[217]

The Chancellor states that he does not know how this happened; but it is easy to see that the romantic view of art, as something irresponsible but at the same time deserving of highest admiration and the uniquely beautiful product of creative will, would appeal to such a spirit. The boy's determination led to a prolonged conflict, and his procedure was typical of his later tactics against the German Republic, for he deliberately sabotaged all studies but art, geography, and history, since he considered only these studies worth while.[218] The doctrines that Fichte and Schelling had propagated still rationalized the hatreds and hopes of the Pan-German schoolteachers, who molded his youthful mind.

His desire to become a painter persisted through adolescence, although he discovered an even greater interest in architecture.[219] When his parents died, he took himself to Vienna and there attempted to gain admission to the academy of art. Although he had rated himself the best artist in his class at school, to his shocked surprise he failed to pass the entrance examination, and he was advised to try the architectural school. But the subjects he had neglected as a matter of stubborn self-expression were required for admission there, so that he could not prepare for an architectural career, either.[220] In Vienna he first worked as a laborer and then as a free-lance painter for five miserable years.[221] He found that work as a draftsman and painter of water colors left him still fresh at night to steep himself in the political and social dogmas embodied later in *Mein Kampf*.[222]

Although Hitler's artistic ambitions had been frustrated by official judges, he did not cease to regard himself as an artist. He continued to paint, in spite of a public rebuke, and he thus prepared himself to act as an artist on a scale larger than the back streets of Vienna.

Later, while condemning expressionist and cubist painting, he could praise the work of Boecklin, an admiration which he shared with the former Kaiser; he asserted that the artist was not a fool, like the modernists, but had also, like himself, received divine grace, an arbitrary but heavenly inspired mandate to work his own will.[223]

He practiced a technique of design and adopted the doctrines of romantic idealism in the beliefs that he entertained regarding the significance of that occupation. In his early plans for the National Socialist party he also brought his experience as a painter to bear on problems of propaganda and agitation. He first asserted the superiority of pictures over printed words,[224] but after his own success as an orator he held that the spoken word was superior to both pictures and printed words as a means of influencing the masses.[225] The difference between a poster advertising an art exhibition and the pictures displayed in the gallery seemed to him to illustrate the gap between what interests the educated and what appeals to the masses.[226] Red was selected as the dominant color in his political posters because it attracted most attention and it also annoyed his enemies.[227] He took particular pride in designing the new flag and the party insignia; although the flag of the Republic had employed the colors red, white, and black, he finally decided to use them also, but in a new pattern. The party emblem, a white circle containing a black swastika, against a red field, was also a product of his artistic judgment.[228]

At first he had thought that his talent for architectural design was a by-product of his ability in painting and drawing;[229] but when he visited Vienna, he was more interested in the museum building than in the pictures it contained, and he was fascinated by the Parliament building, the Ringstrasse, and the Schillerplatz.[230] Later he decided that German art was to be known only in Munich, and he delighted in its streets and buildings most of all.[231]

He was prevented by the adverse decision of the authorities from pursuing a professional career as an artist, but his determination led him to continue painting. His lack of adequate preparation seemed to bar him from practicing architecture, but again his will to disregard any opinion but his own enabled him, as master of the Reich, to engage with profound satisfaction in city-planning and designing of buildings on a vast scale.[232]

His attacks on degenerate art, as he terms it, are connected in his mind with his racist doctrine.[233] Bolshevism, it seemed to him, was expressed by futurist, cubist, and dadaist art. Like Plato, he would extirpate such trends in art to avoid corrupting the youth.[234] German art at the time he wrote *Mein Kampf* impressed him as an obvious proof that German civilization had deteriorated after the war; as the grandeur of the age of Pericles was represented by the Parthenon, so the decadence of Germany was to be seen in cubist paintings.[235] Art, he believed, had prospered in the small German cities, after the Wars of Liberation, when the romantic movement flourished; but the growth of great urban centers later in the century had been attended by a decline in art. Under the Republic, Hitler declared, the state was governed by sordid money-seekers, and there was no appreciation of the heroic either in public life or in art.[236]

In accordance with such views, the platform of the National Socialist party, drawn up in 1927, presented as its Article 23: "Regulations are needed to govern the press."[237] The Reich Chamber of Culture was later instituted to exercise strict control over periodicals, books, the radio, motion pictures, the stage, architecture, painting, and sculpture. The principles approved by Plato and the doctrine of the Academy were combined in subjection to the creative will of the romantic-idealist dictator. That was good and to be admired which the artist, Adolf Hitler, declared to be good. Nothing else might exist.

RACISM AND ART

According to Fichte and Schelling, the course of history is the record of how absolute will has objectified itself. The Aryan or Nordic German is for Hitler the same thing as Fichte's normal folk; it alone is destined to embody and achieve civilization, and the German folk cannot be or do otherwise. Inferior races exist only to be conquered and to serve the superior; their function is to pull the German plow.[238] Buildings and pictures are such manifest signs of genius that anybody can recognize these, its visible manifestations; and, although the fact may be less readily admitted, the German race is eternally endowed with creative ability.[239] Genius may be hidden in a beardless youth, but in times of stress he will reveal himself as the hero he is.[240]

While people generally do not realize this truth, the German Chancellor wrote, human culture is dependent on the German race, and any admixture of alien blood causes degeneration of the chosen strain. A crossing of German blood with that of inferior races is a sin against the absolute will, against divine reality, against God Himself.[241] The purity of the superior race must be carefully assured, and if only the mentally and physically healthy of this people were allowed to propagate, six centuries of selective breeding by the Germans would result in the reformation of all humanity.[242]

By divine right of the creative will of the race responsible for all humanity, Hitler announced, the National Socialist party therefore undertook to secure for the German race the lands that it needed and to which it was entitled. Present sacrifices to obtain control of the earth's surface were sanctioned by benefits which future generations of pure-blooded peasants would reap, for only by war could Germany gain more soil and increase the number of German lives. If a decline in the German population and therefore in the real hope of humanity was the only alternative to extension of its territory through force, to seize additional lands was the clear duty of Germany, since she was the mother of all human life.[243]

The myth of the normal folk was devised by Fichte, but he modeled it on the Garden of Eden and the Old Testament doctrine of the chosen people. It was incapable of logical justification, historical illustration, or other kinds of proof and was frankly admitted to be an arbitrary act of grace. But for Fichte and Hitler it was as though Adam and Eve had never sinned and had never been expelled from Paradise. As the first parents of the normal folk, they were divine creative will; they had made the Eden in which they found themselves and had left it of their own free will, to struggle with the soil and settle upon it a race of pure-blooded German peasants. The knowledge of good and evil they acquired consisted in realizing the evil of life in a luxurious garden and in foreseeing the good which would result from forsaking the comforts of Paradise to subdue the whole earth and populate it with the normal folk.

Fichte's stimulating flattery of the German people, deifying its passions, achieved conspicuous success in 1813 and again in 1870. A general repudiation of his doctrine in 1918 served no purpose but to develop a leader who, in 1939, could voice the romantic dogma in a form much cruder than the phrases of the critics and philosophers who had originated it. The German romantic-idealist view places artists and those who care for art in a position which is peculiarly embarrassing. But if Hitler's understanding of art is wrong, incorrect as well as evil, what may we believe without assenting either to his ideas or to his practices?

VI

Classical Explanations of Art

I T IS often supposed that something new is necessarily more progressive and modern than something old, but the physical expansion of a revitalized barbarism did not establish the justice of its claims by the recent origin of its aggressions any more than it did by its appeal to the primitive resource of armed strength. Its intellectual penetration should be viewed as sceptically as its assaults are energetically resisted. The novelty of its power and the surprise of its strategy did not entitle it to immediate submission; the fact that other ways of life have endured for ages did not require that they be at once abandoned. Whether ancient or modern, ways of thinking and living must be surveyed and analyzed to be understood and appraised, and any such initial prejudice prevents a fair estimate.

Germany, the European country least touched by classical ideas, has in recent times pressed upon its neighbors and overrun their frontiers as savagely and persistently as ever it did during the age of migrations. After those inroads it cost civilization in the West a painful struggle, lasting almost a thousand years, before the classical heritage could be regained and the human spirit liberated. A renewal of the Dark Ages once more threatens, but strength may be found in classical sources to prevent complete submission.

As the German leader has discovered in the artist a justification of his aims, we may well inquire what explanation the thinkers of ancient Greece offered for art and the artist. They were the first to speculate on such topics, and their discoveries deserve our close attention. The sanity of their approach did not prevent them from engaging in daring adventures, for their spiritual conquests endured long after the Greek states had ceased to exist as political entities, surviving alike the hordes that swept away the Roman Empire and the succeeding incursions from the north.

Analysis of their ideas relating to art and the artist has a value for us greater than a merely accurate account of a curious system, long superseded; it gives us the knowledge of how our own cultural ancestors lived and what ideas they found adequate to their existence.

Even when we have discarded the many elements in their thought which were appropriate to the world in which they lived but are no longer sufficient for ours, there still remain solid and enlightening principles which serve to justify our way of life against the ideals and customs of barbarians. In the organized speculative thought of the Greeks, if we are willing to overcome habitual prejudice against things ancient, we can discover something more important than the satisfaction of a philologist's curiosity or materials for a correct chronicle of the dead. We may still profitably look to the words of such men as Plato, Plotinus, and Aristotle, for they reflected on the real objects before them and reached decisions that even today may successfully be set up against the fallacies of German writers from Leibniz to the present.

At this point it should be recalled that the Greek word, now often translated as "art," was one from which our words "technique" and "technology" are derived. That Greek term found a Latin equivalent in *ars*, from which English and the Romance languages secured "art" and various similar forms. In German the word that corresponded to both was *Kunst*. Not before very recent times did these terms cease to mean "technique, developed and orderly skill." When they acquired the connotations of the more extensive phrase *beaux-arts*, they afforded a supposed proof of the truth of German philosophical idealism. On the root of self-centered and self-satisfied rationalist idealism there was grafted the stem of romanticism, and the eventual fruit of this growth was disaster.[244]

The classical thinkers had no term to indicate a classification such as "arts of design," and they could not have conceived such a formula as *beaux-arts* to be seriously intended. What they did analyze was the concept of "technique," the rationally constituted and developed capacities by which men make things and know what they are doing.

For that reason we have to exercise caution in dealing with ancient statements, not to read into their words thoughts that never occurred to their minds. But we can examine what they had to say of things we should now call works of art, and we can analyze those remarks on topics which we today should place under the head of aesthetics. There can be no doubt that works of art produced in ancient Greece were of intense interest at the time they were made, and they still command widespread admiration. The speculation of great thinkers who participated in the same culture has also rarely lacked devoted students; if its unique function as a remedy against the epidemic of barbarism were more widely realized, perhaps classical studies would again be earnestly and seriously pursued.

In this connection the attitude of leaders of the romantic movement toward classical antiquity presents a strange contradiction. They appear to have been the first to realize the basic importance of the temporal sequence in relating human experiences. They provided a new and comprehensive approach to the humanities and gave greater significance to history than ever before.

But their thoughts about ancient art were still dominated by the eighteenth-century views of rationalist idealism, perpetuated in all readers of Winckelmann. The romantic idealists were prone to interpret ancient art and ancient thought about art as if Plato, Aristotle, and Plotinus had also submitted to the whole set of prejudices developed from the end of the sixteenth through the eighteenth centuries and embodied in the formula *beaux-arts*.

By going behind these conventional but erroneous opinions to the original sources, we not only recover the proper historical perspective in which ancient speculation developed, but we also find the corrective needed against the idealism which, founded upon the *beaux-arts* dogma, eventually was invoked to justify the German program of world conquest.

SOCRATES

The father of Socrates was a stone-carver, and he himself practiced that trade.[245] Our knowledge of his views comes chiefly from Xenophon and Plato; but, while it is probable that Xenophon did not fully grasp all that he had heard, it is certain that Plato magnified the historic individual Socrates to make him a literary and philosophic ideal, so that there is more of Plato than of Socrates in the words attributed to the latter in the dialogues. It is more convenient to study the record preserved by Xenophon when we wish to consider Socrates and Plato separately.

Yet Plato agreed with Xenophon in grouping artists with nurses, barbers, cooks, and similar occupations.[246] When Socrates raised questions which we should today discuss with regard to art, the philosopher investigated the activity of a maker of armor as an example.[247] The conclusion he then reached was that the beautiful was the good, the useful in particular, and he accepted the compound term *kaloska-*

gathos, "beautiful-and-good," as a solution, although he perceived the paradox in such an answer.

As he was a poor man, Socrates professed himself unable to deal with problems of economics; and he introduced, as better equipped to do so, a person named Ischomachus, to whom he said the word "beautiful-and-good" could properly be applied. He had become acquainted with this man during his research into the significance of the terms "good" and "beautiful."[248] He had occupied himself only to a limited extent, it was said, with good architects, good painters, sculptors, and others of that sort, for they were usually low persons whose bodies were disfigured by their toil and whose minds were not refined.[249] He plainly considered aesthetic value as having to do with physical appearance only, while ethical values related to character and the mind.[250] It is significant that in the age of Socrates beauty of figure and goodness of character were expected to be combined in one person. The relations between the two qualities were not, however, to be clarified by simply preserving both words in a popular, telescoped formula.

An attempt that Socrates made to solve the problem was not very successful. He gave this explanation of beauty: That which is beautiful in itself is the good or the useful; the beautiful is that which serves a good purpose.[251] He at once admitted the ironic implications of such an answer when he pointed to his own flat nose, with wide nostrils, and his thick lips as beautiful, because they were efficient in smelling and kissing![252]

Socrates also accepted the popular Greek doctrine of imitation. When he was advising the painter Parrhasius, he mentioned another artist—perhaps Zeuxis, who had made a picture of Helen—as having combined in one figure the beauties found in a number of different models.[253] In the same conversation Socrates informed Parrhasius that the visible expressed or imitated the invisible, but the artist was unable to understand how something visible could imitate the invisible.[254] The source of these two important notions—imitation and the "beautiful-and-good"—was simply popular usage. While Socrates suspected the validity of these views, he still retained terms that had general approval.

Socrates seems to have esteemed neither artists nor works of art. According to Xenophon, "Painting and colored decorations of the walls deprive us, he thought, of more pleasure than they give."[255] Socrates, indeed, was primarily a moralist, and his interest in aesthetics and in art was only incidental to other concerns. But the contrast between his ethical views and those of the romantic idealist is in itself significant.

It never occurred to Socrates that an artist could expect exemption from the customary ethical responsibilities assumed by other men. His own conduct makes it clear that he considered every member of the Athenian community under an obligation to fulfil his duties to his fellow-men. Whatever he did, his actions and their results were subject to ethical, as well as aesthetic, judgment. His claim to the unfailing respect of subsequent generations has rested upon his sturdy defense of rational ethics against the ingenious and deductive arguments of the sophists.

Like all Athenians he was familiar with the brutal aggressions of tyrants in certain Greek city-states. Athens still faced the constant menace of a Persian Empire motivated by a wilful policy intent upon crushing the liberties of free men. Socrates and his contemporaries never doubted that such ideas and practices were evil, to be expected only of irrational and wicked men.

PLATO

Throughout the history of Western civilization the influence of Plato has been so great that an eminent philosopher has recently said that European philosophy consists of a series of footnotes to Plato.[256] The literary and dramatic qualities of his dialogues, their concentration on ethical ideals, the stimulating way in which conflicting opinions are presented, and the inconclusive endings of many such conversations all help to account for their persistent effectiveness. While Plato had no system to present, his works have been an inspiration even to those who, like Aristotle, differed from him on important points. Two elements in his thought are particularly significant in the present connection: his theory of Ideas and his theory of art, for his theory of Ideas eventually led to the *beaux-arts*, while his theory of art has always provided a difficulty for those who admired both Plato and art.

As is well known, Plato was more than unfriendly to art—he was bitterly hostile to it.[257] This presented an embarrassing dilemma to thinkers who, in the nineteenth century, accepted the *beaux-arts* dogma. How was it possible that Plato, whose words surpass all others' in homage to beauty, should have waged a sustained campaign against art unparalleled in serious speculation? How could Plato have done this if art and beauty are the same thing?

Many and ingenious were the sophistries by which it was hoped to ease such a painful situation. He was antagonistic only to false tendencies in the art of his times, it was said. Again, it was claimed that his repeated attacks on art were simply examples of Platonic irony. He himself was no minor poet, yet he would expel the poets from his ideal commonwealth; and the reason for this, it was alleged, was because he sacrificed all, even poetry, to his philosophic duty. It is more just to Plato and to ourselves to suppose that he meant what he said, when there is nothing to the contrary in the context. Through study of the place of his views on art in his work as a whole, we may even find that Plato was at least consistent with himself in this regard and that it was the nineteenth century that suffered from obvious incoherence in its thought about art and beauty. For Plato, at any rate, there was no contradiction in loving beauty while he hated painting.

ART AND NATURE

The reasons for Plato's attitude toward art may be found by examining his answers to what were for him three fundamental problems: What is the relation of art to nature? What is the relation of art to truth? What is the ethical function of art? Each of these questions was raised and carefully considered; the replies that he made left no other conclusion possible than to reject art.

Like Socrates and Xenophon he accepted the principle of imitation without further analysis.[258] Although other prevalent concepts were subjected to penetrating criticism by the eager minds whose activity Plato reported, there was no close examination of imitation itself.

The Greeks seem to have set great value on the concept of imitation because they never ceased to be surprised that such a thing was possible. They did not expect stones or walls to look like human beings and other objects. Yet a statue or a painting, things made by men, had a wonderful resemblance to human beings while still remaining a stone or a wall. The delightful similarity between two such different things as a man and a statue was for them a fascinating relation. They felt that they had no right to expect it, but there it was. They prized this strange but pleasing situation, calling it imitation, and were then led by its success in this instance to employ it in explaining other problems where it was really not relevant.

In any event, Plato combined the two concepts of imitation and of art or technique to establish the imitative arts. Among them was music, but architecture was not included; in Plato there is little mention of the latter, and he probably held it to be a useful craft,[259] although today music seems to us to be no more imitative than architecture.

Productive techniques he had divided into two kinds: useful and imitative.[260] He observed that there was nothing more clever or amusing than works of imitation,

and so we recognize that he who professes to be able by virtue of a single art to make all things will be able by virtue of the painter's art to make imitations which have the same names as the real things, and by showing the pictures at a distance will be able to deceive the duller ones among young children into the belief that he is perfectly able to accomplish in fact whatever he wishes to do.[261]

Another classification of the productive techniques was into divine, which is responsible for natural forms, and human technique, which results in artificial forms.[262] Natural imitations of divine products were to be found in mirror reflections and dreams, while human art could imitate technical products, such as houses.[263]

Plato's adverse judgment of pictures as imitations was repeated when he said of a portrait of a carpenter that it "would deceive children and foolish men and make them believe it to be a real carpenter."[264] At the same time he declared that language was not concerned with imitation, as were music and painting.[265] In another passage he decided that painters, musicians, poets, rhapsodists, actors, chorus dancers, and theatrical managers were all superfluous in the state.[266]

It is obvious from these and other statements that to Plato's mind the most conspicuous aspect of art was its function as an imitation. This explained the relation of the work to a model in nature, and such a view seemed to him to demand that art be censured.

ART AND TRUTH

Painting was especially offensive to Plato, for its capacity to imitate troubled him most. As he was a philosopher, he felt it his business to inquire also into the truth or accuracy of artistic representations. Since the model and the imitation were similar only in some respects that seemed unimportant to him but were quite different in other, more fundamental, points, he judged that art gave us untrue imitations.

As did the idealists after him, Plato disdained the understanding derived from empirical practice in general, and for that reason cooking was inferior to medicine, "since it has no account to give of the real nature of the things it applies, and so cannot tell the cause of any of them.''[267] Cooking was an irrational procedure; even worse, it was immoral, for it merely flattered, having no regard for what was really good or bad for those who ate its products, unlike the physician who does care about physical health.[268]

Analysis in a scientific manner was far different from empirical practices and habits.[269] Manual techniques, such as those we call arts of design, clearly rested on empirical routines; even medicine, agriculture, and some other callings in which there was a rational element, possessed little certainty.[270] The imitative craftsman, relying on skilled experience, could have no genuine understanding of whether the things he depicted were beautiful and right or the contrary,[271] and music, for example, was largely a matter of guessing, not of true knowledge. The imitative techniques and their products were merely playful, where medicine, agriculture, and gymnastics were at least serious.[272]

Plato's dislike for painting caused him to call conjecture, the lowest type of understanding, by a name that may be given as "picture-thinking,"[273] in contrast with principles achieved by dialectic, such as were employed in geometry.[274] At precisely the opposite poles from the artist was the philosopher, for the dialectician was "the man who is able to exact an account of the essence of each thing."[275]

He considered only those techniques true which depend on mathematics, and thus he could praise housebuilding and shipbuilding.[276] The carpenter who employed instruments and made measurements to obtain accuracy was engaged in a technique which was more scientific than most.[277]

The imitative arts, on the other hand, were related to an inferior part of the soul, and their products were also inferior.[278] As if there could be any doubt regarding his attitude, Plato expressly declared that when he spoke of beauty in shapes or figures, he did not mean animals or pictures, as most people did, but the regular geometrical shapes. "For I assert that the beauty of these is not relative, like that of other things, but they are always absolutely beautiful by nature."[279]

Plato's opinion of the truth to be found in art is to be understood in relation to what he judged to be true knowledge. For him "the knowledge which has to do with being, reality, and eternal immutability" was true, and dialectic "has the greatest regard for clearness, exactness, and truth."[280] Consequently, "that fixed and pure and true and what we call unalloyed knowledge has to do with the things which are eternally the same without change or mixture, or with that which is akin to them; and all other things are to be regarded as secondary and inferior."[281]

The Platonic Idea[282] alone fulfilled the requirements of absolute truth, and sensory patterns in nature were themselves imitations of the ultimate Idea, while the imitation that the artist produced was at a third stage removed from the real.[283] Perspective, or change in shape according to distance, was a weakness of vision; and scene-painting, because it appealed to the inferior side of human nature, was in the same class with witchcraft and juggling.[284] The painter's works were phantoms, not realities;[285] and if the painter had true knowledge of the things he imitated, he would devote himself to the reality instead of imitating it. In any case the artist's labor was superfluous, for better imitations were to be secured by swinging a mirror about.[286] He declared, finally, that the man "who believes in beautiful things, but neither believes in beauty itself nor is able to follow when someone tries to guide him to the knowledge of it," was not awake; he was asleep and dreaming.[287]

Plato himself asserted that written discourses, in comparison with the spoken word, were not to be taken seriously;[288] and even in antiquity critics pointed out that Plato wrote dialogues that imitated conversations.[289] But his theory of art as imitation and his theory of knowledge as a penetration beyond natural objects to the realities that they imitated compelled him to reject art as untrue and lacking in intellectual value.

ART AND GOODNESS

Believing that art was an imitation of nature, and an inferior, derivative, unreal, and untrue one, Plato's decision as to its moral value was inevitable. To persuade readers of the truth of his views he cited works of art, as nearly all philosophers have done. In the *Republic*, for example, there is a long passage in which the procedure of the painter is paralleled in detail to show how the philosopher should depict the perfect commonwealth, since "no city could ever be blessed unless its lineaments were traced by artists who used the heavenly model."[290]

But in most instances Plato thought that the imitative techniques served to amuse rather than to instruct;[291] while the effect might be good, it was much more frequently evil.[292] When they presented unworthy images of the gods, that was an instance of their generally immoral influence.[293]

The guardians of the state, he claimed, should not be skilled in the imitation of many things,[294] and moral censorship of the imitative techniques was to be exercised in order to assure their proper education:

> Is it, then, only the poets that we must supervise and compel to embody in their poems the semblance of the good character or else not write poetry among us, or must we watch over the other craftsmen, and forbid them to represent the evil disposition, the licentious, the illiberal, the graceless, either in the likeness of living creatures or in buildings or in any other product of their art, on penalty, if unable to obey, of being forbidden to practice their craft among us, that our guardians may not be bred among symbols of evil.[295]

He admitted, however, that the techniques most necessary to human welfare were humble trades that brought no reputation for wisdom;[296] although imitative techniques were pursued for the sake of diversion, they also failed to achieve wisdom.[297]

The legislative control of art, as in Egypt, where, according to Plato, the styles in painting and sculpture had remained unchanged for ten thousand years, was approved.[298] His references to sculpture were less fretful than those to painting, but he made them simply to illustrate his points and to make his dialogues more vivid, without attaching intellectual value to either sculpture or painting.[299] Plato gave prolonged attention also to problems of education, but in the *Laws*, where the liberal education of youth was prescribed in detail, no attention was paid to training in art; the young were to learn to read and write and to play the lyre, with three years each—and no more—for acquiring skill in letters and music.[300]

Since the essence of art for Plato was imitation of nature and the imitation that art afforded was untrue, it was but natural that he should judge art generally evil, from the ethical point of view. But Plato's theory of the Ideas also involved the principle of imitation and, in his judgment, provided additional reasons for hostility to art.

PLATO'S THEORY OF IDEAS

Among other Ideas, Plato analyzed beauty, the central concept of what we now investigate as aesthetics. He examined the view of Socrates that the beautiful was the useful and the definition that it was profitable pleasure, rejecting both on logical grounds;[301] nevertheless, in his discussion of the imitative techniques and of regulations to control them, he concluded that only profitable pleasures were to be permitted.[302]

The elements of beauty he found to consist in the measured and the proportioned, the symmetrical and the harmonious; but the reasons for which he approved these qualities were ethical.[303] Plato also praised what is simple, unmixed, and pure; but these, too, were terms applied to the intangible, invisible soul and expressed moral virtues that he admired.[304] Beyond the beauty of bodies and even of souls there was an absolute beauty, to which alone such words as "real," "eternal," "immutable," "pure," and "true" could be applied.[305]

Plato's favorite explanation of the relation between the eternal Idea and the temporary instance with which we ordinarily deal was taken from the popular understanding of art as imitation, in spite of his having condemned art for that reason. He was concerned with establishing the reality of ethical ideals on a logical basis; and on that ground he found that works of art were necessarily inaccurate and incomplete, untrue and deceptive, tolerable as a concession to the weakness of the average mentality only when severely restrained. Imitation accounted for the inferiority of works of art; but at the same time he adopted it as a principle to rationalize the connection between passing patterns in experience and permanent realities for the mind.

As inferiority was attributed to works of art because they imitated models in nature, so natural objects were, in their turn, lower in rank than the Ideas because they also were not the eternal realities but merely their imitations. To secure the superiority of his logical abstractions, Plato did not hesitate to repudiate art, for in that way he gained a plausible illustration. To make his comparison symmetrical, art had to suffer.

His repeated attacks on the imitative technique indicate that, while his arguments might win assent, they were unable to persuade. He found it necessary to renew the attack at intervals because it was not easy to convince all his hearers that art must be condemned to secure the permanence of ethical ideals. Aristotle later, with more respect for the truth of things as they are, revised the theory of imitation to provide a worthy place for art in the world of experience.

The relation between a work of art and its model, Plato thought, gave clear proof of a metaphysical principle; the modern idealists conclude that introspection affords incontrovertible evidence for an evaluation of art and the artist just the opposite of Plato's. But Plato's theory of the Ideas is the eventual origin of the term adopted by later idealists; and, although an account of how the Idea became transformed into the idea of art has already been given, the theory itself should be more closely examined.

To the ancient thinker there appeared to be no alternative between an unreliable, shifting world of sensations and a fixed, eternal realm of thoughts. In the world of reflection the universals discovered by Socrates were hypostatized and made more real than sensory objects. Plato's report of the nature of the Ideas is less consistent than his conviction that they existed; and to affirm their reality he was willing to risk discrepancies between his various descriptions. Any hesitancy in admitting the truth of his theory he put down to our partaking of the accidental and casual and to our inexperience.[306] He was more fully aware than many of his followers of the logical objections that can be made to it, but he insisted upon the eminent reality of the Ideas as a matter of what we should now call "faith."

Plato found in the doctrine of Heraclitus, who held that all things are essentially unstable and in a perpetual flux, a statement of the view directly opposed to his own.[307] He agreed that the properties of sensory objects were always changing and never at rest.[308] He accounted for this by saying that sensations resulted from bodies that struck the soul; the perpetual motion that agitated these bodies constantly obstructed it.[309] Irrational opinion could be based on sensations, but the properties of the self-subsisting Ideas were such that reason could deal with them confidently. In one passage Plato set forth the difference in these words:

We must agree that one kind is the self-identical Idea, ungenerated and indestructible, neither receiving into itself any other from any quarter nor itself passing anywhither into another; invisible and in all ways imperceptible by sense, it being the object which it is the province of reason to contemplate; and a second kind is that which is named after the former and similar thereto, an object perceptible by sense, generated, ever carried about, becoming in a place and out of it again perishing, apprehensible by opinion with the aid of sensation.[310]

To make this theory of the Ideas vivid and persuasive, it was set forth in rich, metaphorical language, and at the same time the Ideas were assumed to be the grounds of logical analysis and the goals of ethical action. Yet he himself said that the myths and figurative language in which he expressed his belief were not to be taken literally.[311]

Plato refrained from giving to his theory the precision and sharp definition with which he delineated his scheme for the perfect commonwealth. For example, he asked what made beautiful things beautiful and answered that they were made beautiful by absolute beauty, that is, the Idea of beauty. But, he said, whether this was due to the presence of beauty or to participation in it was of less consequence than firm adherence to the principle, even if it was perhaps foolish.[312]

Although he would not permit them to destroy the theory of the Ideas, Plato was aware of the difficulties in explaining the relation of Ideas and of the corresponding instances in sensory experience.[313] He often accounted for it on the basis of imitation, as already noted, and to his mind the inferiority of art to nature seemed to prove the superiority of the Ideas to nature. An alternative metaphor to illustrate the relation was that of participation.[314] But in either case, so far as Plato separated the Ideas from immediate objects in experience, to assure the immutability of the Ideas against the transience of such objects, he left the way open to insuperable objections. An effort to heal the breach is to be seen in his doctrine of the communion of Ideas in one another, with the reservation that some will mingle with others and some will not.[315]

Plato realized the defects of both imitation and participation as explanations of how the Ideas and their imitations or participants were connected. But he persisted in believing that the Idea is a "colorless, shapeless, intangible, truly existing essence with which all true knowledge is concerned, ... visible only to the soul." The region where the Ideas exist is beyond even the heaven where the gods abide, and by them the very gods are nourished.[316]

In the *Parmenides* Plato himself stated some of the more obvious reasons for rejecting ways in which he had declared that the Ideas and the phenomena of experience were connected:[317]

Are there Ideas for all things, not only those of ethics and mathematics, but the ridiculous, vile, and worthless things?

If there are such Ideas, since philosophy cares not for popular opinion, how can an Idea be present in a number of participants without ceasing to be apart from them or becoming separated from itself?

How can the indivisible Idea be divided among many objects?

How can the Idea be one when its relation to each thing in which it participates is a different Idea, and the number of relations for each Idea is thus infinite?

If all other things partake of Ideas, are they not all made of thoughts; but how can this be, if such things are not thought of?

How can the Ideas exist as patterns and other things be imitations of them, if the relation between the Idea and the imitation involves some Idea other than the one imitated?

If each Idea is one and distinct from concrete things, does it not follow that the Ideas cannot be known, for they do not exist in us?

If such absolute Ideas exist but are not relevant to our world, how can God know or govern the world?

The intricate convolutions of the systematic analysis pursued by Plato in the *Parmenides* led him to conclusions similar to those of Kant regarding the transcendental synthetic unity of apperception. It was also quite unintelligible: "Whether the one is or is not, the one and the others in relation to themselves and to each other, all in every way, are and are not, and appear and do not appear."[318]

Plato, however, considered that the Ideas were essential to discourse and dialectic; they were needed as the secure grounds of logic and ethics. The only alternative, it seemed to him, was an irrational chaos of sensations. To protect the integrity of the Ideas he degraded the familiar world of sensation to a deceptive shadow of the inaccessible and unknowable. Since sensations were continuously changing and human technique was employed to change things, but reality must not be changing or changed, sensation and technique were essentially unreal, untrue, and evil. The techniques of imitation, by their very nature, since they presented patterns of sensation, which imitated natural objects that were already inferior to the Ideas, must be rejected.

PLATO AND THE IDEALISTS

Plato's Idea was thus a metaphysical construction, but, beginning with the Romans, it was transformed into a psychological phenomenon. Those who effected this alteration usually gave works of art as illustrations of their interpretation, for the idea or mental image in the artist's mind preceded the execution of the actual work of art. The same extraordinary attributes which Plato had given the Idea were, however, retained for the idea when it was connected with the arts of design, and the idea of beauty was made their essence. Later, when an alliance between letters and the arts of design was fostered through the Academy, the classification *beaux-arts* was devised; and this led to the establishment of aesthetics as a philosophical discipline, to deal with the various problems that resulted from all these assumptions. With introspection of the self as the sole and unchallenged reality and with the arts of design as evidence of the relation between the self and sensory experience, the materials required for the elaboration of idealist systems, both rationalist and romantic, were available.

But Plato was not responsible for the abuse of his views by the ideal-

ists; and the differences between his convictions and those of the idealists from Descartes through Hitler are far more significant than their
common use of the word "idea." Plato never resorted to introspective
analysis of his own soul as the last secure object of thought; he did not
appeal to an inability to doubt his own existence as an impregnable
axiom. He did not undertake to prove the existence of God as the
necessary conclusion of the idea of a perfect being. The ensuing difficulties did not drive him to the fantastic view that the world consists
only of ideas, that the ultimate reality is the self-created will, and
that, as there is only one world, there can be only one absolute I.
Plato would have considered such beliefs worthy of a vain, arrogant,
and arbitrary oriental monarch but unworthy of a rational mind living in a community of free men, all of whom must co-operate in dealing with nature. To him such systems would have appeared to be
vicious dreams indulged in to justify irrational animal impulse.

The idealists retained Plato's own disdain for sensation and his contempt for technique. But he did not contradict himself by making the
artist the archetype of creative will—an I become absolute. His imitative techniques were identical with neither the arts of design nor the
beaux-arts. He studied both natural and technical products when he
sought a definition of beauty; it was not the exclusive right of a particular group of techniques.

That a statesman making a historic decision should call himself an
artist would have been for Plato a logical absurdity, an evil attitude,
and an ugly gesture.

The fundamental assumption of idealism which could reduce the
world to thoughts was not unknown to Plato. He stated it and sum-
marily rejected it. He put the theory in this way: "Well, then, Parmenides, does not the necessity which compels you to say that all
things participate in the Ideas, oblige you also to believe either that
everything is made of thoughts, and all things think, or that although
they are thoughts, they exist without being thought of?"[319] This possibility was introduced for consideration, but it was not deserving of
protracted analysis; he rejected it as "quite unreasonable" and so obviously absurd that it required no extensive refutation.

Thus Plato was himself an idealist in the sense that he held fast to
ethical ideals at all costs and that he established the Idea in the vocabulary of philosophy. But he was clearly not an idealist as that term
describes the philosophy which has prevailed in Germany from Leibniz to the present day.

Hitler himself showed little interest in the views of those who at least attempt rational discussion of this or any other speculative problem. He viewed with derision the inability of serious thinkers to rouse the masses to sacrifice themselves for a ruler. He accepted and applied the doctrines of romantic idealism, but he had not troubled himself to analyze its principles in intellectual terms.

Yet there are several points on which Plato and the German Chancellor are in apparent agreement. Plato also held that written words are unimportant compared with the spoken word. But there is a difference in their reasons, for Plato's objection to written words and set speeches was that the reader or listener had no opportunity to object or ask questions.[320] Hitler's voice, magnified by loudspeakers, allowed the subjects of the Reich no alternative but to listen and applaud. He did not permit critical examination of his romantic-idealist dogmas but relied upon their emphatic and unquestioned reiteration.

Another point where Plato and Hitler seem to have something in common is censorship. But here we must remember that Plato advocated such measures for the sake of properly educating the philosopher-statesmen who were to govern the state in the interest of justice. By the German Chancellor it was enforced as an aid in the execution of his absolute will. Justice was not his concern, for he was the creative artist and what he did was beautiful.

PLOTINUS

The immediate disciple of Plato was Aristotle, and Plotinus did not work out a system incorporating elements from both until centuries later. But there are advantages in considering Plotinus first, for he assimilated many of his important views from the Platonic dialogues and integrated them in a coherent, symmetrical structure. The Platonic aspect of his philosophy is so conspicuous that the differences between Plato and Plotinus were not clearly understood until the nineteenth century.

Plotinus is traditionally known as a Neo-Platonist, and that designation is warranted, on the whole. The doctrine of the Ideas persists in his thought, while the Aristotelian methods, which he employed in relating his fundamental concepts to one another, attract less attention. This does not mean that the philosophy of Plotinus is simply a fusion of the views of his two great predecessors, for there are numerous factors in his conclusions which were alien to both; but the point is that he did effect a synthesis of their characteristic contributions to speculative thought, and he thus affords a convenient transition from one to the other. Plotinus, in fact, preserved the best in Plato and Aristotle, for he agreed with Plato that value is what matters most in the world and with Aristotle that no philosophy lacking rational order can be valuable.

Neo-Platonism was an attitude congenial to the idealists in modern times, but their knowledge of it was drawn usually from patristic, mediaeval, or Renaissance sources rather than from Plotinus. The latter's methods of analysis and presentation were so difficult that his influence was generally indirect, until scholars, stimulated by romantic idealism, made the original source accessible.

In the age of Plotinus intellectual interest concerned itself mainly with questions of ethics, but they were not approached as they had been in earlier days. The founders of Western philosophy had conceived of ethics as dealing with human action in a context of other human beings. By the Alexandrines it was discussed as if it related to an individual isolated and apart from society. Their aim was salvation of the self, and popular opinion held that it was to be attained through ritual and ceremonial.

While Plotinus shared the Alexandrine estimate of the end to be achieved, he did not concur in the methods favored. Compared with his contemporaries and followers, Plotinus was himself free from superstition, as can be seen in his attacks on astrology and Gnosticism; but, ironically enough, in later times some have looked to him for support in occult practices. His moral idealism was, as in the case of Plato, the principal reason for influence in his own day; but his systematic scheme, with its dominant position for the Ideas, found adherents among the philosophical idealists.

TECHNIQUE

One of the essential concepts in the philosophy of Plotinus was that of technique, and in his evaluation of this principle he relied upon Aristotle rather than upon Plato. But, since the Renaissance translator used the Latin *ars* as the equivalent of the Greek word for "technique," the thinkers of the romantic era understood it in the sense of *beaux-arts*. In that way Plotinus became an authority upon whom the doctrines of romantic idealism could be based; but how mistaken such an interpretation was can readily be seen by examination of various passages in Plotinus that indicate what meaning the term had for him.

Technique was, in the first place, a very comprehensive term, including even arithmetic.[321] Beauty and ugliness, he asserted, related to dispositions of the soul toward corporeal things, and these qualities thus belonged both to physical objects and to the soul; the same could be said of techniques.[322] He compared the organs of senses, such as touch and vision, with the tools used by technicians; they also came between the judge and the object judged, as when a carpenter applied a rule to a plank to see if it was straight;[323] and the technician also had to exercise the calculating intelligence about his actions only when some difficulty arose.[324] Like Aristotle, he affirmed that technique introduced form into matter.[325]

In one place Plotinus classified techniques into three groups: those which resulted in the production of an object, like architecture; those which aided natural processes, such as medicine and agriculture; and those which affected the soul, making it better or worse, as did rhetoric and music.[326] He employed the adverb derived from technique to indicate something done with technical success or skilfully, when he spoke of the body as a dwelling constructed with technical success to be a mansion for the soul[327] and again when he attacked Gnostic belief in magic incantations skilfully performed.[328]

The relation between technique and the process of nature was one which deeply impressed Plotinus, for he concluded that life itself was a technique. Every life was an action, not an accidental event, but a movement with a design or form; like a dancer's routine, life was also a technique.[329] He even found in this parallel a suggestion for solving the problem of evil, for he reconciled the activities of evil men in this world by saying that all men were playing parts in a great, universal drama and the design of the whole spectacle was good. Roles played by good and by evil men were like the two opposite parts of the chorus who nevertheless performed by one technique.[330] When he explained why all things were not equally good and beautiful, Plotinus compared the rational order of nature, which produced evil as well as good things, to the painter who did not represent a living creature as all eyes and nothing else, for although other parts were less beautiful, they were still necessary to the whole. But here Plotinus did not expressly mention the painter; he referred to the producer of representations as a technician.[331]

In arguing against the Gnostics, Plotinus pointed out that the processes of technique differed from those of nature in that technique was subsequent to nature and the world.[332] Elsewhere he repeated that technique came after nature, it imitated nature, and produced, in comparison, worthless playthings, achieving nothing but likenesses with all its resources;[333] and in this passage Plotinus seems to have had special reference to representative art, echoing Plato's prejudice in this connection. But even here he found an excuse for nature's failures, saying that defects in natural products were like those of technique, because in both cases they resulted from lapses on the part of the creator as he contemplated the original model.[334]

Elsewhere, in opposition to Plato, Plotinus rejected the argument that technique was inferior to nature on the ground of the latter's logical and temporal priority. But his censure was probably limited to representative art and, in any case, referred to products rather than to the power by which they were created. His defense of technique against Plato's disdain took this form:

If anybody despises the techniques because they produce by imitating nature, it must be said at once that natural things imitate things other than natural. Next, it must be realized that they do not simply imitate visible things, but proceed directly to the ultimate principles or designs from which nature derives her own results. Furthermore, they produce many things on their own account, and supplement the deficiencies in natural things, since they themselves possess goodness and beauty. Phidias made his Zeus, not after any model present to the senses, but grasping him as he would be if he wished to be seen with the eyes.[335]

The metaphysics of Plotinus found a place in the rational order for both nature and technique, as can be seen in several passages where both concepts are considered. He stated:

Every created thing, technical as well as natural product, is a creature of wisdom and wisdom always directs its making. But if anything operates according to wisdom herself, let us consider the techniques as examples. The technician often proceeds to the very wisdom of nature, in accordance with which natural objects come into being, which is not one wisdom composed of many deduced principles; it is a unique whole, not put together in a unit from many parts, but rather breaking up into many parts of one whole.[336]

Technique was, indeed, introduced in his ultimate philosophical principle when he said of the One :[337]

It seems then that the wholeness in each thing aspires to the Good, for so far as it attains the Good, it also achieves Oneness, and it is more or less one insofar as it is good. This is true of natural things and also of techniques, for each technique produces its results to this end, so far as it is able and so far as its objects permit. . . . . Of Being itself, we say, this whole, one Being, and affirm it as the One, indicating its close association with the Good.[338]

While Plotinus often introduced illustrations drawn from sculpture, painting, and architecture, he did not refer exclusively to those fields when he spoke of technique, as many idealists have assumed. They were examples of a more general concept, one so important that it was needed for his basic view in philosophy—the union of wholeness and of value in the One. He also included natural as well as technical products when he attributed ethical as well as aesthetic quality to objects; and he never supposed that any product was essentially lacking in ethical value or that certain techniques, such as the arts of design or the *beaux-arts*, possessed aesthetic value and nothing else.

Plotinus employed examples from the arts of design so frequently that the romantic idealists, swayed by the *beaux-arts* doctrine, could mistakenly infer that his theory of technique had exclusive reference to them. Before we examine a number of these illustrations, cited to make philosophical points more persuasive, we should note that when Plotinus asserted, with Aristotle, that technique introduced form into matter, he did not use the term "form" to signify what it so often means today.

Until the rise of rationalist idealism, with Descartes, it indicated the concept reciprocal to matter. The form of an object was its intelligible aspect, but there could be no form without the matter of which it was composed. Form took the place of the Idea, and it was a principle far more comprehensive than its modern interpretation as mere shape.

Currently we speak of a routine observance as formal, while valid evidence is referred to as material. This is a complete inversion of the original intention, but it is consistent with the philosophy of Descartes, for the form of an object is identical with its shape when it is regarded solely as a tactile pattern. Since the Cartesian view held that this was the only kind of form that extended substance could have and that, besides extended substance, nothing but unextended thinking substance existed, shape was the unique manifestation of form in objects. But objects include other aspects than shape, and works of art are a type of object, not identical with objects in general. Form, on the other hand, includes the whole object apprehended, not shape alone. To understand the classical concept of form in the Cartesian sense of shape is to create many unnecessary problems and to miss the valid relations which shape alone does not include. Constantly bearing in mind that Plotinus and Aristotle did not restrict form to shape, we may profitably consider more closely some of the numerous references made by Plotinus to works of art.

SCULPTURE

Technique was a central concept in the thought of Plotinus because it served to illustrate what he held to be the relation between the intelligible or spiritual and the sensory worlds. His favorite examples were drawn from sculpture, because in such objects he found sensory patterns whose form was achieved by technique. The form was significant in such cases as every form must be, but it was secured by human action guided by intelligence, rather than by natural process; and these objects provided vivid confirmation of his views. They were familiar to the ancients; they were persistent patterns for the senses of touch and vision, and they possessed exceptional significance.

One of the most influential passages in Plotinus, which affected Michelangelo and many others, rests upon an example from sculpture and elucidates the claim that technique introduces form into matter:

Let us take, if you will, two pieces of stone placed side by side, one rough and untouched by technique, the other changed by technique into the statue of a god or some man, of a Grace or a Muse and of a man, but not just any man, rather of one composed by technique on the basis of all handsome men. It is clear that the stone which has become a beautiful form through technique is beautiful not because it is a stone, for in that case the other would be equally beautiful, but because of the form that technique imposed. The matter did not possess this form, but it was in the designer before entering into the stone, and it was in the workman, not because he had eyes and hands but because he had a share in technique. Therefore the beauty was in the technique and much superior, for the beauty that is in technique did not pass into the stone but remained and another lower beauty came from it. Even this did not remain intact and as it would be, but only so far as the stone permitted. If technique makes a thing similar to what it is and possesses—for it makes a thing according to the principle by which it works—it is in greater degree and more truly beautiful, possessing the beauty of technique which is greater and more beautiful than that which is external to it. For as it entered into matter it was extended in space and the more it became weaker than that which remains at one. Everything that extends into space is dissipated, as strength loses in force and heat in warmth and power generally loses in potency, so does the beautiful lose beauty. Every productive principle in itself must be superior to its product.[339]

Plotinus thus found in a comparison between a finished statue and a rough block of stone a convincing example of how technique imposes form on matter. He also concluded that, since technique is responsible for the beauty of form in sculpture, technique itself must be still more beautiful.

This passage was used by the romantic idealists to justify their deification of the artist, ignoring the context in which it occurred and the particular doctrines that it exemplified, according to Plotinus. Goethe himself translated it into German, while protesting against the claim that the beauty of a product is inferior to the technique by which it was produced. Other thinkers of the romantic era cited the text to show that the artist is the arbitrary, irresponsible Creator, where Plotinus had explicitly used the illustration to show that the sculptor's procedure is a rational, orderly one, imposing form on matter,[340] and that technique must be more beautiful than any of its products.

Further references to sculpture were made to afford evidence of more special and characteristic views. He compared contemplation of the One and of the manifold with the vision beheld in the sanctuary and the statues seen on the way to the temple.[341] The same figure was used to show the superiority of the ecstatic vision over experience of beauty and virtue in concrete things.[342] In another passage he spoke of contemplation of statues in a palace and of its living master; similarly, when the soul possessed the intelligible, it abandoned everything else.[343]

Statues were again mentioned to make vivid his ethical teachings. According to Plotinus, the soul achieved wisdom by contemplation of herself; purification from extraneous additions was like the cleaning of statues that had become covered with rust and dirt.[344] He advised his hearers to be like sculptors, removing superfluities, chiseling, polishing, and cleaning, to discover the beauty of their own souls.[345] Although Plotinus here set an example for the introspective analysis characteristic of idealist philosophy in modern times, he did not found the romantic doctrine of the artist's nature.[346]

PAINTING

Far more than in his discussion of technique or of sculpture, Plotinus displayed the influence of Plato in what he had to say of painting; but even here he saw that painting was a defective illustration of the point that Plato and he had in mind. With the author of the dialogues, he asserted: "Would anybody capable of contemplating truth prefer the image of truth? The more stupid children, those who are incapable of learning and speculation, are reduced to manual techniques."[347]

Yet facts of the technique of painting were called to testify to many of his conclusions. He claimed that when we find fault with the world for containing ugly and evil as well as beautiful and good things, we are like those who lack skill in the technique of painting but blame a painter for not spreading beautiful colors everywhere and for giving appropriate color in each place.[348] Speaking of the relation of the intelligible world to the world of sensation, he said that they were not separated any more than the reflection in a mirror could exist apart from the thing it reflected. But "the world of sensation is the image of that intelligible world in the same degree that an image of a living creature preserves the creature itself, that a painting or a reflection in water are identical with the object before its representation in water or a picture."[349] In another passage he continued to display the influence of Plato when he called the world of sensation "a shadow, and on this thing which is itself a shadow there is the representation of living creatures and the appearance of reality."[350]

But he seems to have been aware of defects in the example of painting as an illustration of philosophical points, for he reported the objection that it was not necessary for a portrait to be always connected with its model; the image survived apart from the thing represented. For that reason images in mirrors or in water and cast shadows were better analogies, since they were made by the object itself.[351]

Finally, he explicitly indicated a higher rank for sculpture than for painting when he spoke of intelligible beauty and said that in the beyond the gods do not contemplate logical propositions or mathematical theorems. All things there are as real as beautiful statues, "not pictures of statues, but real ones."[352]

ARCHITECTURE

Of architecture Plotinus had little to say, but here again certain remarks continue the Platonic tradition. He gave architecture a higher rank than the techniques of imitation because of its connection with geometry. "All the techniques that produce an object of sensation, such as architecture and carpentry, derive their principles and thoughts from beyond, so far as they employ symmetry." On the other hand, "all the techniques of imitation, painting and sculpture, dance and pantomime, are products of the world of sensation, for they have a sensory model."[353]

In his essay on the beautiful he employed an illustration that did not rest directly on the Platonic view mentioned above, and this passage had a considerable effect on the Mannerist and Academic theory of art. He wrote:

A faculty of the soul, disposed towards it, recognizes beauty, and there is no faculty surer in judging what belongs to it, even when the rest of the soul judges also. Perhaps it also pronounces in accordance with the form within the soul, using it as a standard in judgment, like a rule used to decide if a thing is straight. But how can the physical beauty be in accordance with the beauty that is prior to physical things? How does an architect find that the form of the external house corresponds to the form of his internal house and he calls it beautiful? Because the external house, apart from the stones, is the internal form, but divided by the external mass of matter; the indivisible being of the form manifests itself in manifold parts.[354]

Plotinus recognized an objection which was made to this view, when he argued against the Gnostics and affirmed that his principle did not sever the soul from the body but kept them together. He made his reasons clearer when he spoke of two men living together in a fine house, one of whom condemned it entirely but still remained there, while the other found that it had been produced by skilled technique and awaited the time when he was to leave, needing it no longer.[355]

In this way it becomes obvious that Plotinus held a theory of technique in general which derived from Aristotle and assumed great importance in his own system. He was unsympathetic to painting but approved of architecture for Platonic reasons. He admired sculpture most of all and often summoned its testimony on behalf of his views. By technique he did not mean the arts of design alone, much less did he have reference to any such classification as the *beaux-arts*; but what he had to say of technique applied to painting, sculpture, and architecture because these were all specialized skills.

THE SYSTEM OF PLOTINUS

The place of technique, an Aristotelian concept, and of the Ideas, adopted from Plato, in the system of Plotinus is important, since he incorporated these as fundamental principles in the rounded, coherent scheme by which he harmonized the characteristic views of both his great predecessors. Plato had already outlined the dialectical process by which the soul ascended to the eternal Ideas, while Aristotle had stressed form and matter as the outstanding aspects of reality, and he had also introduced the notion of physical movement as the distinguishing factor in nature.

Plotinus sought to overcome the disastrous separation of the Ideas from sensory experience and to secure coherent relations between the absolute, the world of spirit or intelligence, and the world of sensation by extending Aristotle's rule of motion to the entire universe. He asserted that these realms were connected as stages in one descending process, each being an overflow from the next higher, and the procedure of technique seemed to him convincing proof of this relation.

The comprehensive scheme of Plotinus is set forth in the *Enneads*, an edition of his works prepared by his disciple Porphyry, consisting of six parts of nine books each. In addition to linguistic and literary difficulties in these treatises, there is the method of presentation to deal with. Each book seems to be the report of one or more seminar sessions, and it often begins with a statement, usually from Plato, expounded, analyzed, and evaluated in discussion with a trained audience. Plotinus composed his works late in life when his system was already worked out in his own mind, and they assumed a consistent, central position with reference to which the several topics taken up were always treated. For these reasons, the *Enneads* are not progressive expositions of his doctrine so much as clarifications occasioned by the questions or objections of his audience. Obscurity and repetition make the comprehension of his works difficult, but they present the same fundamental views throughout.

For several centuries before Plotinus the transcendence of God had been progressively emphasized, and he posited the One as beyond existence.[356] The term "One" was used to stress its simplicity and absence of parts and its lack of positive attributes, since no qualities could be asserted to inhere in it. The One was identical with the Good, not as one Good or the good One, but absolutely.[357] As the first in the scale of being, the One could not be said to think, so that intelligence was the second stage of reality, but the first existing thing.[358] With intelligence began the division of the One into the manifold; the distinction between subject and object exhibited this trend.[359] Intelligence was, at the same time, identified with the Demiurge, the Creator of the world, as the ultimate physical cause.[360] The intelligible world included the Ideas or eternal forms, of individuals as well as of universals.[361] But these Ideas were immanent in intelligence, not apart from it, so that intelligence and its Ideas could be distinguished only in analysis.[362]

The manner in which each lower stage derived from a higher was not emanation as usually understood, for Plotinus denied that the higher lost some of its substance to the lower, which derived from it.[363] The lower was immanent in the higher, and its existence depended on its superior.[364] The process relating the different stages of reality was not voluntary but an action due to the necessity that the imperfect should be subsequent to the perfect.[365] An analogy to illustrate this situation was the sun, which radiated light and heat, without loss of substance, while remaining undisturbed and undiminished.[366] The dependence of the lower on the higher was exemplified by the mirror.[367] According to Plotinus, the activity by which the superior produced the inferior and by which the lower remained immanent in the higher was seeing, vision, or contemplation.[368]

Below intelligence was soul, the world-soul of Plato, which contemplated intelligence and from it secured that degree of reality which the world of appearance possessed.[369] But soul also inclined to that which was below it and created the world of sensation; it was identical with nature.[370] Individual souls were distinct but not separate from soul, and like it they contemplated what was below as well as what was above them.[371]

The world of appearance derived from soul, but on the lower side it was restricted by a negative principle which was matter.[372] Matter was, however, the nonexistent and therefore had no qualities;[373] but since the One, the first, was identical with the good, matter was similarly evil, as the last.

Individual souls were analyzed into intelligence, a sensory life, and matter.[374] Practical activities, including techniques, were considered inferior to theoretical contemplation. So far as they were connected with the phenomenal world, they were unimportant;[375] but so far as they involved logic and intelligence, they were commendable.[376] The religious motivation of his system appeared in the doctrine that above all sensory experience and intellectual analysis was ecstasy—immediate contemplation in union with intelligence,[377] where absolute beauty was to be found.[378]

THE TREATISE ON THE BEAUTIFUL

With this outline of his metaphysical system in mind, we may now turn to those passages in which the aesthetic theory of Plotinus was set forth, since it not only was consistent with his general attitude but constituted the culmination of the upward ascent. His analysis of beauty is to be found in two of the fifty-four books into which his work was divided; one of them was devoted to the beautiful in general,[379] while the other was concerned with intelligible or spiritual beauty.[380] But the treatise on spiritual beauty is not paralleled by one on the beauty of the sensory world, which means that he and his audience did not have sufficient interest in the matter to discuss the beauty of nature or of technical products, such as art. The essay on the beautiful was, after all, but a logical introduction to the treatment of spiritual beauty. Nevertheless, within these limitations, imposed by the temper of the times, he employed materials taken mainly from Plato and Aristotle, and he succeeded in accomplishing a task they had not undertaken. He was the first systematically to examine the concept of beauty and to achieve aesthetic principles which were philosophically established in their own right.

In the treatise on the beautiful he began by pointing out that it was present in sensory patterns, but it occurred also in things that were not sensory, such as professions, sciences, and virtues. Was beauty a single principle, and, if so, what was it? Virtue was always beautiful in itself, but physical things were sometimes beautiful and sometimes otherwise, so that physical existence and beauty were different things.

Before developing his theory further, he paused to demolish the popular belief that beauty was the result of putting parts together, by showing that on this basis the parts must also be beautiful. Again, simple things which were not composed were often beautiful. For this and other reasons, beauty could not be due to proportion or to consistency. Finally, how could intelligence itself be beautiful if proportion were the principle of beauty?[381]

Beauty in physical objects was instantly perceived, for when the soul discovered something similar to its own nature it was delighted, but it rejected ugly things as alien to its own essence. Both sensory and intelligible objects were beautiful because they participated in a form, but matter without form was the absolute ugly. Form was the source of wholeness in an object, and thus physical objects became beautiful by participation in a principle of divine origin.[382]

The soul, Plotinus declared, had a special faculty for the perception of beauty, which it judged by comparing sensory patterns with the beauty of form which it possessed within itself. Various examples showed that beauty in sensory objects derived from form, which descended on matter and gave it order.[383]

Just as we could not appreciate beauty in sensory objects without the senses, so we were able to grasp spiritual beauty because we already possessed it. As the contemplation of spiritual beauty was higher, it was more delightful, and those who were moved by it were lovers.[384] Spiritual beauty belonged to the soul and was truly real, while ugliness in the soul came from mingling with matter; but it could recover its beauty by purification and the rejection of alien matter.[385]

The virtues were thus attained by purging of the soul, by elimination of matter, and through union with divine intelligence. Matter was the first evil and ugliness in itself, but the One was both the good and the beautiful; goodness and beauty were there identical. The good was attained by purification, and the perception of it was beautiful.[386]

In the ascent to the divine, the soul aspired to the good which all men desired, but the soul that beheld absolute beauty, pure, beyond the sensory and spiritual worlds, possessed the supremely valuable.[387]

To attain the ecstatic contemplation of absolute beauty, we should flee from the senses and sensory beauty to the real world from which we came, closing our eyes in order to exercise another kind of vision.[388] In practicing this ascent, we should begin with the contemplation of fine callings, good deeds, and the actions of virtuous men, and not by contemplation of things made by technique, Plotinus explicitly declared. Then the soul should perfect itself until it became free from any admixture, for to enjoy the vision of divine beauty the soul must itself become divinely beautiful. In this way the soul would rise to the intelligible world and behold the beauty of the Ideas which derived from intelligence. Finally, beyond even intelligence, the soul would find beauty and the ultimate good which was the source and principle of beauty.[389]

From this summary of the treatise on the beautiful by Plotinus, the aspects of his thought which were congenial to the idealists can be readily marked, but the elements which they ignored should also be noted. Contemplation of the self or the soul was, for the idealists, a secure foundation for speculative thought. Plotinus was reassured by the beauty which he found there; the rationalist idealists supposed that they discovered in their estimate of their own souls an incontrovertible truth. But today we see that the self was simply one among a vast number of objects available for contemplation; judgments with regard to it were no more and no less guaranteed to be true than those with regard to the other objects. While Plotinus perceived beauty in his own soul, the romantic idealists often seem to have found in their selves something ugly and evil, from which they expected to escape by practicing the *beaux-arts*. Such a classification of techniques would have been abhorrent to Plotinus, who held techniques in general as tainted with inferiority, except for the convenient way in which they connected the several worlds that he distinguished. He was a more consistent idealist, for he passed as soon as possible from the beauty or truth of sensory things to the sources of those qualities and did not suppose that certain techniques were exempt from the contamination of matter. The mystic ascent which he expounded was a familiar program; and, while he personally was an ascetic, a man of recognized virtue, the mystical element in romantic idealism could easily justify any evil consistent with sensationalist materialism.

THE TREATISE ON INTELLIGIBLE BEAUTY

The treatise on intelligible beauty by Plotinus was one to which that on the beautiful was an introduction, but it repeated some of the points already made. It also depended for its materials on well-known passages in the Platonic dialogues[390] and began with that comparison between a marble statue and a rough block of stone which has already been mentioned in connection with references to sculpture made by Plotinus. Next he made the claim that technique paralleled nature rather than functioned subordinate to it, which has been cited when discussing his theory of techniques. Proceeding, then, to natural products, Plotinus asserted that the beauty of sensory objects derived also from form imparted by a superior principle, just as the beauty of technique was higher than that of things achieved by means of it, and the soul had within itself an example from which it might rise to intelligible beauty.[391] Contemplation of intelligible beauty, from which that of nature derived, accounted for the happiness of the gods.[392]

From this Plotinus advanced to conclusions not contained explicitly in his preceding treatise. He claimed that the wisdom of the technician must come from intelligible wisdom. He then took an opportunity to attack the Platonic theory that the earth was a gradual product of the Demiurge,[393] because, he said, this world developed from the superior intelligible world which was simultaneously its beginning and end, lacking nothing.[394] The primary beauty of the intelligible world was the source of beauty in this visible world, and it was wrong to criticize beauties here, for they were inferior only because they were not the superior from which they derived.[395]

Such considerations led Plotinus to conclusions which made aesthetic value the basic factor in his metaphysics. He said: "Yonder [in the intelligible world] active power alone possesses being, alone is beautiful, for where would beauty be if deprived of being, or being if deprived of beauty? To lose beauty is also to lack being." But he added immediately: "Here [in the world of sensation] there is deceptive being, an image that requires a borrowed beauty in order to appear beautiful and even to be."[396]

The gods and those who grasped beauty in the intelligible world found that their object was not external but divine and identical with the very self.[397] Plotinus then traced the ascent again, claiming that lack of sensory experience in its culmination was not ignorance but union with the true self.[398] He concluded this treatise with allegorical references to the genealogy of the gods, to illustrate the nature of beauty in the intelligible world, and summarized: "When we know ourselves we are beautiful, but ugly when we ignore ourselves."[399]

THE AESTHETIC IN THE PHILOSOPHY OF PLOTINUS

After we have noted the consistency of the two treatises on beauty by Plotinus with his general metaphysical structure, we realize that it was he who gave the aesthetic a place of unprecedented importance in philosophy, since he identified it with the absolute. Far from being limited to a theory of art, he had in mind the logical and aesthetic value of concepts; and even when these were dissipated in the undifferentiated absolute it was still beautiful.

The consequences and implications of this point of view were considerable, but his position was in agreement with the intellectual climate of his age. The Alexandrine school, known to us through the works of Plotinus, developed in an atmosphere heavy with defeat. In the whole civilized world there was then no escape from frustration. Hopeless and disillusioned, no longer expecting that genuine satisfaction could be gained through dealing with sensory objects, men still were intent upon ethical problems. But faith in the efficacy of human action having vanished, moral values were sought in religious beliefs and mystical rites rather than in constructive efforts. The intellectual concerns of the times were predominantly religious, and salvation was earnestly desired through the mediation of some power intervening between untrustworthy sensation and remote, impassive divinity.

Plotinus, however, did not simply elaborate notions current in his day by devising a new plan of salvation or inventing novel rituals. He attempted to justify religious feeling through an Aristotelian, purely rationalistic scheme. He adopted the division of the world into the absolute—the realm of spirit or intelligence and of the soul, with its counterparts of ecstasy, mind, and sensation in human experience—and matter as the limit of the descending scale; but this was a plan common to the whole period. What distinguished him from the Gnostics and the other Neo-Platonists was his resolute rationalism.

The aspect of his system which is often called "emanation" was also a prevalent explanatory concept, as familiar as is evolution today, although it is more properly termed a "theory of procession," as Plotinus understood it. But Plotinus rejected evolution in the modern sense, for against the Gnostics he argued that the world was eternal, not a historical product but a continuous, final, and self-contained reality. This view was in agreement with astronomical and cosmological conclusions then prevalent, and it also agreed with the general theory of history in antiquity. His philosophy afforded no principle of progressive development or evolution in time; his metaphysics did not view the past and the future as extensions of the present. Instead, his metaphysics expounded the internal structure of the present world, discovered through introspection of the soul, now identified with the divine, in its own eternal, present moment.

The flight of the solitary soul to absolute solitude was achieved by excluding sensation, using progressive comparison of memories and concepts, finally, to surpass reason and experience. For Descartes the self-evident existence of the soul, invulnerable to every doubt, was something on which he could construct a philosophical system, while to Plotinus the obvious beauty of the soul, perceived by a mind compelled to turn its attention inward, seemed equally certain. Plotinus found undeniable evidence of the reality of beauty in his own soul; but when the object known to be pre-eminently beautiful was his own self and when knowledge of this beauty was the most obvious instance of truth, then ethics was bound to be subordinate to aesthetics, with logic subservient to both. In spite of his prolonged discussion of intelligence or spirit and his adherence to the methods of rationalism up to, but not including, the very last step, the ultimate, mystical goal was beauty. Without attributes, the One was identical with the good as the end to be achieved, and it was beauty when attained. As a description of a sequence of psychological states in human experience this might have been acceptable, but as an analysis of metaphysical relations it had inevitable defects. Logic was likely to dissolve in sentiment, and the unknowable One was not distinguishably different from vague, intense well-being, which was not even conscious of itself. The hope of rationalism is the discovery of orderly relations, but the result of the intellectual labors of Plotinus was to liquidate reason itself.

This aspect of the thought of Plotinus has been traced to Plato by Aristotelians, who look upon Plato's recourse to poetic imagery and myths as mysticism; but it has been blamed on Aristotle by Platonists, who see an example of self-destroying rationalism in the concept of the Unmoved Mover. Those who interpret Plotinus as a natural development of Greek thought in either of these directions are opposed by those who find in him the intrusion of a specifically oriental factor, connected with the cultural confusion of the times. But it may have been a case where Greek thought reached a stage that had become permanent in the East.

This trait in the speculation of Plotinus brings out an interesting difference between the three greatest Greek philosophers. Plato had so keenly insisted on ethical value that his theory of knowledge was not convincing, while the dependence of aesthetic value on the moral good left it with little independent interest. Aristotle, his successor, was so concerned with methods to understand the given that his ethics sometimes seem but an organized system of prudence. While he recognized the distinction between the ethical and the aesthetic, he did not pursue it. Plotinus, finally, discovered such conclusive aesthetic value in the object of introspection that his ethics and logic depended on it. In effect each thinker selected one of the primary values—the ethical, the logical, and the aesthetic—as a foundation to which he subordinated the others.

PLOTINUS AND THE IDEALISTS

Something has already been said about the relation of Plotinus to the idealists as one of their sources, but further consideration will show how the Greek tradition preserved him from lapsing into the mistakes typical of his admirers among the modern idealists. Like him, the romantic idealists gave a position of extreme importance to the aesthetic, subordinating the good and the true to the beautiful. Idealists, both rationalist and romantic, turned to their own souls as objects of whose properties and relations they could be certain.[400]

But Plotinus retained many sound principles native to the tradition in which he shared. He never had the arrogance and intolerance required to assert that his own divine will created the universe. If he had a low opinion of sensory objects in comparison with intelligible realities, he had just as little esteem for the human soul in comparison with what lay beyond and above it. Technique was for him not an obstacle, a way to exercise the will by struggling with self-created opponents, but a parallel in the human sphere to the processes of nature. It provided a clear example of the upward ascent to the One.

Although Plotinus was, like Plato, hypostatizing the categories and making the sequence of psychological states a model of how ultimate reality was constituted, more frequently than any of the leaders of Greek thought he cited works of sculpture, painting, and architecture as persuasive examples to support his arguments. He went further than Plato in analyzing the artist's activity and in drawing inferences from his observations. He was particularly fond of sculpture, and to emphasize the vivid reality of the ecstatic vision he could think of nothing more appropriate than statues.

But he never supposed that all we can know is our own ideas, and he could not think of the Ideas as simply patterns inside the head of the artist. He discussed architecture, sculpture, painting, the dance, poetry, and music as techniques, but he did not have any comprehensive term, such as *beaux-arts*, to include them all, for he would promptly have rejected the belief that any or all of these techniques and their products were exclusively beautiful. In his theory of beauty he explicitly considered such things as virtues and professions, which are not sensory patterns, as well as natural and technical products that do present sensory data. Nor was he concerned to claim the privileges of the poet for the painter.

The ethics of Plotinus stressed purification from evil to recover the soul's original, beautiful integrity. But his understanding of history was not that of an infinitely expansive development, in which the absolute I made itself manifest. His doctrine of the descent or procession and of the ascent of the soul to the One was a circular, self-contained, eternally repeated process. The succession of states of being from the One to the lowest limit of matter was a necessary, inevitable overflowing of reality. The soul regained the solitude of the absolute by a course of purification and abstraction. But, to employ Kantian terms, for Plotinus the task of the empirical I was mainly negative and the transcendental One was not an I; it was even not conscious.

When the romantic idealists discovered Plotinus, they sought support in him for the position which they had established. His emphasis on aesthetics was congenial to them; and, although he did not have special reference to the academic classification of the *beaux-arts* when he analyzed the concept of technique, they supposed that he had. The introspective approach to intellectual problems on the part of the rationalist idealists, but even more the search for aesthetic value by the romantic idealists, led them to approve the self-centered contemplation of his own soul by Plotinus as something of which he could be quite certain.

Having observed how Plato's theory of the Ideas was perverted by modern idealism, how the theory of technique set forth by Plotinus was held to rationalize the *beaux-arts* dogma, and how his estimate of the place of the aesthetic in philosophy led to conclusions that he never anticipated, we may now turn to Aristotle. Ever since the sixteenth century, when his *Poetics* was recovered, he has had an important influence on the theory of art. But in his other works, also, principles can be found which overcome the weaknesses either found in Plato and Plotinus or else developed from their thought. A theory of art based upon Aristotle is, indeed, still the one followed in practice, whatever the values and functions attributed to it.

ARISTOTLE

Plato's works have come down to us practically intact; they are polished literary productions, and some at least of his dialogues have attracted fascinated readers in every age. But Aristotle's finished compositions have not survived, and the writings that we today possess are lecture notes and outlines, either his own or those of his students, often combined in rather incoherent fashion by editors who put together in one treatise topics that had slight connection with one another.[401]

Except for their scientific and philosophical interest they would find few readers today; and of his works, that one which is now most frequently studied is a brief discussion of tragic poetry, a minor part of his whole achievement.

As in his treatment of poetry, when Aristotle referred to painting, sculpture, and architecture he retained more of Plato than is usually admitted, but his endeavor was to understand the given fact rather than to correct the ethical foundations of his times. As a result, his comments on art and aesthetics, viewed in the light of his criticism of the Platonic Ideas, have provided for art a legitimate and proper place in the world of human experience.

ARISTOTLE AND PLATO

Aristotle's speculative enterprise was no less original than Plato's, but his method was to analyze and classify, to reflect on the implications of experience, rather than to degrade the world in the interest of abstractions outside it. Instead of finding in the principle of imitation a reason for denying philosophic importance to art and admitting only a dependent, derivative value in sensory objects, Aristotle directed his efforts to examination of the existing world as one that included art; he could thus offer an explanation of the facts of technique and of aesthetic value in technical products.

Plato adduced the evidence presented by works of art when they represented models, to illustrate his theory of Ideas; but he then condemned art and repudiated the belief that it could have genuine truth, goodness, or beauty, in order to reserve these attributes exclusively for his abstractions. Aristotle, on the contrary, could accept the principle of imitation and admit that works of art might possess those admirable qualities. He had less to say about painting and sculpture than he did about poetry, perhaps for the reason that in the opinion of Aristotle's contemporaries whatever could be said of an imitation could also be said of the thing imitated, and it would have been an unnecessary duplication to survey other imitations also.

It was Plato's aim to secure the Idea of the good as the ultimate reality against every changing circumstance, but his attempt succeeded only in placing it on an inaccessible level, with the properties of a logical abstraction, claiming that the experienced world was its inferior. Aristotle applied more thorough logical analysis to observed facts, furnishing more adequate instruments to understand accessible realities. These comprised art as well as ethical value, which he placed firmly in the center of human relations, a world with which we are all acquainted.

Although he did not expand the remark, Aristotle also made a logical distinction, which eventually led to a definite separation of aesthetics from ethics in the thought of Plotinus. The confusion between the two in the minds of such thinkers as Socrates and Plato was aided by a limitation of the Greek language as then employed, for *kalos* indicated the admirable both in ethics and in aesthetics. It had the same ambiguity as the English word "fair," which may mean beautiful in appearance when applied to a girl but signifies something just and generous when used with reference to an individual's acts or judgments.

IMITATION

For Aristotle, imitation was, to begin with, a principle to separate the products of certain techniques from those of others. He included instrumental music along with poetry and the drama among the imitative techniques,[402] on the ground that music imitated human character.[403] He mentioned works of painting, sculpture, and poetry while he asserted that it was sweet and pleasant to learn about things and admire them; therefore, whether the thing imitated was attractive or not, in relating an imitation to its model we were bound to learn and might enjoy the object.[404] When we remained unacquainted with the model, our pleasure could be due to the execution, the color, or some similar cause.[405]

The historical origin and psychological function of the techniques of imitation pointed to their necessary existence as a contribution to experience. Indeed, to make imitations and to learn from them was a distinguishing trait of mankind; in this, men were superior to the other animals.[406] Our natural tendency to make imitations and our ability to learn while we delight in them, Aristotle thought, rescued the imitative techniques from charges of insignificance and intrinsic inferiority that Plato had preferred. Having defined and justified them, he suggested various principles to mark subdivisions of the general classification.[407]

Aristotle analyzed imitation in general rather than resting content with Socrates and Plato after borrowing a term from popular usage. He expanded and refined its meaning so that it no longer was restricted to the copying or repetition of an original. He held that imitation depended on similarity between the imitation and what was imitated; this was a qualitative relation, he said, not a quantitative one such as equality, inferring that imitation in the popular sense was merely quantitative.[408] It was awareness of similarity that made it possible for us to enjoy imitations and to learn from them by means of reasoning. He explained the relation of techniques and reasoning to experience in this fashion:

Thus the other animals live by sensory impressions and memories and have but little share of experience, but mankind also lives by means of technique and reasoning. It is from memory that men acquire experience, because many memories of the same thing finally result in having the effect of one experience. Experience seems similar to knowledge and technique, but men acquire knowledge and technique through experience.[409]

Imitation was, first of all, a basis for classifying certain techniques. Against Plato, he held that it was not intrinsically inferior. A product of imitative technique differed from most things that men make because it was similar to some things that men could not make; but there was no inevitable ethical inference from this fact. Against the dogmatists of the Academy, centuries later, and against the romantic idealists, he would have said that there was also no necessary inference as to aesthetic value.

Aristotle's view gave to imitation a value far beyond that of its original popular meaning as reproduction or duplication. The prior distinction, however, before objects could be assigned to the classification "techniques of imitation" was technique itself. Aristotle held this to be a principle of extraordinary significance, for technique was the specifically human and intelligible factor in the world.

TECHNIQUE

To realize the importance of technique in this philosopher's organized thought, we should observe that Aristotle's *Poetics* and his *Rhetoric*, probably even his logic, were not composed as purely intellectual exercises but had conspicuous practical ends in view. To understand, to appreciate, and to produce the sort of things to which these lectures were devoted seemed to him a not unworthy activity. His analysis was to show the intelligible relations characteristic of such specialized performance; but to understand them should be an aid to improved production.

Plato himself had held that those techniques which exhibited rational principles were superior to others. In one connection he said:

> Are not arithmetic and certain other techniques of the same kind, regardless of their application, abstract knowledge? . . . . But the knowledge found in carpentry and manual crafts in general is inherent in their exercise, and through them are produced objects which previously did not exist. . . . . In this way, then, divide all kinds of knowledge into two classes, calling one the practical and the other solely intellectual. [410]

Following this division, Aristotle concluded that "the object of theoretical knowledge is truth, while that of practical knowledge is action."[411] He classified the virtues in similar fashion as intellectual and moral or pertaining to character. The intellectual virtues were further divided into the scientific and the calculative; the calculative were not exercised with regard to things invariable[412] but were invoked in the exercise of technique. By this means Aristotle undertook to reconcile Plato's aim to achieve impregnable knowledge of eternal things with the sophists' objective, which was to gain success in a constantly changing world.

Aristotle viewed the parallel between technique and natural process as connected with the factor of imitation: "In general, techniques either, on the basis of nature, carry things further than nature can, or

they imitate nature."[413] Certain techniques applied to natural products made them more useful to men, by carrying natural process further than nature did, as was the case in cooking. Other natural products were already so well developed that technique imitated them, as
could be seen in portraiture.

He also discussed inspiration or imagination, which for Plato had
been perhaps a divine, but surely an irrational, factor in experience.
He advised the dramatic poet to imagine his characters and their situations as vividly as possible for a very practical reason: "In construct-
ing plots and completing the effect by the help of dialogue the poet
should, as far as possible, keep the scene before his eyes. Only thus, by
getting the picture as clear as if he were present at the actual event,
will he find what is fitting and detect contradictions."[414]

Enthusiasm, an emotion or state of the soul, he discussed in connection with music and said that hearers were thrown into the same state
of feeling represented by the imitation.[415] He even considered abnor-
malities of the imagination, such as the visions of the mad, showing
how they differed from normal memory and recollection.[416] The satisfaction found by lovers in things vividly recalling the beloved was
mentioned,[417] and other references to imagination[418] show that he approached its problems as proper to elementary psychology.

While, on the one hand, Aristotle developed the concept of imitation, making its essence the quality of similarity, on the other, he still
retained the term as relevant to objects where similarity existed but
not as the result of imitative action. For that reason, when the *Poetics*
was recovered and studied intensively, the concept of imitation provided exceptional difficulties for critical theory; but when the doctrine of the *beaux-arts* emerged, it lost ground, and its rationalistic
character was so alien to romantic idealism that it has now practically disappeared among responsible thinkers.

The emphasis which Plotinus placed on technique was, however, a
principle that he accepted from Aristotle, and it has often been successfully revived in opposition to idealism, by more recent philosophers.

ARCHITECTURE, SCULPTURE, AND PAINTING

Of the particular techniques afterward combined under the name
"arts of design," Aristotle gave no systematic account, after discussing the concept of technique in general and developing implications of
imitation. But various incidental references are of interest.

Architecture was not considered by either Plato or Aristotle to be an imitative technique. It was frequently referred to by the latter as a conspicuous example of human constructive enterprise, and some of its aspects were brought in to support his arguments.[419] He used this sort of illustration to show what he meant by a material cause,[420] and he also laid down certain architectural requirements of city-planning.[421]

To sculpture he gave greater attention, saying, among other things, that Phidias and Polyclitus were examples of wisdom in the fields of techniques.[422] He pointed out that the sculptor exercised a special skill and that a statue could be made of bronze, to illustrate that an object could have several distinct causes; and in describing the four principal causes or necessary conditions of a product, he mentioned sculpture in connection with both material and formal cause.[423] He named Polyclitus when he claimed that an agent could be indicated by a characteristic,[424] and he probably had in mind that sculptor's excellence of proportion when he spoke of virtue as a mean between excess and deficiency.[425]

Aristotle did not see in painting, as did Plato, the leading witness to the deceptiveness, untruthfulness, and unreality of art. For him Zeuxis and Polygnotus were representatives of painting, as Polyclitus and Phidias were typical of sculpture. Accordingly, when he analyzed tragedies that did not excel in the study of character, he compared Zeuxis, who was lacking in this respect, with Polygnotus, who was remarkable for his success in it.[426] He stressed his view that in tragedy the plot was primary and character was secondary by saying that lovely colors, when smeared at random on a surface, were not so attractive as drawings in black and white.[427]

Again, while offering a defense for the representation in tragedy of apparent impossibilities, he said: "For poetic effect a convincing impossibility is preferable to that which is unconvincing though possible. It may be impossible that there should be such people as Zeuxis used to paint, but it would be better if there were; for the type should improve on the actual."[428] This point, obviously, was made as part of his defense of poetry against the attacks of Plato, but the doctrine of idealizing imitation was afterward developed from it by critics of the Mannerist period, in an attempt to reconcile imitation and the Idea. In his analysis of ethical differences in works of art, Aristotle held that "Polygnotus depicted men as better than they are, and Pauson worse, while Dionysius made them as they are."[429]

When Plato listed the subjects to be included in a liberal education, he could find no place for drawing; but Aristotle made express provision for it, and he appeared far more confident of its value than he was of that of popular music. He reported that it was one of the customary subjects in the normal curriculum, "reading and writing and drawing being taught as useful for the purposes of life and very serviceable."[430] Drawing was a desirable accomplishment, for "drawing also seems to be useful in making us better judges of the works of artists."[431] He later gave a broader reason for such study, saying that it trained the ability to appreciate beauty in sensory objects, natural as well as technical:

And it is also clear that some of the useful subjects as well ought to be studied by the young not only because of their utility, like the study of reading and writing, but also because they may lead on to many other branches of knowledge; and similarly they should study drawing not in order that they may not go wrong in their private purchases and may avoid being cheated in buying and selling furniture, but rather because this study makes a man observant of bodily beauty.[432]

BEAUTY

Aristotle definitely recognized the difference between ethics and aesthetics, for he said: "Goodness is distinct from beauty for it is always in conduct that goodness is present, whereas beauty is also in motionless things."[433] Although he did not write a treatise devoted to aesthetics, as he did for ethics, and we have no work of his dealing with painting, sculpture, and architecture, like his books on rhetoric and tragic poetry, he was at least aware of the basic consideration that makes aesthetics possible as a field of philosophy. He did not follow the view, accepted largely by his predecessors, that moral good and aesthetic value are identical.

The main characteristics of beauty, he said, were "orderly arrangement, proportion, and definiteness."[434] But these traits were not to be found in works of art alone, for Aristotle demanded that there be a limitation of magnitude in the city-state to secure orderly government: "Certainly beauty is usually found in number and in magnitude, but there is a due measure of magnitude for a city-state as there is also for all other things—animals, plants, tools."[435] As universal qualities, it is clear, the various kinds of beauty that he admired were to be looked for in things natural, as well as in products of technique.

DEFENSE OF ART

Color and figure were two aspects of all visual objects, and therefore of works of art, analyzed by Aristotle. He discussed color and color-harmony as sources of pleasure,[436] and he examined the relation of vision to light;[437] a short treatise, assigned to Aristotle but probably by a member of the Peripatetic school, consists of many collected observations and some theories regarding the matter.[438] Figure and color were for Aristotle the two elements of visual impression; and in paintings, he asserted, they were needed for signs or indications of character but did not by themselves possess it. He asserted that paintings, however, could have an effect on character, and for that reason ``the young must not look at the works of Pauson but those of Polygnotus.''[439]

Such statements show that Aristotle never conceded the exemption of art and the artist from the responsibilities incurred by other human beings who made things, but art was not therefore intrinsically bad in its effects. Observations similar to those which he made with regard to tragic poetry might also have been extended to art, since he formulated a deliberate defense of the drama against the censures of Plato. The latter had condemned representation by means of art, where its explanation as imitation could be tested, in order to reserve imitation as a relation between the eternal Ideas and sensory objects, where it had to be taken on fatih.

In answer Aristotle compared history and tragic poetry, for both he and Plato found ethical value in men's conduct and actions, with which history was concerned. He claimed: ``The real difference is this, that one tells what happened and the other what might happen. For this reason poetry is more philosophical and serious than history, because poetry gives general truths while history gives particular facts.''[440]

Even more famous is the phrase in the definition of tragedy which has proved such a fruitful source of controversy: ``through pity and fear relieving these and similar passions.''[441] Whatever its precise translation and interpretation, it is clear that Aristotle believed there were in the drama forces making for moral improvement rather than for corruption.

Plato had charged that imitation made works of art inferior, the third stage away from reality. Aristotle replied by making a logical and psychological analysis of the class of real things to which the drama belonged. Plato had rejected imitative art as untrue, and his disciple maintained that it offered a truth superior to the recorded fact. Finally, Plato believed that drama had an evil effect on the audience, but Aristotle claimed that, on the contrary, such an experience purified it of weaknesses.

ARISTOTLE ON THE PLATONIC IDEAS

Aristotle, as we have just seen, had high regard for technique; he interpreted imitation so that it surpassed the popular notion of duplication; and he defended the techniques of imitation against the attacks of Plato. His hostile analysis of the Platonic Ideas is fully as important.

After nineteen years of study with Plato, Aristotle was probably well informed as to the doctrine of the Ideas then taught in the Academy. We have already noted that Plato was unable to offer convincing replies to his own objections to the theory; but he retained it, in spite of its logical defects, since he thought the Ideas necessary for reasoning and discourse. He could think of no alternative to them but a chaos of sensations and an irrational flux. Without them he felt that there would be no proper objects of ethical endeavor.

But Plato's own reservations were not observed by his followers, either in the Academy or among the Neo-Platonists. They continued to hold that the Ideas existed beyond the limits of time and space, far removed from any actual experience. They still explained the relation between the Ideas and sensory objects by means of imitation and participation. Idealist adherents in modern times have charged that Aristotle misunderstood his master's doctrine; as a rule, they have attempted to explain away Plato's own objections to the theory. The customary procedure has been to attribute to Plato the very views that Aristotle stressed as his own, believing them to be insuperable differences between himself and the Platonists.[442]

Aristotle's general line of argument was that the Ideas could not exist in separation from individual, particular things. He showed in detail that the Platonic doctrine could not be proved, that the reasons advanced on its behalf were unsound, and that it was an impediment to philosophical investigation.

Socrates, he pointed out, had not conceived of universals and definitions as existing by themselves, apart from things actual, but the Platonists asserted their independent existence, giving the name of Ideas to them. Such an attitude did not render speculative problems more amenable to reason but made the task one of insurmountable complexity.[443] It at least doubled the number of things that had to be explained, for "the Ideas are as many as, or not fewer than, the things in search of whose causes these thinkers were led to the Ideas." It was probable, even so, that there would be more Ideas than there were particular things. For each sensory object there was a corresponding

Idea apart from it, and for things not sensory there was one Idea or common denominator to include the many occasions on which it occurred.

The arguments by which the Platonists undertook to prove the existence of Ideas were defective and unsound, according to Aristotle. Some of them proved nothing, while others would lead to the conclusion that Ideas existed for things when they could not conceivably do so. Since there were to be Ideas for all things considered by the sciences, there would be Ideas for negations, and there would also be Ideas for things that had ceased to be. But if the Ideas were transcendent and continued to exist independently and if particulars were related to them by means of imitation and participation, how was it possible for things that did not exist to continue imitating or participating in Ideas?[444]

It was held that there were Ideas of things other than substances or existing individuals, but if things participated in Ideas, the latter must also be substances. The same name, shared by both the Idea and the particular, must mean the same thing for both. If the definition of a particular and of the corresponding Idea were the same, a separation of the two led to unintelligible distinctions.[445]

To explain that the Ideas were patterns, Aristotle declared, "is to use empty phrases and poetic metaphors, for what is it that makes particular things after the Ideas as models?" Besides, a thing could exist or become without imitating something else; for example, a man could become like Socrates without imitating him, whether or not Socrates then existed; and this would also be true even if Socrates were immortal.

The Platonic theory required a different Idea or pattern for each predicate of a particular thing, hence there would be a multiplicity of patterns for a single thing. Furthermore, it would be necessary to have Ideas on which Ideas would themselves be patterned, so that an Idea would be both the copy and the original of itself.[446] Finally, Aristotle analyzed the later explanation of the Ideas as numbers and rejected it also.[447]

He summarized his objections to the theory of Ideas by saying of the Platonists:

They not only treat the Ideas as universal substances, but also as separable and particular. . . . . The reason why those who hold substances to be universal combined these two views was that they did not identify substances with sensible things. They considered that the particulars in the sensible world are in a state of flux, and that none of them persists, but that the universal exists besides them and is something distinct from them. This theory . . . . was initiated by Socrates as a result of his definitions, but he did not separate universals from particulars; and he was right in not separating them. This is evident from the facts; for without the universal we cannot acquire knowledge, and the separation of the universal is the cause of the difficulties which we find in the theory of Ideas.[448]

ARISTOTLE'S THEORY OF CAUSES

To replace the theory of Ideas, Aristotle developed the theory of form. He held that the essence of the particular was its form and the particular was an individual, a whole whose parts could be distinguished only through abstraction. Matter was the general reciprocal of form; but, while form and matter could be distinguished in the individual, they could not be separated in the actual object; neither form nor matter ever existed apart from its reciprocal term.

All actual forms were products of either natural process or human technique. Products of technique, among which he would have included those of design, could always be accounted for on the basis of four types of cause: formal, material, efficient, and final.[449] He did not limit form to shape, nor did he virtually restrict cause to one kind— the efficient—as did the Cartesians. Following his example, the theory of causes may be illustrated by works of art.

The four categories were classifications of indispensable conditions required for the production of such objects. A statue could always be analyzed in these terms. The formal cause would be the plan or design according to which the piece of sculpture had been made. Later thinkers have seen that this formal cause was itself a product of imagination, of which memories were the matter; but the artist planned his work in accordance with the opportunities and limitations of the technique in which he was skilled. The orderly application of tools to sensory materials was, for the technician, an acquired skill, but one so familiar with practice that it became a specialized habit. Aristotle did not suppose that an absolute will could create without materials and orderly process. In his sustained effort to understand the relations of the real, he could not ignore the data of sensation or the orderly sequence of technique.

It was, therefore, consistent with Aristotelian tradition when sixteenth-century critics found in drawing a specific technique by which the several processes proper to painting, architecture, and sculpture could be grouped together in the class "arts of design," afterward abbreviated to "art." Design meant, first of all, the imagined plan, and in this sense it was common to all constructive human efforts. But design also indicated the particular technique of drawing, and in this sense it served to distinguish all members of this class from the products of other techniques.

The material cause of a statue was the bronze, marble, or wood of which the work was constructed. Such kinds of matter, before they were taken in hand by the sculptor, had other forms, but they acquired a new one given by the artist. Unlike the romantic idealists, Aristotle did not make the mistake of fancying that the artist could carry out his design without materials to transform, nor did he suppose that the artist himself created his own materials in order to exercise his creative will. Again, Aristotle did not fall into the idealist error of asserting that all we know are our ideas, for he was acquainted with innumerable objects so familiar that he did not have to invoke concepts to explain what he already understood. Concepts were necessary to discourse; but, even though he was a philosopher, Aristotle realized that writing and reading, speaking and hearing, did not comprise the total range of human experiences. In case an object was not fully understood, an appeal to the concepts representing the four kinds of cause would, if thoroughly pursued, yield the knowledge desired. The technician, also, had recourse to concepts and employed the calculative intellect to remedy the situation, when tools or materials did not function as expected or when the result hoped for was not realized.

He could admit the existence for imagination of forms and concepts to which no actual sensory pattern then existed. But in order to account for the emergence of new forms he did not find it necessary to assume that natural objects were also simply products of his imagination. That objects could lose their status as forms to become matter of a new form was not for him a logical impossibility or an unhappy actuality. It was something to be observed every time an artist created a new work out of previously existing materials; and the created object, because it was the result of a process, could always be understood in terms of a material as well as a formal cause.

The statue was also to be explained in relation to its efficient cause. The sculptor used tools upon his materials, carrying out his imagined design as well as he was able. He could eliminate various alternatives and determine the arrangement of his work in advance, as far as he deemed desirable, by means of drawings. In dealing with a specific individual object, such as a statue, explanation by means of vague, general causes, assumed at the same time to be efficient, would not be enough. The force of gravity, a type of economic structure, or similar reason would be inadequate to account for the actual product as an individual. That universals could themselves function as efficient causes, according to the belief of many idealists, would scarcely have seemed plausible to him. To assume that the transcendental I, itself a remote and abstract universal, could perform as an efficient cause would have been fantastic.

Aristotle knew well that men do not make things solely by taking thought, by imagining forms. Designs and plans, things hoped for in imagination, precede and accompany the exercise of technique. A sensory pattern can be achieved by a human being when he employs sensory materials. A mythical transcendental I—a universal abstracted from the continuity observed by each man in the course of his own experiences—even if granted existence, could not, any more than the individual series, of which it was assumed to consist, transform without something that already existed to be transformed. To relieve this transcendental I of the need of orderly procedure in achieving its designs and to claim either that it created its materials at the same time that it achieved its new forms or that all forms were imaginary and imagined forms had no matter was to postulate the impossible on behalf of the incredible. Abstractions do not act as efficient causes; individual men alone or in co-operation are the efficient causes of paintings, statues, and buildings.

Last of all, a statue might be explained in terms of final cause, the end or goal of the work performed, the resultant product for the sake of which the sculptor had imagined a design, applying then his tools to materials in a sequence of orderly operations. Like nature, technique also often failed fully to achieve its desired goal; but, on the whole, Aristotle thought, the fact of technique helped us to understand natural process also. There was an intelligible sequence of stages in the development of any natural product, just as there was in the steps by which a statue was created. As any resulting product of natural or technical process exhibited an order in its parts and as the sequence of stages by which it came into being also displayed a cumulative tendency, so Aristotle held that the final object must also represent a type of cause. Any orderly action implied an ordered result, and this he termed the final cause.

Aristotle's four causes or principles of explanation to account for the form of any actual product were consistent with the positive doctrine of relativity. Often, as by the ancient sceptics, relativity has been judged an insuperable obstacle to true knowledge. As every object of awareness must be in relation to other things but, it was supposed, true knowledge would possess an object independently of any relations, thus genuine understanding was impossible. The positive doctrine of relativity holds that, since the real is always in relations, we can acquire true knowledge of a present object by ascertaining how it is related. Relativity, as a positive appreciation of the inevitable relatedness of things, is a most reliable assurance that adequate knowledge can be gained. To connect a sensory pattern produced by technique, such as a statue, with its formal, material, efficient, and final causes is to discover specific relations of genuine significance. To analyze how aspects or parts of a present object are related to one another is to find out how it is with regard to the category of final cause.

VII

Contributions to an American Philosophy of Art

SO FAR we have justified the need of Americans for a philosophy of art consistent with their other basic insights. We have traced the natural history of art, seeing how the Idea was transformed from a metaphysical absolute into a mental image, which was claimed to be the essence of art, while still retaining its divine attributes. We have noted how the Academy was instituted to improve the social prestige of artists, how the concept of the *beaux-arts* was evolved to support their claims, and how the field of aesthetics was developed to deal with the problems that ensued. We have also examined the concept of design as the one that actually obtains in practice even now.

Next, we traced the course of rationalist idealism in relation to art, through Descartes, Spinoza, Locke, Leibniz, and Berkeley, culminating in Kant. After that we analyzed the romantic idealism that superseded it through Herder, Schiller, Schlegel, Wackenroder and Tieck, Fichte, and Schelling. The views of Hitler were seen to be the most conspicuous recent expressions of romantic idealism in art.

Contrasted with these were the views of Socrates, Plato, Plotinus, and Aristotle. Their discussions were found to offer no ground for the usual German idealist interpretations of the ancient philosophers with regard to art. Indeed, they still provide sound principles which can well be adapted toward a realistic, American philosophy of art.

This work has been entitled a "preface," since it does not pretend to be a complete philosophy of art but simply presents some historical data and critical comments which are preliminary to that purpose. The misrepresentations and erroneous conclusions of the German idealists have been exposed, and the constructive elements suggested by classical sources will now be reviewed in summary form. After that, certain basic considerations, deemed essential to a comprehensive American rationalization of art, will be put forward.

IMPLICATIONS OF THE CLASSICAL TRADITION

When we use the term "art" to signify the techniques or arts of design, we imply that its products present patterns of sensory data and that these patterns are significant and valuable as a result of human, ordered actions.

Aristotle might well have accepted the classification "arts of design," since it was an extension of the method he had already applied, in considering different types of technique and grouping them according to some principle of distinction. He had gone far toward superseding imitation in the sense of copying and had seen that the quality of similarity was not limited to the imitative techniques but was a necessary factor in the identification of any object and in the acquisition of knowledge. To identify an object by assigning it to a class of which it was a member was the initial step in understanding it. To know it in terms of similarity to other things was an indispensable and preliminary step before it could be judged with regard to those qualities in which members of a class might differ from one another.

It would not have occurred to Aristotle, any more than it would to Socrates, Plato, or Plotinus, that a group of techniques and their products could be established with beauty as their essence or distinguishing trait. The products as objects of human awareness must necessarily be subject to logical and ethical, as well as aesthetic, judgment. By virtue of the fact that works of art could be explained as goals or ends of human effort in terms of final cause, they could not escape the possibility of valid ethical judgment. Because they resulted from orderly processes and presented an intelligible order in the product, they offered opportunities for reliable logical judgment. Since a work of art could be intelligible as an orderly product and valuable as a result of human enterprise, it was also, then, to be judged aesthetically.

Music, the dance, poetry, and similar designations are names for organized patterns of sensation produced by technique whenever they are the actual and immediate objects of human interest, attention, or effort. To include these, together with the arts of design, in one vague group called "fine arts" or *beaux-arts* is to submit to the academic dogma of the seventeenth century. It implies that the *beaux-arts* and beauty are one, that art and aesthetics are the same thing, which is an illogical claim and contrary to familiar experience.

In spite of the confusions naturally resulting from the *beaux-arts* dogma, we still succeed in practice when by the name "art" we mean the techniques of design and their products. When we have to do with an art school, with art history, a museum of art, or an art exhibition, we properly rely on that definition in our actions. We have clear recollections of the sort of thing with which we have dealt; we have justified expectations as to the type of object we shall find; and when we are in the presence of the objects and activities designated by "art," we adopt appropriate attitudes and pursue proper courses of action.

It is for the very reason that the designation "art" does not and cannot include positive aesthetic value in conspicuous degree as an essential attribute that aesthetic judgments can be and are exercised with regard to works of art. If *beaux-arts* means that its members are always beautiful, it is not a genuine and valuable classification; and if the claim is reduced to the modest assertion that objects belonging to it are liable to aesthetic judgment, in that case it does not differ from the products of every other technique or from any object whatever, and the name is misleading.

A work of art presents an organized pattern of sensory data, and it is a product of technique. The senses for which such an object offers occasions of ordered experience are chiefly those of vision, touch, equilibrium, and direction. The way in which these data are composed as matter of a form secures for them, as a rule, a high degree of temporal persistence. The Greeks' sculpture and architecture survive, long after their music and drama perished with those who first created and enjoyed them.

Because they are products of human technique as well as vivid, durable patterns, they are significant of their human origins and are means whereby human experience can be recorded, communicated, and appreciated. The Greek way of life differed from that of the German romanticists, and the significant differences are preserved in the works of art they both made. Inevitably and necessarily, the maker of a work of art records his preferences and his judgments of value in the thing that he has achieved. The intense cultural significance of a Greek statue derives from the fact that it is a durable, vivid sensory pattern and that the traits in which it is distinct from other works of sculpture correspond to the characteristics of the environment from which it sprang. Today we cannot hear the voice of Plato, and not a single word written by his own hand still exists; but the very marks of tools used by Greek sculptors, builders, and painters are even now available to our immediate observation. The connection with the makers of these durable, vivid, and significant objects is therefore more direct and intimate.

The human imagination, again, is something whose exercise cannot be completely inhibited by any code of censorship or prison guard. The hope of better things, to be achieved through orderly human action, is warranted by the relative freedom of art. A Greek statue is a permanent witness to what can be done when men are free from tyrants and despots and to the truth that men do not prosper only under totalitarian regimes. Best of all, it testifies to the justified belief that because better things have once been actual, they may be made so again. Change is irresistible; and, with change, evils may be abolished and remembered or imagined goods may be realized. Works of art, on the whole, represent men at their constructive best; and when the times are base, they still hold forth grounds for rational confidence, because what men have once done they may do again.

A work of art, then, may be durable, vivid, significant, and a secure warrant of freedom. The romantic idealists, overlooking the sensory reality and technical origin of art, found in the artist a perfect type of self-created creator, without moral or intellectual responsibility. Such a foundation for an irrational philosophy was credible, provided only that the *beaux-arts* dogma had first been accepted.

According to the romantic view, based on the *beaux-arts* doctrine, when a man calls himself an artist and believes that his technique necessarily produces beautiful things, he is a privileged creature. He is a law unto himself, as independent of human control as a flood or a cyclone. When art is the same thing as beauty, the artist exists in a separate sphere, freed from the restraints of ethics and logic.

But nothing could have been more abhorrent to the founders of Western civilization, for they were already familiar with the principles of absolute Persian monarchs and other barbarians. Aristotle exhibited outstanding merits of the Greek mind, and his attitude has become so generally approved that it is optimistically called common sense.

Fanaticism, brutality, and passionate ignorance are wholly apart from such an attitude. Since works of art are not the products of blind, irrational force, art provides no evidence that such is the way of the artist. As a technician he respects his materials and works according to a rational procedure. As one who practices the arts of design, the artist produces a durable, vivid, significant record of human experience, and what he makes testifies to human freedom from slavery perpetual and complete. Art does not flourish through the suffering and death of the artist's fellow-men; the artist prospers through contributing to the happiness of the living.

To summarize this defense of art against the idealists who misrepresent its nature so that it can be cited as evidence for their special philosophy, valuable traits found in the ancient thinkers whom we have considered can be condensed into three or four phrases.

The characteristics of the earliest recorded systematic thought about art which have a direct relation to basic American insights are, first of all, moral idealism and intellectual naturalism. Of almost equal value are Aristotle's concepts of technique and of causation.

Moral idealism was the essential note in Plato, and his anxiety to preserve ethical ideals against opportunist and unscrupulous popular leaders induced him to condemn art, believing that if his ethical ideals were to be eternal Ideas, they must be removed from the flux of circumstance. In order to assure the security of his Ideas, all actual things had to be only their copies. To prove the superiority of Ideas to actual instances, art, which he considered primarily imitative, had to be condemned, so that the relation of nature to the Ideas would parallel that of art to nature. Thus, even in his arguments against art, he was moved by a zealous ethical idealism.

Aristotle, treating things from the point of view of an intellectual naturalism, could esteem art as beneficial to mankind, for he also was animated by ethical ideals, but they were practical. Dealing with nature as it is, we can hope to gain a greater measure of happiness for men by analysis of the facts before us, to discover genuine relations between them and, through technique, improve the human lot. The contribution of Aristotle was a comprehensive technique for analysis of concepts and for dealing with human relations. His concern with technique, as the orderly sequence of actions, transforming materials to fit them to human needs and make men better, is something congenial to the American point of view.

A contribution of Aristotle which has in the course of time been neglected but would be more sympathetically viewed by Americans if it were more thoroughly grasped was his theory of causation, demanding four principal causes or groups of necessary conditions to explain any actual product. In modern times the tendency has been to select one alone, the efficient, neglecting the rest; but, at least in the realm of human values, none of the four can be omitted.

EXPERIENCE

The term "experience" is a favorite one among American pragmatists; but here, as in many of their sounder views, the origin is to be sought in Aristotle, who in his *Metaphysics* declared:

It is from memory that men acquire experience, because the numerous memories of the same thing eventually produce the effect of a single experience. Experience seems very similar to knowledge and technique, but actually it is through experience that men acquire knowledge and technique; for as Polus rightly says, "experience produces technique, but inexperience chance." Technique comes into being when from many notions of experience a single universal judgment is formed with regard to like objects. . . . . It would seem that for practical purposes experience is in no way inferior to technique; indeed we see men of experience succeeding more than those who have theory without experience. The reason for this is that experience is knowledge of particulars, but technique of universals; and actions and the effects produced are all concerned with the particular.[450]

Aristotle contrasted experience with wisdom or philosophical knowledge, and in general it covered what was called the "empirical" by the later rationalist idealists. The American pragmatists were attached to empirical experience because of their hostility to merely verbal statements and to the belief that knowledge consists of symmetrically related series of words. In their anxiety to demolish the system of Hegel—the chief exponent of such views—any weapon was a good one, with the result that in many cases their arguments are inconsistent with one another, even when advanced by the same writer. The desire to avoid the rationalist excesses of Hegel led to overemphasis in the opposite direction, as instanced by the reduction of all values to the moral, the interpretation of moral value as the utilitarian, and the substitution of an outmoded biology for metaphysics.

Because many translators of Aristotle[451] have used the term "art" in its general sense of "technique," where the original, indeed, employs the term "technique," pragmatist philosophers have been prone to adopt Aristotle's explanation of technique as the explanation of art; but, since they limit the values which art may have to the utilitarian or instrumental, the results are not convincing. In their praise of technique, however, they are likely to apply to it the term "art," in which they preserve the implications of *beaux-arts*, so that all techniques are admirable because they are *beaux-arts!* At the same time, the theoretical limitation of value to the utilitarian has made it possible for some younger disciples to declare that what makes a picture beautiful is its effectiveness as propaganda.

The realist insight can be successfully preserved if we assert that experience is always experience of objects. When I experience, what I experience is objects. Existing things need not be experienced in order to exist, but anything actually and immediately experienced is an object. To be an object requires the activity of experiencing. For Americans, therefore, an explanation of art must begin with a consideration of objects belonging to that class, instead of with a concept of the *beaux-arts*, which leads only to confusion.

Classes or universals are established, as Aristotle pointed out, "when from many notions of experience a single universal judgment is formed with regard to like objects." The similarity observed to hold between numerous objects creates concepts or universals because, as he explained, "the numerous memories of the same thing eventually produce the effects of a single experience."

It is mainly when the present object is strange, unfamiliar, disturbing, or dangerous that we seek to classify it through reference to other things with which we are already familiar and to which it is in some degree similar. We customarily employ memories condensed into word or verbal concepts, instead of demanding the actual presence of objects which they indicate, because of their frequent adequacy for the purpose of identification and explanation. But, having gained a satisfactory designation for an object, we need not repeat the operation every time we discover an object belonging to that class.

The vast majority of objects with which we have to deal demand no such reference, for we know what the object is without asking ourselves or others, and we act in accordance with our justifiable expectations. We do not ask ourselves or others what the object is, for we have already become acquainted with it.

A REALIST DEFINITION OF ART

But since the understanding of art as *beaux-arts* is so prevalent, art must be redefined in the sense of the "arts of design," abbreviated to the one word "art" by Winckelmann. The class consists of objects that have been produced by design, meaning by that term the image presented before the artist's mind through imagination, as well as drawing, the specific technique required to produce such objects and distinguishing them from music, dancing, poetry, and other classes. Art includes products of the techniques of architecture, painting, sculpture, and the minor arts.

Judgment as to what things belonging to this class shall be preserved and exhibited in museums, homes, churches, and other structures or in parks and conspicuous sites is a matter not dependent on the class to which the objects belong but on the qualities discovered in them. The broad, comprehensive class of qualities which we call the "aesthetic" is not limited to works of art or even to products of technique in general but pertains to any object as such.

All experienced objects are not exclusively sensory, nor are even sensory objects wholly so. But when we have to do with a work of art, we may be sure that it offers a sensory pattern, produced by technique through design. The point at which to begin in accounting for objects belonging to that class is with a succession of examples rather than with a false concept of the *beaux-arts*.

The concept, or condensed definition of art, should inform us what we shall always find in a work of art when it is an immediate object of experience. This concept should be true. The idea signified by the word "art" as a sign ought to be true so that it will eliminate false, misleading expectations. It ought not to present internal contradictions, and its structure should result in a coherent whole. It ought also to be coherent with the remainder of our tested concepts.

If we doubt either that the definition is true or that some object is a work of art, we can always apply tests to verify the validity of the definition or the propriety of the classification. Testing a claim that a flower is a work of art, we must reject it because we see that the object has not been designed or achieved through technique by an artist. We can also see that a melody is not a member of the class "art" but belongs to music. It is planned but not designed with the aid of drawing; and, while it is a sensory pattern, the sensory data are not of the kinds to which art is limited.

Art does not compose audible data but only those of vision, touch, equilibrium, and direction; and we should bear in mind that to be a work of art only those types of sensation are required. If, on the other hand, we seek out one of the objects illustrated in a history of art so that it becomes the immediate object of an act of experiencing, we find that the definition holds. The same view will be confirmed as true if we visit an art school, an art museum, or an exhibition of art.

The concepts of experience and art here outlined are consistent with one another and aid in understanding the nature of both. But the notion of sensation, as it relates to art, is one that also requires clarification.

THE SENSORY ASPECTS OF ART

One expectation, that will always be satisfied when we have an object properly designated a "work of art," is that it presents a pattern of sensations. An understanding of sensations is then required which makes analysis of the work in those terms possible, without admitting the materialist view that objects consist of nothing but combinations of sensations.

A specific type of sensation is never experienced alone, and such a situation as the experience of a naked, isolated sensation never occurs; but types can be distinguished, even if their actual separation is impossible. The senses required for experiencing a present work of art are four in number: vision, touch, equilibrium, and direction.[452]

Each of these senses can be referred to the persistent object which is the body. Parts of that reliable pattern can be called the organs of various senses or, to say the same thing in different words, sensations can be localized. When those parts function under appropriate conditions, sensations of very distinct kinds occur; but when those conditions are disturbed, such sensations are absent. We see with our eyes, and those organs can be localized as in the head, at the top of the body, at the front of the head, and related to one another as right and left eyes. We hear with our ears, which are to be found on either side of the head. We can touch our eyes and ears, although we cannot see our own eyes or hear our own ears directly. But we can, as just noted in the case of the eyes, locate them in the bodily pattern in terms of the sense of equilibrium, so that the organs of any sense can be localized in terms of sensations other than those pertaining to themselves alone. We can see our hands, the instruments by which most discriminating data of touch are secured, just as we can touch our eyes. Senses can therefore be localized and distinguished as related to organs without whose effective functioning sensory data of the corresponding kinds are not discovered in experienced objects.

Besides localization, there is another important distinction among the senses. Extending the powers of vision through use of a microscope, we see that the ends of nerves which terminate in the several organs also possess distinct shapes. Thus the nerves of vision have shapes indicated as rods and cones, present in the retina—the back interior wall of the eye. The nerves of pain are much more primitive but still distinct from those of any other sense. The skin contains nerves for types of sensation distinct from that of touch or pressure; but nerve terminations of that sense are also found in other places, such as the joints and elsewhere. The inner ear is the seat of nerve terminations without which we have no awareness of equilibrium or direction. Those of direction are found in the semicircular canals, while those of equilibrium are located in the vestibule leading to the spiral cochlea as well as to the semicircular canals.

That sensations do not occur singly is also easily established. If, for example, I have an orange as a visual object, it is in front of me (datum of equilibrium), and from previous experience I know how its surface will feel (remembered data of touch); and if I should doubt this correlation of vision and pressure, I can immediately extend my hand (datum of direction) to verify that expectation and confirm or reject it. When I find an orange in front of me, it must be a recent event; and either I approached the object or it was brought toward me, and in both cases the shape of the orange became progressively larger (datum of direction).

A work of art is limited to the data of these four senses. A picture does not produce sounds. For a building to be hot or cold is an accident of the sensory pattern required to make it a work of architecture. The data of smell are not required to be present in order that an object shall be a statue.

Because sensations are never found isolated and completely separated from one another but always simultaneously with other types, the actual set of relations prevailing among them is a pattern or, in the work of art, a composition.

In a natural object the pattern or system of related differences in sensory data is a product of processes independent of human intervention; but in a work of art it is a composition arranged by an artist. From this point of view, therefore, what the artist does is not to determine whether or not the observer shall see, but what data he shall see and in what spatial order he shall see them.

IDEALIST ERRORS REGARDING SENSATION

The idealists were prone to accept several erroneous assumptions about sensation and to face perplexing problems as a result. The tactile reduction was usually accepted or implied as a matter of course, but this is so important that it deserves separate discussion. The beliefs that sensations occur in isolation or that apprehension of sensory data must precede knowledge of any other kind led to endless problems, of which the following are examples.

If the data occur independently, how can they ever be brought together? If knowledge of sensory data precedes all other knowledge, how can any other kind ever be had?

Assuming that the data were initially isolated and not already in relation to one another, the philosophers borrowed an explanation from art. The theory of association in psychology and views of the mind such as that of Kant, who considered it primarily synthetic or formative, reduce to this: As the artist takes a blank panel or canvas and puts together his pigments in a certain scheme which he plans and imposes on his materials, so the mind takes its sensory data as materials and composes a pattern of them. This led to the inference not only that the plan was devised by the subject but that it also resided solely in his mind, so that the artist, as well as every other man, could have no genuine acquaintance with an independent, objective pattern.

But, as already noted, sensory data never occur in complete separation; they are always arranged in a specific order or system of differences, at the same time the data of distinct senses are intelligibly related. The problem of how to bring them together does not arise, for they are already together in some way, whenever the sensory object is present in immediate experience. For technique the problem of process in relation to materials is how to transform materials which already have forms; it is not how to give formless materials something which they do not already have in their own right.

The assumption that sensory knowledge precedes and is the ultimate source of all other things in awareness is also open to serious criticism. Even a very young infant is aware of data of touch and equilibrium; his senses of taste and smell are also active, while familiar gestures express pleasure in patterns of such sensations, as well as well as pain, at a very early age. The correlation of visual data with those of touch and direction occurs at a very early age, and awareness of their differences is even earlier. Knowledge of precise and communicable concepts awaits ability to hear and speak words, but the knowledge of relations holding between sensory data is practically simultaneous with their perception.

The belief that experience is for the infant entirely a buzzing, bewildering confusion is almost as extreme as the view that preceded it, whereby the child at some fairly early age, from six to sixteen perhaps, becomes suddenly a fully developed man, completely acquainted with the absolute standards of right and wrong and responsible for all his actions, as he is presumed to have knowledge of all their consequences.

If the connection of ideas with language is ignored or denied, it is a genuine difficulty to tell how knowledge and concepts can ever be acquired. The idealist solution, usually, was to turn the tables and assert that knowledge consists wholly of ideas, that we know only ideas, including those of sensation, and not the things to which they relate or which they represent, if there are such things outside the ideas which are perceived.

Experience is continuous, and it is vivid and acute at periodically connected intervals. Certain regions of this continuous possession of objects are distinguished as sensations, but they do not comprise the whole of experience. Because experiencing is itself not an object, we ought not to conclude that all objects are simply ideas; nor, because we have bodies or persistent objects of sensation, need we assert that only sensory objects really exist.

PERSPECTIVE AS AN IDEALIST PROBLEM

If it is assumed that sensory data are independent, because the organs of sensation can be separated as tactile patterns, the question arises: How can they work together? If the anatomist can extricate the eyes or sever the hands from the body, how is it that what we see and touch are not identical? A man sitting at a large circular table sees it as an irregular ellipse. Ought he not to see and touch it so that it will yield identical patterns? If he could, he would have only one sense. Since he has at least touch and vision, when the table is an immediate object, it must necessarily appear to touch as circular and to vision as elliptical. By virtue of this fact he can reach out and grasp an object at the opposite side of the table, or he can walk around the table and stand there because he can order his successive sensations in a regular and reliable way. In action men are not surprised by the fact that we have wide and confident experiences through the known interrelations of sensations. The advantage of having more than one sense is that the depth and breadth of experience stretches far beyond that possible with only one. Philosophers have often created artificial problems by adopting erroneous presuppositions.

The problem of perspective is often put this way: Why does a thing which is the same size look larger when it is nearer than when it is far away? The answer is that while the object is, in tactile terms, the same pattern, the area on the surface of the retina taken up by the image of the object varies with the distance of the object from the lens. Measurement has primary reference to tactile units, although it is most often directly based on data of vision when the object is within tactile range. "Larger" or "smaller" then means a determination with respect to tactile experience. The lens of the eye provides an aperture through which light converges from the whole surface of the tactile object, whether near or far, and it is then spread out again on the retina. The area of the image in tactile terms of measurement, as fractions of an inch or centimeter, varies in regular fashion so that distant things take up a very small share but near objects a greater one. This occasions no distress in the thoughts of ordinary men, although it is relied on by idealist philosophers in their professional capacity, for it enables men to order their experiences. If an object is approaching or if I am approaching an object, the reliable changes in the data of vision and touch as related to the data of direction certify the fact.

THE IMAGE INVERTED ON THE RETINA

Some trouble is also often discovered when the inverted image on the retina is considered. Because of the function of a lens, as we see on the ground-glass back of a studio camera, the image must be upside down. How, then, do we see it right side up? If we see things upside down and are mistaken in the belief that we see them right side up, how can we credit the evidence of the senses in any case?

This problem might well be called the dilemma of the little man who isn't there. There is a relic of primitive animism in the presuppositions of the problem. It is assumed that the image on the retina is somehow observed by an observer inside the head, who gazes at it upside down. There is no such little man. In experiencing objects as visual we do not look at the back of our retinas. We see by means of our eyes, but we do not see our own eyes, either inside or out or from behind. With regard to the standard relations of visual data with those of other senses, it makes no difference which way the image lies on the retina, provided it is always the same way. In that case the data of equilibrium and direction can always be correlated with the visual image. If we can see our feet on the ground and our hands above them, nearer our eyes, it makes no difference which way the image lies with reference to the body as itself an object of sensation, so long as positions are constant.

These and other so-called illusions are often employed by philosophical idealists in an attempt to establish the utter unreliability of the senses in contrast with nonsensory ideas. A sceptical analysis of sensation, based upon divergence between the data of the senses, is the usual destructive preliminary to construction of an idealist system. The ephemeral status of sensory patterns compared with the assumed constancy and unalterable character of ideas is also stressed.

THE ASSUMED SUPERIORITY OF IDEAS

But on closer inspection the idealist philosophers do not seem to have been completely accurate in their estimate of the superiority of ideas to sensations. Since ideas or concepts are not sensory objects, it is sometimes more difficult to observe that one's own ideas or those of another are themselves subject to change, probably no more and no less unreliable than sensory patterns. In some instances ideas have been more damaging to whole societies than the occasional errors of individuals in judging things seen or touched.

Through memory, however, numerous examples can be found of vivid, trusted concepts that in their present state have undergone notable change. Revision of ideas and of evaluations is, indeed, a necessity of intellectual life. The difference between Arabic numerals and the letters employed to designate numbers by the Greeks and Romans points to a profound alteration in the stock of concepts available to those who employed these different systems. Almost anybody can, by comparison of the meanings which he attaches to certain words with those given by the dictionary, discover that he errs in regarding those words as signs of the concepts that he has until then entertained when confronted with them in reading. College courses in poetry consist largely of an attempt to induce undergraduates to read closely and accurately enough so that they will not misunderstand what the poet writes or completely fail to grasp a good deal of his work.

Furthermore, there is such a thing as the history of a given language which is not simply a record of advance from ignorance to perfect knowledge. It is a series of transformations, of changing concepts, whose various stages have been preserved in documents. Slang displays a constant effort to emphasize familiar ideas, as the customary words become less forceful with use, while the same word may possess almost opposite meanings in the course of time.

If an American is to feel that he is dealing with something worth while, he had better not suppose that the sensory data of his object are mere illusions when his object is a work of art. Neither need he suppose that his experience is limited to relations between his body and other tactile objects. He does not have to take refuge in materialism to escape idealism. A responsible, hopeful, and self-respecting man may, on the whole, trust his senses, because objects that offer occasion of sensation are real in their kind.

THE TACTILE REDUCTION

The tactile reduction is one of the most important phases of the traditional view, because it has long impeded systematic thought. It is the bias which manifests itself clearly in Cartesian dualism, with its two substances; and it is the usual point of departure for the problem of the relationship of body and mind, as that difficulty is usually stated. By "the tactile reduction" is meant the reduction of all sensations to species of touch, or even of all experienced objects to tactile forms.

The sense of touch or pressure has several striking aspects which afford superficial justification for such a radical simplification. In the first place, it is comprehensive, so that all parts of the skin have terminations of this particular type of nerve in greater or less abundance. This means that we are always aware of it when we are being touched by some other body, and we know that we are in contact with other things practically all of our waking hours. For this reason we are likely to think of our own and other bodies as primarily tactile patterns, without criticizing this plausible conviction.

Again, this sense has a reciprocal activity, so that organs of touch are aware of one another in their own terms, something which is not true of other senses in the same way. We can touch our own hands and our tongues touch and are touched by the interior of the mouth, but we do not hear our own ears or see our own eyes.

Finally, although the sense of vision has a wider range, as does hearing, for they make us aware of things at some distance, we are accustomed to confirming doubtful cases by means of touch.

The range of touch is limited, since its objects have to be, so to speak, within arm's reach; but when unfamiliar relations of vision and other senses are presented, we rely on touch when we can bring the object near enough.

This reliance on the data of touch as solving perplexities about visual objects is justified in so far as the body is a tactile pattern; and such it is during waking moments at least, for we always can feel our feet on the ground while we stand or sit and have similar contacts in other positions. But the conclusions derived from this fact must all be sustained if all sensations are to be species of touch or if all things to be real must be tangible. We should then recall certain considerations which limit reference to this sense as the model or source of all the rest and the possible ultimate substance.

While the data of touch are continuous and comprehensive, the data of equilibrium are almost equally so. Although we are constantly aware of aspects of equilibrium in sensory patterns, disturbances of its normal relations are so rare that we do not often attend to it and ignore other sensations. Wherever we have tactile experience we ordinarily have experience of the other also. When we fall from a height or dream of doing so, the fear we feel occurs because familiar data of touch are absent, and, although equilibrium is still active, it has none of the well-known tactile facts with which it is normally related.

Again, the sense of touch has a reciprocal activity, but the regular relations of visual and tactile patterns, in our own bodies at least, compensate for this deficiency elsewhere. We see our own hands when we move them and gain data of touch. The normal human being is completely relaxed and motionless only on rare occasions and then for but a brief space of time. During motion or change in the spatial context the senses of both equilibrium and direction are active and afford vital data.

If we confirm doubtful tactile patterns by means of touch, we far more frequently accept visual data as adequate for tactile knowledge also. We know enough about most tangible things simply by looking at them, without ever touching them.

It would seem, therefore, that comprehensiveness, continuity, and reciprocity are to be accepted with definite reservations as establishing the primacy of touch. Nevertheless, it has been customary to sustain the claims of touch on genetic grounds, claiming that it is the origin of all other sensations or that all other sensations are its varieties. But the skin or surface of the body has organs for at least three other types of sensation; and if presence in the skin is the ground for this view, it must be observed that the nerves of another sense may have preceded it in origin there. It is possible that the nerves of some senses, such as those of equilibrium, are closely connected with touch in origin, as well as in present function. But the contrary is clearly true of others. Sensitiveness to light and to odors is of the chemical order of reactions and not of the tactile at the level of direct experience. The most elementary organisms respond to chemical and electrical changes in their environment where there can be no question of tactile data in any genuine sense.

The most damaging testimony against the presumed primacy and priority of touch is the fact that there is another more rudimentary, more widely diffused sense, and that is pain. Since irritability is one of the basic characteristics of living matter, prior even to tactile awareness, and since pain is a developed, but still primitive, system of nerves to yield data of irritation, it seems likely that pain would deserve to be considered initial and ultimate if order of origin were all that needed to be taken into account. But before any one sense can be given such pre-eminence, and even if a conclusion of rank in immediate experience of objects were to be based on priority in prehuman stages of life, certain other points should first be mentioned.

As we have already noted, experience does not consist exclusively of sensory objects, and even sensory objects have integral aspects that are not sensory. Except for supposed facility in analysis and explanation, there is no justification for reducing all sensations to varieties of touch. But the excessive penalties for this easy transformation of all experiences and of all sensations to one alone become all too obvious when we observe the consequences.

When Descartes wished to clarify philosophy and simplify it for rigid and coherent solutions of traditional problems, he reduced the world, as already noted, to two substances; one unthinking but extended and the other thinking but unextended. Unthinking, extended substance was a mere parallel to tactile pattern, although no pattern of tactile data in the complete absence of other sensations was ever an immediate object of experience. Thinking, unextended substance was, by definition, the opposite of tactile substance, but mind or soul was constituted solely with reference to that substance and was usually described in terms more appropriate to things tangible, with the verbal reservation that it could not really be touched. It was like a body in most respects except one, for nobody could lay hands on it—and that is the familiar description of a ghost or disembodied spirit.

In any case, if there are two substantial, independent, and self-sufficient types of being, how and why are they ever related? How can they ever have any actual relations? How can an unextended soul move a tangible body? How can an extended body affect the states or ideas of an intangible soul? That is the familiar mind-and-body problem. But it is an urgent one only if the conventional estimate of tactile patterns as ultimate or primary is accepted, and if it is supposed that the act of experiencing can somehow ever, itself, be an immediate object. Since both these frequent assumptions are far less likely to be true than they are to be false, the problem has hardly deserved the attention it has received from Descartes until recent times.

The concept of substance, usually assimilated to the tactile, also provided a frequent topic of metaphysical discussion. The nature of the ultimately real is a favorite problem, and those who seek an answer have sometimes supposed they had evaded objectionable implications when they made, as the idealists did generally, the tactile an idea without altering its primacy among ideas. In practice, the metaphysical question has sometimes degenerated into this form: To what thing in the world is the world as a whole most like? The tactile reduction amounts to the reply: Something touched. Any conclusion of this type must always exclude or transform other aspects of experience to attain such an economical and, at the same time, comprehensive idea. As a consequence of too narrow a choice, objections by those who insist on the reality of other aspects of experience are always plausible. That an object within the world should be a pattern or model, a clue to that of the totality, would be a pleasant coincidence, perhaps, but the reasons to believe that it exists are not convincing.

Reality is, after all, a relation rather than a substance. Experience of objects, and the genuine question involved in each case is with regard to that object's mode of reality. We may ask: In relation to what is this object real? As it is actually experienced, the object must have some kind of reality, but the precise kind must often be ascertained. The real is what can be truly related, and reality is the universal signifying this trait of any object. Since objects do occur and any object is always in relations, some of which can be more or less accurately ascertained, we are not driven to deduce the reality of an object from the assumed nature of a sole real substance. The internal relations of parts or aspects of the object and its external relations to other things, as both similar and different, make analysis possible and possibly true. The convincing success of geometry in proving by deduction from as few axioms as possible a large variety of implications, based on the relations of those few axioms, inspired the idealists with the unwarranted hope that all real things could be deduced, as its necessary inferences, from the idea of a sole substance.

Owing to an excessive reliance upon the concept of substance as tactile pattern, the rationalist idealists struggled to find an intelligible solution of the problem of dualism. Leibniz in effect made the monads something like hollow spheres with a mind in the geometrical center of each one, and nothing coming in or going out. The coincidence of the experiences of numerous monads was to be explained by pre-established harmony. The central point in the monad was based on the self which he judged to exist within his own breast, while the sphere was a perfect geometrical figure or easily constructed tactile pattern. Locke, who properly declared that our ideas are nowhere, since they are not sensory patterns and do not consist of sensory elements similar to those of the spatial pattern, as is required for location in space, nevertheless made most of his primary qualities those of tangible objects. Idealists such as Berkeley, aware of the impossibility of explaining the world in terms of two substances, indulged in a bold reduction, making the world consist wholly of ideas or immaterial objects. The romantic idealists went still further and declared that unextended substance made itself as well as its objects.

FORM AND CONTENT

Another difficulty which still persists in speculative thought because the tactile reduction is accepted as a presupposition is the theory of form and content. In a work of art, for example, we often hear the tactile form or shape, with its visual equivalents, spoken of as "form," while other equally real aspects or relations of the object, such as aesthetic quality and significant gesture, commonly called "expression," are termed the "contents" of that form.

But only tactile objects can contain or be contained. A pitcher can contain a liquid, but a picture cannot contain beauty. At best, the terms "form" and "content" offer a misleading metaphor which is convincing only so far as the tactile reduction is accepted. In any case, tactile or visual shape is not identical with form in general. Form is the principle of individuation, that which makes an object a uniquely present, distinct, coherent whole. Matter, not content, is the reciprocal of form, since any form is the form of something and that something may be discovered through analysis.

Acceptance of the tactile-reduction and the form-and-content theory gave rise to a standard German formula in aesthetics: If I find a piece of sculpture beautiful but the statue cannot experience beauty because it is only a piece of bronze, and if the beauty which I feel is only an emotion in me and not something felt by the statue, how can

I suppose that the statue is beautiful? The answer was expected to be provided by the principle of *Einfühlung*, or empathy in English. The emotion in me is attributed to the impassive bronze because I feel my emotions into it! Apart from the fact that, logically, this is the problem itself and not an answer to the question, such a widely accepted explanation takes the tactile reduction for granted and refuses to credit the validity of its own experience of beauty in even a tangible object. Conspicuous beauty, it is true, is not an intrinsic aspect of every tactile body. Any such thing has weight, but its weight is not in proportion to its beauty. Yet tactile patterns can always contain in proportion to their internal areas. So, when the question is asked, "How did the bronze statue seem to have a quality which it really could not have, if all realities are tactile and beauty is intangible?" the reply is that it contains that attribute because I, by an act of happy self-delusion, put it there.

ANALYSIS AND SEPARATION

In addition to these consequences of the tactile reduction in the fields of art and aesthetics, there are still more general difficulties. A troublesome puzzle for many analytical thinkers is: How can we be certain of truth when it relates to things that cannot be separated so that they can be examined by themselves and their intrinsic natures ascertained? This problem, again, depends on the tactile reduction.

Analysis is not limited to things whose parts can be separated, and this is true for several reasons. Only tactile patterns can have their parts severed from one another, but no pattern is ever tactile and nothing else. In the first place, the tactile data of an object must be distinguished from others that it presents; and even when parts have been separated, the resulting parts all have at least their tactile dimensions as well as those of equilibrium. If a cube is cut in two, each resulting part will still present the three dimensions of touch; and the terms "left" and "right," which are a dimensions of equilibrium, can still be appropriately applied to each one.

It is even often expected that because some tactile patterns can be put together again, as cakes of soap can be taken out and then replaced in a box, so we can be sure of the nature of separated parts only when we can restore their original order.

Separation is relevant only to tangible objects, and even then distinction from the environment is a prior necessity. Thus, to hold that we can understand the nature of a whole only when it is tangible and we can separate its tactile members is a false inference based on the tactile reduction.

It is, however, one of the most durable and popular of all obstacles to intellectual progress. The alternative is not a gullible obscurantism or some type of idealist mystification. The realist attitude is to find out what sort of thing we have to deal with in immediate experience before we proceed to invert the order of analysis and lament that our efforts are doomed, that our knowledge is but one of illusions, because we have illegitimately limited the kind of object that can be known.

Since works of art always offer patterns of sensations and since they are not composed solely of tactile data but of other sensations as well, we see that for any serious study of art the tactile reduction is neat and parsimonious; but its effect is to impoverish the world of genuine and valid experience. An American philosophy of art ought not to labor under the burden of intolerable difficulties laid upon it by this arbitrary simplification. What it should do, after critical examination of the evidences for this assumption, is to reject it so that we may enjoy art without intellectual reservation, without judging that truth has nothing to do with art and cannot have, because all the world, except for tangible things, is a deceptive mirage. To that end, after outlining a theory of sensation, we should consider what quality is. We must know something of the nature of quality before we can see how art can possess aesthetic quality and whether it can properly be judged for ethical and logical value as well.

THE QUIDDITY OF ART

The strong penchant of the idealists to find an object of indubitable certainty in the self alone has led to the customary discovery of qualities there also as uniquely true. But the self is no more and perhaps less accurately known in respect to its qualities than are other objects.

The initial requirement, when a new object is experienced, is to find out what it is, to investigate its quiddity. Before we can deal with an object, we must somehow classify it. Giving names to things is the most obvious instance of this need; and whenever a noun is properly used, there is an example of satisfying this demand.

Of a thing identified as a work of art, we know that when it is an immediate object it is composed of sensory data related in an organization, achieved through human action by means of design, and not an immaterial image or a universal quality. We can go further and determine with greater or less accuracy when and where it was produced and by whom, and, if it is a representation, what it represents, provided that our initial designation is accurate.

When once an object has been properly identified or its quiddity sufficiently established, there is no persistent need to invoke concepts or to seek an accurate name for it, since the task has already been accomplished. Only when others ask questions, or we assume that they do, must we resort to ideas to convey information, or only when for some reason the name we have so far used becomes untenable must improvement be sought.

QUALITY IN ART

No actual object, including works of art, it will be observed, ever lacks qualities in immediate experience. Quality is not something added or a separable aspect of an object. Only when the tactile reduction is admitted as an article of faith does the relation of qualities to objects present a genuine difficulty. If tactile extension is the ultimate, substantial reality, we have to ask: How can a flower be graceful? How is it possible for a flower to have color? If it is fragile, of very recent origin, and ephemeral by nature, how can it be real? These all involve the belief that only the changeless and the permanent are real and that tactile patterns alone are identical for all men, so that the primary or essential qualities are those of things tangible.

But all its qualities are integral aspects of an identified object. Qualities are the qualifications of something in actual experience and that something is what the object is. To ascertain that objects never lack qualities we can take such an extreme example of abstractions or universals as the multiplication table. Our ordinary feeling about that table is one of confidence and trust; we employ it habitually, fully believing the set of relations among quantities that it asserts. However, when it comes to algebra, many young people at the beginning find it hard to believe that the product of two minus numbers is identical with the same numbers when they are plus. Often they can never put quite the same trust in this principle that they accord the multiplication table, and they accept it as an academic fiction.

It must be noted, however, that the relations of quiddity and quality found in an object are not irrevocably bound in that order. In language this is shown by the relations of adjective and noun, whereby the word that was previously the substantive may become the modifier, and vice versa. If an object is identified as a square and then seen to be green, it is properly called a "green square." But when the object is greenness present in a number of shapes, and one instance is to be distinguished from others, such as circles and triangles, then we might speak of the "square green." The phrases "deep oceans" and "ocean depths" illustrate the same point.

This affords another approach whereby the validity of the tactile reduction may be tested. If it were true, the only genuine quiddity would be tactile and all other things would be its qualities, as Locke implied when he established his three ranks in quality. But vision is so much superior to touch in range and precision that by far the larger part of our knowledge is acquired through experiences of that sense. In dominant areas the situation is that a visual pattern is the quiddity and the tactile is the occasional quality. We rarely stop to verify the tactile data, for we can properly rely on established equivalents. The practical problem, therefore, is just the opposite of what the tactile reduction assumes.

DIFFERENCES IN JUDGMENT OF QUALITIES

The broadest general explanation of differences in a sensory pattern, experienced by numerous individuals viewing it from various positions, is perspective. The same rationalization is made for numerous objects beheld by one observer. The comprehensive and ordered relations known as "space" always present a complete frame of reference for patterns composed of the same kinds of sensory data. We are no longer surprised by this situation but, on the contrary, depend on it with confidence, unless we are idealist philosophers, when we are likely to regard it with an alarm assumed for professional purposes.

The variations of visual patterns in relation to those of direction are understood as necessary and orderly. In the representation of such differences, various systems have been devised, and they have a profound significance for the cultures in which they have prevailed. But any system for representing perspective is a set of elements selected from it, and that usual in Europe since the fifteenth century is not identical with the one common in the Far East. Perspective is universally acknowledged in practice, but how it is to be represented depends on the intellectual convictions of those who depict it. Plurality in methods of representation does not affect the basic observation on which they all depend. Distinctly located observers will have patterns before them which vary with their positions in space. From differently fixed points simultaneous observers will have distinct patterns; from the same point various successive observers will have a pattern similar enough to be called the same.

Diversity in judgments of the same object is essentially no more objectionable or incredible than multiplicity in judges and things judged. The vanity of the romantic idealists could not tolerate the actual state of affairs; hence they attempted to reconstitute the world, exalting the empirical me to the status of a transcendental and mythical I, leaving only one experiencer of a unique object created by me. Such a claim, supposed to be justified by the activity of the artist, was perhaps a refuge for wounded conceit, but it should hardly be accepted as a reliable philosophical conclusion.

In judgments of other sensory qualities of tangible things or in evaluations of moral and aesthetic worth in things, the same type of general explanation has not generally been allowed, but it ought to be. The body is not the same in that from every point of view and for different observers it is always the same.

THE SELF AND THE BODY

Furthermore, the body and the self are not identical. The body is a relatively persistent sensory object, but the self is an object that includes memories other than sensory. Its type of reality is temporal rather than spatial, and it is an object which is historical in character; but this does not debar it from having intelligible relations with other objects. When a man refers to his self, he indicates a nonsensory object into which his past experiences have been summarized through memory and imagination. A candid and spontaneous judgment of value will be coherent and usually consistent as an extension of this concentrated self. From the position which the self has reached in time and in relation to its achieved summary of previous experiences, such a judgment is as valid as any representation of perspective relations in space.

However, if the activity of experiencing is wrongly identified with the self and if this self is further identified with the body, many extraordinary consequences ensue. To alleviate these difficulties the theory of emotions appears. The states of the mind are said to be governed by feelings. For the rationalist idealist these are irrational because they disturb his normal calm reasoning; for the romantic idealist they provide welcome and vivid contrasts with monotonous and boring surroundings. But emotion seemed to be an answer to the question: How can qualities be found in tactile patterns external to the body? Emotions were identified as disturbances of the bodily states, and thus, although qualities other than tactile were open to grave suspicion, there was no doubt that vivid experiences could on occasion be had in the body itself.

When the idealist stubbornly insists that a statue can have no genuine qualities other than tactile and that other qualities attributed to it are only emotions, then realizations of color, social and individual worth, as well as aesthetic value, would have status only as species of emotion. Such qualities are not those of other objects but only of the self, and qualities of the self are supposed to be states of the body. German explanations of the difficulties involved ranged from empathy to theories of conscious self-deception. Although they had made the world a complex of ideas, the idea of the tangible still harassed them. However, for philosophy, when it attends to actual objects, the data of all the senses are equally real; they differ in that some have a greater range because they are more discriminating and are therefore more frequently employed.

EMOTION AND QUALITY

Emotions pertain primarily to the body, and they, too, as objects, have qualities. When a very vivid quality is discovered in objects, emotions also take place in the body. But emotion is not the same as quality in general. An emotion of intense longing may easily become, either in another or when it is viewed as a part of the self, a repugnant object. Its quality is negative and offensive, although the emotion took place originally while desirable qualities were being found in an object.

On the other hand, because emotion and the quality of an object in general are not identical, the sentimentalist who regards his own emotions with special tenderness can be satisfied by quickly turning from an object in which he has found unpleasant quality to admire his own state when he was aware of that quality. He can have as his object another person who is in obvious distress, and, without doing anything to remedy the situation, he can at once be filled with satisfaction by admiring his own pity. He finds his pity worthy of admiration. He is more than content because of the nobility he discovers in his own emotion, and at the same time he is spared the expense of effort and participation in another's anguish. It may properly be said that he admires his own pity, but that his admiration felt pity, anger, fear, or any other emotion would not constitute an intelligible statement. Emotions can have quality, but qualities cannot have emotions.

Emotions and qualities are not identical, and normally neither occurs in extreme degree. The body always has some emotion, and all objects have qualities; but sanity and health would deteriorate if extreme emotion or a very high degree of quality were too frequent. The popular expectation that a work of art is not good unless it always arouses intense emotional excitement is unreasonable and contrary to fact.

THE LOGICAL ORDER OF QUALITY

Finally, with regard to quality, there are facts concerning it which are important for its logical treatment. Because tactile objects can be cut in two, it seems to be supposed that positive and negative qualities can be separated in the same way, that a thing is absolutely good, true, or beautiful or, on the contrary, that it is absolutely evil, false, or ugly. A little consideration will show that the situation in any actual instances is neither so simple nor so final.

Recalling the scale of value in color, we remember that there is a coherent series of differences ranging from white to black, or light to dark, with all the intermediate grays. Any instance of color can be identified by reference to this scale, since it will there find a precise position. It will be lighter than the next position on one side and darker than the next position on the other. Taking the scale as a whole and dividing it into three parts, we can begin at the black end going toward white, so that the middle part is then less dark and the white end is the least dark. If, on the contrary, we begin at the white end and proceed in the opposite direction, the middle section is then less light, and the black end is the least light.

The most general indications of quality are the terms "good" and "bad," but these are not connected as exclusive and exhaustive alternatives when they relate to immediate objects but as opposite directions in judgments of value. This is indicated by the three degrees of comparison in English: "good, better, best," and "bad, worse, worst." If we relate these degrees as we did the scale of lights and darks, we can interpret them as dependent on proceeding in a positive or in a negative direction. In the positive direction, good, better, best is the familiar order; but we can also rate those same terms in a negative direction, for good is the worst where there is a better and a best, the better is worse than the best, and the best is the least bad. The familiar terms for negative quality can also be rated in a positive direction, for the bad is the best where there is a worse and a worst; the worse is better than the worst; and the worst is the least good.

When qualities are compared in actual instances they are never absolutes; their quality is relative, for they are, in fact, being related or compared with one another. The relativity of qualities actually experienced was pointed out long ago by Plato when he said that a maiden is more beautiful than an ape but less beautiful than a goddess.

All qualities are real when they are the qualities of experienced objects, but in order to be so they need not be present in the highest conceivable degree. The fact that certain classes of objects, such as works of art, do not always present their qualities in extreme degree and in absolute fashion does not make experience of them chaotic or irrational. On the contrary, since degrees of quality can be discovered through comparison of objects which possess them, quality is a rational and orderly thing. Qualities of actual objects are objectively real, for they really are the qualities of real objects.

Any quality, however, is not experienced in isolation, apart from an object qualified. Triangularity, for example, is not itself to be experienced except as the quality of a figure. Numerous experiences of such a quality lead to the meaningful concept, which is signified by the word "triangularity." But neither the word nor the concept is itself triangular, let alone triangularity. Such concepts permit us to consider things more expeditiously, securely, and economically; and as objects they, too, have qualities. To a student who has just failed an examination in trigonometry, triangles and triangularity probably have definitely ugly qualities. The same thing holds true of beauty as a concept, for it cannot be experienced as other than the quality of an object in actual experience, although we effectively employ it as a concept to signify that quality.

Even the word "beauty" and its connotations may not always be found beautiful. "Sublime" and "picturesque" were words corresponding to certain aesthetic qualities which were esteemed in the eighteenth century; and they were devised not as species of beauty but as alternatives to it, when characteristics of art and nature previously found beautiful no longer satisfied; and, while the old word was retained for those traits, new terms had to be developed to indicate newly appreciated qualities.

This is a view of quality, quiddity, and passion or emotion consistent with a generally realist attitude. So long as the implications of the *beaux-arts* formula are accepted, modern idealists can point to art as a proof of their position, for the very good reason that the name of their philosophy and many of its primary tenets derived from that particular concept. But Americans who are realists in every other department of thought have no compelling obligation to adopt in art what they reject everywhere else. It would be more consistent to entertain a theory of art and of quality which makes that experience a rational thing, with real objects and real qualities.

ART AND QUALITIES OTHER THAN AESTHETIC

The work of art possesses aesthetic, as it also has other types of quality when it is an actual object experienced. Although such qualities are there, they often are present in slight degree and are taken for granted. There is a range of tolerance so that the presence of positive or negative qualities becomes conspicuous only when they differ from familiar types and degrees.

The controversy over the nature of value and the critical examination of the whole question were frequently prejudiced by the fact that the tactile reduction was often admitted as a presupposition without itself being analyzed. Once freed from this oppressive concept, we can look confidently to art for instances of experienced qualities. Although the *beaux-arts* erred in many ways by asserting beauty to be the prerogative of a group of techniques, it at least drew attention to the problem of quality in such objects. A full statement of realist conclusions to be drawn from the occurrence of quality in works of art would take more space than can conveniently be given to it here, but at least some of the main points can be set forth briefly.

Conservative psychology used to employ three terms to designate the elementary aspects of experiencing. Experiencing cannot be an immediate object; but, since it is the having of objects, its nature can be inferred from constant traits of this activity. Since qualities, for example, are always to be found in its objects, it must be capable of doing what it actually and continuously does, in appreciating them, and its main aspects can be distinguished, although not separated.

The main aspects used to be called "knowing," "willing," and "feeling." These terms in the course of time became restricted and did not include the whole of that to which they referred. Knowledge was taken to be true knowledge presented in accurate verbal formulations. Willing came to signify striving conscious of itself. Feeling came to mean what was also called "emotion."

Names which would be more comprehensive as well as neutral were required. Knowing is not always true, and the designation of this aspect of experiencing should include false, as well as true, knowledge. It should not be limited to verbal formulations, for we do know things without repeated and interminable recourse to words or even concepts. Willing does not have reference solely to the self, and what is willed can be directed toward the evil as well as toward the good. Feeling is not simply a matter of pleasure or displeasure in sensations, for qualities are found in things nonsensory as well as in sensory.

The revised terms are "cognition," "conation," and "affection." Each is neutral because it does not signify one direction only in the scale of its respective qualities. It is comprehensive, for it includes every object actually experienced; truth is not restricted to words or beauty to art.

The several basic aspects of experiencing are not equally active at the same time; and when an object discloses quality of one of the three main types, the object's status in that respect may also be distinguished. When an object of immediate experiencing manifests emphatic quality for cognition, it is a "sign." When it does so for conation, it is a "signal." When affection prevails, then it is a "symbol." The same pattern may function successively as sign, signal, and symbol.

Distinction between sensory and nonsensory, between visual and audible, sensory data offers instances of cognition. Patterns for further cognition, conation, and affection depend upon such an initial distinction but entail so little difficulty that it becomes very inconspicuous. That a given object is known to be a visual pattern is itself an act of cognition, and the object functions as a sign; but we rarely close our eyes to make sure that the object is one, in fact, which requires the action of the organs of vision to be perceived.

If we shift our eyes or turn our heads to see a visual pattern which was either on the periphery of the visual field or outside it, that is an act of conation. The object which is brought to attention through our effort is a signal. We are not inert or passive receptacles responding only to tactile contacts. We are active, inquiring, searching creatures, and this means that we exercise conation to obtain most of our experienced objects.

When we know what we have in the object—what it is—and when we have gained its presence, then the activity that prevails is affection. We no longer inquire what it is, for we know; we do not exert ourselves to bring it before us, for we have it; and what we then do is to enjoy it. Enjoyment is not simply pleasure, for pleasure is concerned only with sensory patterns, and enjoyment includes dissatisfaction as well as satisfaction.

All objects of immediate experiencing are objects of cognition, conation, and affection. An attempt to prove the complete absence of any one of these aspects of experiencing an object would itself disclose the presence of such factors in the statement of the supposed proof. The opposite is inconceivable, the fact is presupposed in denial and exhibited in any instance.

The connection of qualities with the fundamental aspects of experiencing should also be discussed, for here again there is a familiar correlation. The broad class of qualities found in an object while experiencing it as a sign through cognition may be designated the "logical"; the group of qualities disclosed by an object as a signal for conation may be termed "ethical"; and those that prevail when it is a symbol for affection are the "aesthetic." Logical, ethical, and aesthetic qualities cannot be denied in the work of art when it is actually an object.

This theory of qualities demands reference to the immediate object, whatever it is. Such a theory may be judged superior to one which would attribute aesthetic value exclusively to art while it relieves the artist of logical and ethical responsibility. Art does not possess a monopoly of beauty, nor is beauty to be found there alone. Since each series of experiences is unique and individual, individual responsibility for the discovery of qualities still remains and cannot be transferred to a formula or to society. To be a living, experiencing being is to find qualities in objects, but experience is of particulars and by particular individuals.

To deny ethical and logical quality to the artist or what he does is to encourage a disastrous program when, as in Germany, this view justifies a national policy of destruction. To be subject to the necessity of finding ethical and logical, as well as aesthetic, quality in things is unavoidable for any being that is human. To deny this necessity is not to abolish it. To regard the statesman as a "political artist," using Fichte's phrase, does not free him really from ethical judgment and deserved condemnation or emancipate his statements and beliefs from logical judgment and proper designation as untrue.

It is well for Americans to realize that qualities logical, ethical, and aesthetic have as much to do with art and the artist as with any other objects. It ought to be possible, and it is, for them to enjoy genuine, positive qualities in their experience of art. Those who cultivate art can enrich their lives, broaden their range of sympathetic understanding, and count on persistent sensory patterns to which they gain ready access. But it is not by means of a deceptive, false formula that they can do so.

The responsibility of the individual for his own experiences of quality cannot be evaded in art or elsewhere. An estimate of the possible influence upon others is not enough; but on examining in memory the actual influence of works of art, one sees that they can be good because they can also be evil. Our knowledge of works of art, as prompt intuition or as slowly acquired information, may be false because it may also be true. We can enjoy beautiful works of art that serve as signs and signals, for the reason that we may also find ugliness in them. Nobody can undertake to perform our experiencing for us; we can share it, but we cannot surrender it.

CONCLUSION

The promises that a work of art always fulfils are few but certain. It will invariably present a pattern of sensations, and these will be vivid as well as persistent. The pattern is in every case produced by a technique connected with drawing. That means some human being, alive like ourselves when he made it, preserved there a record of selections and preferences, a judgment of what he and his fellows found valuable in experience. By virtue of its vivid persistence and technical origin, the work of art presents us with an easily identified type of object. Such truths as these make us confident that when we enjoy art, we have to do with real and really valuable things.

There exists no moral obligation or political demand that would compel Americans to accept an illogical theory of art. A realistic view leads, not to self-delusion and destruction of one's neighbors and their goods, but to secure possession of positive values which can be shared with others securely and peacefully.

Wholehearted belief in a false doctrine and conduct which is consistent with such a belief more often than not lead to catastrophe. Fortunately, in America the *beaux-arts* doctrine has not been consistent with the general pattern of our convictions, nor have our policies been justified by it. A realistic philosophy of art warrants a search for beauty in art, and when we find it we do not deceive ourselves. We deal with realities rather than with illusions. We possess it, keeping faith with ourselves and with our fellow-men, truly and immediately.

Notes

I. INTRODUCTION

(*1*) Heinrich Schmidt, *Philosophisches Wörterbuch* (Leipzig, 1934), p. 17. (*2*) An approving analysis of this situation is found in Edward F. Rothschild, *The Meaning of Unintelligibility in Modern Art* (Chicago, 1934). (*3*) Cf. Herbert Furst, *Art Debunked* (New York, 1936). (*4*) Cf. *Hegel Selections*, ed. J. Loewenberg (New York, 1929), p. 311, where the Preface to Hegel's *Vorlesungen über die Aesthetik* is translated as "Introduction to the Philosophy of Art." The same practice is followed in many other instances; e.g., in the four-volume translation of Hegel's *Aesthetik* by F. P. B. Osmaston (London, 1920), which is entitled *The Philosophy of Art*.

II. THE NATURAL HISTORY OF ART

(*5*) The *Oxford English Dictionary* (Oxford, 1933), under "Art" (I, 467, No. 6.), says: "The application of skill to the arts of imitation and design, *Painting, Engraving, Sculpture, Architecture;* the cultivation of these in its principles, practices, and results; the skilful production of the beautiful in visible forms. This is the most usual modern sense of *art*, when used without qualification. It does not occur in any English Dictionary before 1880, and seems to have been chiefly used by painters and writers on painting, until the present century." (*6*) This development has been studied by Julius Schlosser in *Die Kunstliteratur* (Vienna, 1924), pp. 393 ff.; and by Erwin Panofsky in his *Idea* ("Studien der Bibliotek Warburg" [Leipzig, 1924]). In the latter appeared many important new materials, but both neglected to indicate the connection of a theory of art with German philosophical idealism.

THE IDEA TRANSFORMED

(*7*) *Metaphysics* vii. 7. 4. 1032 b. (*8*) *Metaphysics*, trans. W. D. Ross (Oxford, 1908). (*9*) Cicero *Orator ad Brutum* ii. 7. (*10*) Cf. Panofsky, *op. cit.*, p. 75, n. 35. (*11*) Seneca *Epistolae* lxv. 2 and lxviii. 16. (*12*) Cf. Panofsky, *op. cit.*, p. 30. (*13*) Leone Battista Alberti, *Kleinere kunsttheoretische Schriften (Della Pittura)*, ed. Hubert Janitschek (Vienna, 1877), p. 151. (*14*) *Le Vite de' più eccellenti Pittori, Scultori e Architettori*, ed. Gaetano Milanesi (Florence, 1878–81), I, 168. (*15*) Cf. Panofsky, *op. cit.*, pp. 98–99, nn. 160 and 161. (*16*) *Idea del Tempio della Pittura* (Milan, 1590). (*17*) Panofsky, *op. cit.*, Appen. I, pp. 122–30. (*18*) Giovanni Pietro Bellori, *Le Vite de' Pittori, Scultori et Architetti moderni* (Rome, 1672), I, 3–13. The theoretical Introduction had originally been given as a lecture before the Roman Academy in 1664 (cf. Panofsky, *op. cit.*, Appen. II, pp. 130–39). (*19*) Johann Winckelmann, *Geschichte der Kunst des Altertums* (Dresden, 1674), Part I, chap. iv, ii, pp. 141–57; cf. the complete reproduction of this edition issued by the Phaidon-Verlag (Vienna, 1934), pp. 139 ff.

THE ACADEMY

(*20*) Isocrates *De Permutatione* 2. (*21*) Cf. H. L. Ulrichs, *Über griechische Kunstschriftsteller* (Würzburg, 1887); and L. von Ulrichs, *Die Anfänge der griechischen Künstlergeschichte* (Würzburg, 1871–72). (*22*) Plutarch *Pericles* 1. 2. (*23*) Lucian *Somnium* 9. (*24*) *Lorenzo Ghibertis Denkwürdigkeiten (I Commentarii)*, ed. Julius von Schlosser (Berlin, 1912), p. 4. (*25*) Alberti, *op. cit.*, *passim*. (*26*) *The Notebooks of Leonardo da Vinci*, ed. Edward MacCurdy (New York, 1939), pp. 905, 910. (*27*) Giovanni Battista Armenini, *De' veri precetti della Pittura Libri III* (Ravenna, 1587). (*28*) The first edition of Bellori's *Vite* (1672) was dedicated to Colbert, at the request of Charles Errard, director of the French Academy in Rome. (*29*) Henry Testelin, *Sentiments des plus habiles peintres sur la pratique de la peinture et sculpture mis en table de préceptes* (Paris, 1680). (*30*) G. P. Lomazzo,

Trattato dell'Arte della Pittura, Scoltura, et Architettura (Milan, 1585), pp. 486–87. (*31*) Horace, "Epistola ad Pisones," *Ars Poetica* ll. 361–62: "Ut pictura poesis; erit, quae, si propius stes, / Te capiat magis, et quaedam, si longius abstes." (*32*) Plutarch, *The Glory of the Athenians* 346 F; *How To Study Poetry* 17 F. (*33*) Charles Alphonse du Fresnoy, *De arte graphica* (written 1641–65) (Paris, 1667); 2d ed. by Roger de Piles (Paris, 1673); translated into English by Dryden and published (London, 1695). (*34*) *De arte graphica*, ll. 1–2: "Ut pictura poesis erit; similisque poesi / Sit pictura." This formula was systematically attacked by Lessing in his *Laokoon, oder über die Grenzen der Mahlerey und Poesie* (Berlin, 1766). (*35*) By the eighteenth century, art had attained social recognition also in England (cf. Matthews Pilkington, *The Gentleman's and Connoisseur's Dictionary of Painters from the Year 1250 to the Year 1767* [London, 1770]; cf. also B. Sprague Allen, *Tides in English Taste* [Cambridge, Mass., 1937]). A new publication, containing valuable materials, but disappointing on the whole, is Nikolaus Pevsner, *Academies of Art, Past and Present* (Cambridge, Eng., 1940).

THE BEAUX-ARTS

(*36*) Charles Perrault, *Le Cabinet des beaux-arts ou Recueil d'estampes gravées d'après les tableaux d'un plafond, où les beaux-arts sont représentés avec l'explication de ces mêmes tableaux* (Paris, 1690). The term "*beaux-arts*" occurs in the French language, apparently beginning with the seventeenth century. Thus the *Dictionnaire Général de la Langue Française*, by Hatzfeld, Darmesteter, and Thomas, cites La Fontaine under the word *beau*. It quotes from his *Songe de Vaux* (1657–61) the words: "Oui, beaux-arts, quand je veux, j'étale vos attraits." The well-known dictionary by Littré (Paris, 1878), under the word "art" cites lines from the celebrated drama, *Charles IX*, of M. J. Chenier, produced in 1789: "Le plaisir instruisant par la voix des beaux-arts / Embellira la vie au sein de nos remparts." But neither under "art" nor under "*beau*" is "*beaux-arts*" found in Édmond Huguet, *Dictionnaire de la Langue Française du Seizième Siècle* (Paris, 1928). (*37*) J. B. Dubos, *Réflexions critiques sur la Poésie et la Peinture* (Paris, 1719); English translation by Nugent (London, 1748). (*38*) Charles La Motte, *Essay upon Poetry and Painting* (London, 1730). (*39*) André Fontaine, *Les doctrines d'art en France* (Paris, 1909), pp. 197–203. (*40*) Charles Batteux, *Les beaux-arts réduits à un même principe* (Paris, 1747). German translation by Johann Adolf Schlegel (Leipzig, 1751); cf. also Albert Dresdner, *Die Kunstkritik* (Munich, 1915), p. 317, n. 59; Fontaine, *op. cit.*, pp. 203–7. (*41*) Lionello Venturi, "Per il Nome di Arte," *La Cultura*, I, No. 7 (new ser.; July, 1929), 385. (*42*) Francesco Bocchi, *Le Bellezze della città di Fiorenza, dove a pieno di Pittura, Scultura, di sacri Tempii, di Palazzi i più notabili artifizii e più preziosi si contengono* (Florence, 1591 and 1592). (*43*) Joh. Georg Sulzer, *Allgemeine Theorie der schönen Künste* (2 vols., Biel, 1777; 4 vols., Leipzig, 1786–87); with additions by F. von Blankenburg (4 vols.; Leipzig, 1792–94); 3 additional volumes by Dyk and Schulze (Leipzig, 1793–1803). (*44*) Among similar works published in German during this period may be mentioned: Gottlieb Schlegel, *Abhandlung von den ersten Grundsätzen in der Weltweisheit und den schönen Wissenschaften* (Riga, 1770); Joh. Christoph König, *Philosophie der schönen Künste* (Nuremburg, 1784); Friedrich J. Riedl, *Theorie der schönen Künste und Wissenschaften* (Jena, 1767); while other massive treatises, usually in three or four volumes, were published by Daniel Schubert (Münster, 1781); by Westenrieder (Munich, 1778); by Görny (Salzburg, 1785); by Schott (Tübingen, 1789); by Schneider (Bonn, 1790); and by Heydenreich (Leipzig, 1793–95), all under variants of the title "Theorie der schönen Wissenschaften und Künste." (*45*) Rev. Robert A. Bromley, *A Philosophical and Critical History of the Fine Arts, Painting, Sculpture, and Architecture, with occasional observations on the progress of engraving* (2 vols.; London, 1793–95). (*46*) Francesco Milizia, *Dell'arte di vedere nelle belle arti di disegno secondo i principi di Sulzer e di Mengs* (Venice, 1781, 1792, 1823). Translated into German (1785); into French (1798); into Spanish (1827). (*47*) Anton Friedrich Büsching, *Entwurf einer Geschichte der zeichnenden schönen Künste* (Hamburg, 1781). (*48*) Luigi Lanzi, *Storia pittorica dell'Italia dal risorgimento delle belle arti fin presso al fine del XVIII secolo* (Bassano, 1789). (*49*) The altered title of a French dictionary of art when it appeared in German shows the persistence of the popular estimate even with the new terminology; cf. Claude Henri de Watelet and P. C. Levesque, *Dictionnaire des*

Arts de Peinture, Sculpture, et Gravure (5 vols.; Paris, 1792), which was revised and translated by C. H. Heydenreich as *Aesthetisches Wörterbuch über die bildenden Künste* (Leipzig, 1793–95). (*50*) Quatremère de Quincy, *Considérations sur les Arts du Dessin en France, Suivies d'un plan d'Académie, ou d'Ecole publique, et d'un systeme d'encouragemens* [*sic*] (Paris, 1791). (*51*) Cf. François Benoit, *L'Art Français sous la Révolution et l'Empire* (Paris, 1897); J. Renouvier, *Histoire de l'Art pendant la Révolution* (Paris, 1863); C. Saunier, *Les Conquêtes artistiques de la Révolution et de l'Empire* (Paris, 1902); M. W. Brown, *The Painting of the French Revolution* (New York, 1938).

AESTHETICS

(*52*) Alexander Gottlieb Baumgarten, *Aesthetica* (2 vols.; Frankfurt a.d. Oder, 1750–58). (*53*) Gottfried Wilhelm Leibniz, *Meditationes de cognitione, veritate et ideis* (in "Acta eruditorum" [Leipzig, 1684]); cf. also E. F. Carritt, *Philosophies of Beauty* (London, 1931), p. 57. (*54*) Christian Wolff, *Psychologia empirica methodo scientifica pertracta, qua ea, quae de anima humana indubia experientiae fide constant, continentur, &c.* (Frankfurt, 1732); cf. Carritt, *op. cit.*, p. 81. (*55*) Alexander Gottlieb Baumgarten, *Meditationes philosophicae de nonnullis ad poëma pertinentibus* (Halle, 1735); reprinted by Croce (Naples, 1900); cf. also Carritt, *op. cit.*, pp. 81–84. (*56*) Carritt, *op. cit.*, p. 84. (*57*) *Ibid.*, pp. 83–84. (*58*) "Theoria liberalium artium, gnoseologia inferior." *Liberalium artium* is wrongly translated by Carritt (*op. cit.*, p. 84) as "fine arts." (*59*) *Ibid.*, pp. 84–85. (*60*) *Ibid.*, p. 81.

DESIGN

(*61*) Ant. Francesco Doni, *Disegno partito in più ragionamenti* (Venice, 1549). (*62*) Vincenzo Danti, *Il primo libro del trattato delle perfette proporzioni di tutte le cose, che imitare o ritrarre si possono con l'arte del disegno* (Florence, 1567). (*63*) ("Everyman's Library" ed. [1927]), I, 1. (*64*) Raffaello Borghini, *Il Riposo, in cui della pittura e della scultura si favella* (Florence, 1584). (*65*) Schlosser, *op. cit.*, p. 352. (*66*) Gio. Paolo Lomazzo, *Trattato dell'Arte della Pittura, diviso in VII libri, nei quali si contiene tutta la Teoria e la Pratica di essa Pittura* (Milan, 1584); *Trattato dell'Arte della Pittura, Scoltura et Architettura, diviso in sette libri* (Milan, 1585). It was translated into English by Richard Haydocke and published at Oxford in 1598. (*67*) *Trattato*, pp. 7 ff. (*68*) *Ibid.*, p. 412. (*69*) *Vitruvius: The Ten Books of Architecture*, trans. M. H. Morgan (Cambridge, Mass., 1926), p. 5. (*70*) *Ibid.*, p. 6. (*71*) *X libri de re aedificatoria* (Florence, 1485); cf. Schlosser, *op. cit.*, pp. 105–11. (*72*) Schlosser, *op. cit.*, pp. 112–17, 119. (*73*) On the treatises of Alberti's successors cf. *ibid.*, pp. 361–65, 373–75; Aristotle *Politics* viii. 2. 3–4. 6; 3. 1–2, 1337 b 23–42, 1338 a 13, 1338 a 32–1338 b 8; cf. also Schlosser (ed.), *Lorenzo Ghibertis Denkwürdigkeiten*, I, 5. (*74*) Schlosser, *Kunstliteratur*, p. 358. (*75*) Federigo Zuccaro, *L'Idea de' Scultori, Pittori e architetti, divisa in due libri* (Turin, 1607); cf. Schlosser, *Kunstliteratur*, pp. 345–46, 358; cf. Panofsky, *op. cit.*, pp. 47–53. (*76*) Filippo Baldinucci, *Notizie de' Professori del disegno da Cimabue in qua, per le quali si dimostra come e per chi le bell'arti di Pittura, Scultura e Architettura, lasciata la rozzeza delle maniere greca e gottica si siano in questi secoli ridotti all'antica loro perfezione* (Florence, 1681–1728); cf. Schlosser, *Kunstliteratur*, pp. 417–20, 423–24. A curious parallel to Baldinucci is to be found in a work published in England over a century later: John Williams, *An authentic History of the Professors of Painting, Sculpture and Architecture, who have practiced in Ireland, involving original letters from Sir Joshua Reynolds which prove him to have been an illiterate* (London, 1795). (*77*) Filippo Baldinucci, *Vocabolario Toscano dell'arte di disegno, nel quale si esplicano i propri termini e voci non solo della pittura, scultura ed architettura ma ancora di altre arti a quella subordinate e che abbiano per fondamento il disegno* (Florence, 1681); cf. Schlosser, *op. cit.*, pp. 419–21, 545. (*78*) Cf. Albert Dresdner, *op. cit.*, pp. 117–27; Lionello Venturi, *History of Art Criticism* (New York, 1936), pp. 132–36; Fontaine, *op. cit.*, pp. 98–156. (*79*) This misunderstanding of drawing was congenial to Mengs and Winckelmann. Mengs defined it: "By drawing is chiefly meant the contour or circumference of things with the proportion of their length, size, and form" (cf. *Opere di Antonio Raffaello Mengs*, comp. Niccola d'Azara, ed. Carlo Fea [Rome, 1787], II. 19). But he also spoke of the arts of design in the traditional sense of that term (cf. II, 203 ff.). (*80*) Cf. Pierre Monier, *Histoire des arts qui ont rapport au dessin* (Paris, 1698); Johann Dom. Fiorillo,

Geschichte der zeichnenden Künste (Göttingen, 1798–1808). *(81) Geschichte der Kunst des Altertums* ("Phaidon" ed. [Vienna, 1934]), p. 456. *(82) Ibid.*, p. 486. *(83) Ibid.*, p. 487. *(84) Ibid.*, p. 25: "Die Künste, welche von der Zeichnung abhängen."

III. RATIONALIST IDEALISM

DESCARTES

(85) The slight interest that Descartes (1596–1650) had in the theories of art and aesthetics is indicated by the lack of works discussing this phase of his thought among the many books written about him. One of the few is E. Krantz, *Essai sur l'Esthétique de Descartes* (Paris, 1882); cf. also Benedetto Croce, *Estetica* (5th ed.; Bari, 1922), p. 224. The term "ideist" was used by John Sergeant (1621–1707) in his attack on the idealism of Descartes and Locke: *Solid Philosophy asserted against the Fancies of the Ideists: or the Method to Science farther illustrated with Reflections on Mr. Locke's Essay Concerning Human Understanding* (London, 1697). *(86)* C. A. du Fresnoy, *De arte graphica* (Paris, 1667); 2d ed. by Roger de Piles (Paris, 1673). Nicolas Boileau, *Art poétique* (Paris, 1674) André Fontaine (*op. cit.*) points out that Le Brun derived his theory of the passions from Descartes (pp. 69, 79, 101), and he also shows the influence of Descartes on Roger de Piles (p. 135). *(87)* Cf. *An Anthology of Modern Philosophy*, comp. D. S. Robinson (New York, 1931), pp. 162–63. The translation is from *The Philosophical Works of Descartes*, by E. S. Haldane and G. R. T. Ross (Cambridge, 1912). The quotation is from the first meditation in *Meditationes de prima philosophia, in qua Dei existentia et animae immortalitas demonstrantur* (Paris, 1641). *(88)* Cf. A. Philip McMahon, "Sextus Empiricus and the Arts," *Harvard Studies in Classical Philology*, Vol. XLII (1931). *(89)* From the second meditation (cf. Robinson, *op. cit.*, pp. 169–70). *(90)* From the third meditation (cf. Robinson, *op. cit.*, pp. 183–84). *(91) Principia Philosophiae* (Amsterdam, 1644) i. 7. *(92) De trinitate* x. 14. *(93)* Cf. *Les passions de l'âme* (Paris, 1649); Robinson, *op. cit.*, pp. 187–93. Other solutions found that the efficient cause of co-operation between the body and the mind is God, who occasions changes in the body corresponding to changes in the soul and vice versa. Suggestions of this character were made by Arnold Geulincx (1624–69) and Nicole Malebranche (1638–1715).

SPINOZA

(94) Born, Amsterdam, November 24, 1632; died February 21, 1677, in the house of the painter, van der Spyck. The views mentioned are to be found in his *Ethica, ordine geometrico demonstrata*, published after his death in the *Opera Postuma* (Amsterdam, 1677). The points which later Germans interpreted as supporting their own views were concisely presented by Spinoza in five propositions: (1) Except God no substance can be granted or conceived (*Eth.* I, 14). (2) God's existence and his essence are one and the same thing (*ibid.*, I, 20). (3) Thought is an attribute of God, or God is a thinking thing (*ibid.*, II, 1). (4) Extension is an attribute of God, or God is an extended thing (*ibid.*, II, 2). (5) The order and connection of ideas is the same as the order and connection of things (*ibid.*, II, 7). For the origins and a summary of the system of Spinoza cf. Richard McKeon, *The Philosophy of Spinoza* (New York, 1928). *(95)* Cf. Conrad von Orelli, *Spinozas Leben und Lehre* (Aarau, 1843); Max Grunwald, *Spinoza in Deutschland* (Berlin, 1897).

LOCKE

(96) John Locke (1632–1704), *An Essay Concerning Human Understanding, in four books* (London, 1690) (portions in French, 1688), Book II, chap. i, sec. 2 (cf. *Locke, Selections*, ed. Sterling P. Lamprecht [New York, 1928], p. 111). *(97) De anima* iii. 4. 430 a. *(98)* Cf. Aquinas *De veritate* ii. 3: "Nihil est in intellectu, quod non sit prius in sensu." *(99)* First presented in this form by Aegidius Romanus, according to K. Prantl, *Geschichte der Logik im Abendlande* (Leipzig, 1850–70), III, 261. The phrase is to be found in Albertus Magnus, Bonaventura, and Thomas Aquinas. *(100) Essay*, Book II, chap. xi, sec. 5 (cf. *Selections*, p. 132). *(101) Selections*, pp. 111–12. *(102) Ibid.*, p. 128. *(103) Essay*, Book II, chap. viii (*Selections*, pp. 205–6). *(104) Essay*, Book II, chap. xxiii, sec. 5. *(105) Ibid.* (*Selections*, pp. 205–20). *(106)* Lord King, *The Life and Letters of John Locke* (new ed.; London, 1858), "Descartes' Proof of a God, from the Idea of Necessary Existence, examined"

(p. 316): "So that real existence is but supposed on either side; and the adding in our thoughts the idea of necessary existence to an idea of senseless material substance or to the idea of an immaterial knowing spirit, makes neither of them to exist, nor alters anything in the reality of their existence, because our ideas alter nothing in the reality of things. . . . . Real existence can be proved only by real existence" (cf. Robinson, *op. cit.*, pp. 334-38).

LEIBNIZ

(*107*) G. W. Leibniz (1646-1716), *Nouveaux essais sur l'entendement humain*, written in 1704, first published in 1765; English translation by A. G. Langley (New York, 1896). (*108*) Letter to Bierling, November 19, 1709, in *Die philosophische Schriften von G. W. Leibniz*, ed. C. I. Gerhardt (Berlin, 1875-90), VII, 488. (*109*) He here paraphrased the formula used by Aquinas when he misrepresented Aristotle and said: "Nempe nihil est in intellectu, quod non fuerit in sensu, nisi ipse intellectus." (*110*) G. R. Montgomery, *Discourse on Metaphysics, Correspondence with Arnauld, and Monadology* (Chicago, 1902), Letter XIV, p. 161. (*111*) Gerhardt, *op. cit.*, II, 45; Montgomery, *op. cit.*, Letter VIII, p. 116. (*112*) Montgomery, *op. cit.*, Letter XIV; Gerhardt, *op. cit.* VII, 302. (*113*) Cf. *Principes de la nature et de la grace* (pub. 1718); Gerhardt, *op. cit.*, Vol. VI. (*114*) Montgomery, *op. cit.*, Letter IX; Gerhardt, *op. cit.*, II, 57; Montgomery, *op. cit.*, p. 133, (*115*) Montgomery, *op. cit.*, Letter VIII; Gerhardt, *op. cit.*, II, 43; Montgomery, *op. cit.*, p. 112. (*116*) Montgomery, *op. cit.*, Letter XXII; Gerhardt, *op. cit.*, II, 112. (*117*) First published in the *Journal des Savants*, April 4 and 9, 1696; cf. Mary W. Calkins, *The Persistent Problems of Philosophy* (5th ed.; New York, 1929), pp. 79-96; and G. M. Duncan, *The Philosophical Works of Leibniz* (New Haven, 1908), for summaries of the monadology. (*118*) Cf. Robinson, *op. cit.*, p. 292, sec. 32. (*119*) George Santayana, *Egotism in German Philosophy* (London, 1916), p. 104. (*120*) Cf. George Santayana, *The Realm of Matter* (New York, 1930), p. 170.

BERKELEY

(*121*) George Berkeley, Bishop of Cloyne (1685-1753), *Alciphron; or, The Minute Philosopher* (Dublin, 1732); French translation (1734); German (1737), Cf. E. F. Carritt, *Philosophies of Beauty* (London, 1931), pp. 74-81; *Berkeley*, ed. Mary W. Calkins (New York, 1929), discreetly omits this passage. (*122*) Carritt, *op. cit.*, pp. 76, 80-81. (*123*) *Ibid.*, pp. 77, 79. (*124*) *A Treatise Concerning the Principles of Human Knowledge* (Dublin, 1710), containing the first part; 2d ed., revised (1734). Cf. Calkins, *Berkeley*, pp. 124-25; cf. also *Three Dialogues between Hylas and Philonous* (London, 1713); translated into French, (1750); into German (1756); cf. Calkins, *Berkeley*, p. 304. (*125*) Calkins, *Berkeley*, pp. 125-26. (*126*) This is the conclusion reached in the *Principles* and the *Three Dialogues*. (*127*) George Santayana, *The Life of Reason, or Phases of Human Progress* (New York, 1905), I: *Introduction and Reason in Common Sense*, 112-14.

KANT

(*128*) Christian Wolff (1679-1754). (*129*) David Hume (1711-76), *Treatise on Human Nature* (London, 1739-40), translated into German (1790-91); *Philosophical Essays Concerning Human Understanding* (London, 1748), translated into German in 1755 by Sulzer, and again in 1793. (*130*) Immanuel Kant (1724-1804). Francis Hutcheson (1694-1746), *Enquiry into the Original of our Ideas of Beauty and Virtue* (London, 1725); translated into German (1762) (cf. Carritt, *op. cit.*, pp. 70-72). Henry Home, Lord Kames (1696-1782), *Elements of Criticism* (Edinburgh, 1762), translated into German (1763), and reviewed, perhaps by Kant, in 1764 (cf. Carritt, *op. cit.*, pp. 94-95). Archibald Alison (1757-1839), *Essays on the Nature and Principles of Taste* (Edinburgh, 1790) (cf. Carritt, *op. cit.*, p. 107). (*131*) *Kritik der Urteilskraft* (1st ed., Berlin, 1790; 2d ed., 1793; 3d ed., 1799), Part I, third moment, sec. 16 (cf. *Kant, Selections*, ed. T. H. Greene [New York, 1929], pp. 399-400; also Carritt, *op. cit.*, p. 116). (*132*) Carritt, *op. cit.*, p. 111. (*133*) Cf. E. F. Carritt, "The Sublime," in *The Theory of Beauty* (London, 1923), pp. 219-58. (*134*) Accordingly, he wrote *Kritik der reinen Vernunft* (Riga, 1781; 2d ed., 1787); *Kritik der praktischen Vernunft* (1788); and *Kritik der Urteilskraft* (1790). (*135*) "Transcendental Analytic. Section II. Transcendental Deduction of the Pure Concepts of the Understanding," *Critique of Pure Reason* (cf. Greene, *op. cit.*, pp. 74–77). (*136*) Greene, *op. cit.*, pp. 77–79. (*137*) Cf. M. M. Rader, *A Modern Book of Esthetics* (New York, 1935), p. 147, reprinting George Santayana, "The Mutability of Esthetic Categories," *Philosophical Review*, Vol. XXXIV (May, 1925). (*138*) Cf. "Of the Paralogisms of Pure Reason," Greene, *op. cit.*, pp. 165–81. (*139*) Cf. "On the Ground of the Distinction of all Subjects into Phenomena and Noumena," *ibid.*, pp. 145–55; and Mary W. Calkins, *The Persistent Problems of Philosophy* (5th ed.; New York, 1925), pp. 254–55. (*140*) Cf. Greene, *op. cit.*, p. 40; "The General Problem of Pure Reason," *Critique of Pure Reason*, Sec. VI. (*141*) Greene, *op. cit.*, p. 39. (*142*) *Ibid.*, p. 45. (*143*) *Ibid.*, pp. 45–56. (*144*) *Ibid.*, p. 56. (*145*) Cf. Greene, *op. cit.*, pp. 375–82; "Analytic of the Aesthetic Judgment," *Critique of Judgment*. (*146*) Greene, *op. cit.*, pp. 392–407. (*147*) *Ibid.*, p. 407, "Explanation of the beautiful derived from this third moment." (*148*) *Ibid.*, pp. 416–17. (*149*) *Ibid.*, p. 382: "Explanation of the beautiful resulting from the first moment." (*150*) *Ibid.*, pp. 417–33 (*Critique of Judgment*, secs. 46–50). (*151*) *Ibid.*, pp. 422–25 (sec. 48): "Of the relation of genius to taste." (*152*) *Ibid.*, pp. 425–30 (sec. 49). (*153*) Cf. Ernst Kris and Otto Kurz, *Die Legende vom Künstler* (Vienna, 1934); Edgar Zilsel, *Die Entstehung des Geniebegriffes* (Tübingen, 1926). (*154*) Cf. A. Philip McMahon, *The Art of Enjoying Art* (New York, 1938), pp. 111–71. (*155*) Cf. Benedetto Croce, *Estetica* (5th ed.; Bari, 1922), Part I, chap. xvi, pp. 130–40, "Il Gusto e la riproduzione dell'arte"; Part II, chap. iii, pp. 206–23, "Fermenti di pensiero nel secolo XVII." (*156*) Cf. A. Philip McMahon, *The Meaning of Art* (New York, 1930), chap. ix, pp. 235–54, "Is Art the Product of Genius?" (*157*) Greene, *op. cit.*, pp. 434–35 (*Critique of Judgment*, sec. 56). (*158*) *Ibid.*, p. 437 (sec. 57). (*159*) *Ibid.*, p. 436. (*160*) *Ibid.*, pp. 436 and 438.

IV. ROMANTIC IDEALISM

HERDER

(*161*) Johann Gottfried Herder (1744–1803), *Vom Erkennen und Empfinden der menschlichen Seele* (Riga, 1778); *Ideen zur Philosophie der Geschichte der Menschheit* (Riga, 1784–91); *Briefe zur Beförderung der Humanität* (Riga, 1793–97). (*162*) *Kritische Wälder oder Betrachtungen, die Wissenschaft und Kunst des Schönen betreffend* (Riga, 1769). (*163*) *Plastik: Einige Wahrnehmungen über Form und Gestalt aus Pygmalions bildendem Traume* (Riga, 1778). (*164*) *Kalligone* (Leipzig, 1800). (*165*) *Verstand und Erfahrung, Vernunft, und Sprache: Eine Metakritik zur Kritik der reinen Vernunft* (Leipzig, 1799); cf. also Max Schasler, *Kritische Geschichte der Aesthetik* (Berlin, 1872), p. 473. (*166*) Cf. Schasler, *op. cit.*, p. 474; also Robert Zimmermann, *Geschichte der Aesthetik* (Vienna, 1858), pp. 428–29. (*167*) *Kalligone* (*Sämtliche Werke* [Berlin, 1878], Vol. XII), pp. 308–17.

SCHILLER

(*168*) Johann Christoph Friedrich Schiller (1759–1805); cf. E. Kühnemann, *Schillers philosophische Schriften und Gedichte* (Leipzig, 1910). (*169*) Cf. *Über Anmut und Würde*, first published in 1793, and *Briefe über die ästhetische Erziehung des Menschen*, published in 1795. His poem, "Die Künstler," appeared in 1789. *Die Horen*, a periodical founded in 1794, in which Schiller and Goethe collaborated, produced the letters before they were issued in a book. (*170*) The theory of the *Spieltrieb* is set forth mainly in the *Briefe*.

FRIEDRICH SCHLEGEL

(*171*) His first influence was exerted through the aphorisms which appeared in the periodical *Athenäum* (1798–1800), which was edited by Friedrich Schlegel (1772–1829) and his brother, August Wilhelm, (1767–1845). In 1799 he also published *Lucinde*, a novel in which philosophical speculation was combined with amorous episodes. (*172*) Cf. his *Über die Sprache und Weisheit der Indier*, published in 1808. (*173*) Cf. *Kunstanschauung der jüngeren Romantik*, ed. Andreas Müller (Leipzig, 1934), pp. 220–21. Schlegel's book on painting appeared as *Gemäldebeschreibungen aus Paris und den Niederlanden in den Jahren 1802-1804*, revised in Vol. VI of his *Sämtliche Werke* (Vienna, 1823); cf. also Ricarda Huth, *Blüthezeit der Romantik* (Leipzig, 1899), pp. 338–45. (*174*) His *Philo-*

sophie des Lebens appeared in 1828. There is a translation in "Bohn's Library" (1847), by the Rev. A. J. W. Morrison (cf. Robinson [comp.], *An Anthology of Modern Philosophy* [New York, 1931], p. 509). *(175)* Robinson, *op. cit.*, p. 511. *(176) Ibid.*, p. 512. *(177) Ibid.*, p. 520.

WACKENRODER AND TIECK

(178) Wilhelm Heinrich Wackenroder (1772–97), Ludwig Tieck (1773–1853). After 1825, Tieck concluded the standard German translation of Shakespeare which had been begun by A. W. Schlegel. *Herzensergiessungen eines kunstliebenden Klosterbruders* was published in Berlin in 1797, while *Phantasien über die Kunst für Freunde der Kunst* came out in Hamburg in 1799. *(179)* Cf. Wilhelm Waetzoldt, *Deutsche Kunsthistoriker* (Leipzig, 1921), I, 217–32; also Rudolf Haym, *Die Romantische Schule* (Berlin, 1906), pp. 120 ff. *(180)* The sources on which Wackenroder drew, often reproducing their words verbatim in German, were Vasari, Bellori, Malvasia, Leonardo da Vinci, Felibien, Sandrart, Schiller, Hamann, and Mengs (cf. P. Koldewey, *Wackenroder und sein Einfluss auf Tieck* [Göttingen, 1903]). Other studies of his sources and influence have been published by H. Wölfflin, E. Dessauer, O. Walzel, and Ph. E. Gulzow. *(181)* Cf. Andreas Müller, *Kunstanschauung der Frühromantik* (Leipzig, 1931), p. 15. *(182) Ibid.*, p. 20. *(183) Ibid.*, p. 26. *(184) Ibid.*, p. 49. *(185) Ibid.*, p. 66. *(186) Ibid.*, p. 71.

FICHTE

(187) Johann Gottlieb Fichte (1762–1814); his *Grundlage der gesamten Wissenschaftslehre* first appeared in 1794. It thus preceded Schlegel's aphorisms (1798–1800), Wackenroder's *Herzensergiessungen* (1797), Schiller's *Briefe* (1795), and Herder's *Kalligone* (1800). *(188) Versuch einer Kritik aller Offenbarung* (1792). *(189) Reden an die deutsche Nation* (Berlin, 1808). *(190) Die Grundzüge des gegenwärtigen Zeitalters* (Berlin, 1806). *(191)* Fichte emphasized his doctrine of the will as follows: "But self-active reason is will. The law of the super-sensual world must, therefore, be a Will:—A Will which operates purely as will; by itself, and absolutely without any instrument or sensible material of its activity; which is at the same time both act and product; with whom to will is to do, to command is to execute; in which therefore the instinctive demand of reason for absolute freedom and independence is realized. . . . . This Will binds me in union with Himself; He also binds me in union with all finite beings like myself, and is the common mediator between us all. This is the great mystery of the invisible world, and its fundamental law, in so far as it is a world or system of many individual wills:—the union and direct reciprocal action of many separate and independent wills; a mystery which already lies clearly before every eye in the present life, without attracting the notice of any one, or being regarded in any way wonderful" (from *Die Bestimmung des Menschen* [Berlin, 1800], trans. William Smith, *The Popular Works of Fichte* [1848–49]); cf. also Robinson, *op. cit.*, pp. 558–59 and 560. *(192) Egotism in German Philosophy* (London, 1916), p. 76.

SCHELLING

(193) Friedrich Wilhelm Schelling (1775–1854). Cf. Alfred Rosenberg, *Der Mythus des 20. Jahrhunderts* (Munich, 1930). *(194)* Cf. *Werke*, VII, 350 (from *Über das Wesen der menschlichen Freiheit* [Landshut, 1809]). *(195) Vom Ich als Prinzip der Philosophie oder über das Unbedingte im menschlichen Wissen* (Tübingen, 1795). *(196) Abhandlungen zur Erläuterung des Idealismus der Wissenschaftslehre*, originally published (1809) in a periodical edited by Fichte and Niethammer. *(197) System der transcendentalen Idealismus* (Tübingen, 1800), trans. Thomas Davidson (1867); cf. Robinson, *op. cit.*, pp. 569–70. *(198)* "The whole system falls between two extremes, of which one is denoted by the intellectual intuition, the other by the aesthetic intuition. . . . . The one thing to which absolute objectivity is given, is art. Take away, it may be said, the objectivity of art, and it ceases to be what it is, and becomes philosophy; give philosophy objectivity, and it ceases to be philosophy and becomes art. Philosophy attains the highest, but it brings to that point, so to speak, only a fraction of the man. Art brings the whole man as he is to the cognition of the highest, and this is the eternal distinction and marvel of art" (from the *System der transcendentalen Idealismus;* cf.

Werke, II, 630). *(199) Vorlesungen über die Methode des akademischen Studiums* (Stuttgart and Tübingen, 1803); trans. E. S. Morgan (1881); cf. Robinson, *op. cit.*, pp. 571–76. *(200)* Cf. Bernard Bosanquet, *History of Aesthetic* (New York, 1910), p. 329. *(201) Werke*, III, 349.

THE PERSISTENCE OF IDEALISM IN THE THEORY OF ART AND AESTHETICS

(202) The influence of idealism, both rationalist and romantic, on many subsequent theories of art and aesthetics may easily be discovered by examination of the views of those who succeeded Schelling, in such accessible works as the following: E. F. Carritt, *Philosophies of Beauty* (New York, 1931); Melvin M. Rader, *A Modern Book of Esthetics* (New York, 1935); Bosanquet, *op. cit.*; Benedetto Croce, *Aesthetic* (London, 1922); the Earl of Listowel, *A Critical History of Modern Aesthetics* (London, 1933); Katherine E. Gilbert and Helmut Kuhn, *A History of Esthetics* (New York, 1940). *(203)* Johannes Caspar Schmidt ("Max Stirner"), in his *Der Einzige und sein Eigentum* (Leipzig, 1845), carried some of the consequences of the romantic-idealist view to extremes. On publication it was at first confiscated but was soon released as too absurd to have any effect (cf. G. Santayana, *op. cit.*, pp. 99–103). Schopenhauer in *Die Welt als Wille und Vorstellung* (Leipzig, 1819) attacked Kant and interpreted the will in a fashion which refuted many of the conclusions of Fichte and Schelling with regard to art and aesthetics (cf. Santayana, *op. cit.*, pp. 108–22). *(204)* Dependence on romantic-idealist philosophies has been shown for Marxism in general and for communism, fascism, and naziism in particular. The theory of the totalitarian state was well developed by Fichte and Adam Müller, although the connection between the organization of the Prussian state and Hegel's absolute is more familiar (cf. G. A. Borgese, "Romanticism," in *Encyclopaedia of the Social Sciences* [New York, 1937], XIII, 426–33).

V. THE ABSOLUTE ARTIST OF ROMANTIC IDEALISM

HITLER BY NATURE AN ARTIST

(205) Documents concerning German-Polish Relations and the Outbreak of Hostilities between Great Britain and Germany on September 3, 1939 ("British Blue Books" [New York: Farrar & Rinehart, 1939]). Cf. *Life*, VII, No. 16 (October 16, 1939), 35–42; *New York Times*, September 22, 1939, p. 12. *(206)* First paragraph of telegram, dated August 25, 1939, from Sir Nevile Henderson to Lord Halifax. *(207)* Seventh paragraph of the same telegram. *(208)* In a supplementary report, dated London, September 20, 1939, issued as pp. 251–82 of the *British White Paper: Germany No. 1* (1939), Sir Nevile Henderson further refers to the conversation of August 25, on p. 262, where he says: "Though he spoke of his artistic tastes and of his longing to satisfy them, I derived the impression that the corporal of the last war was even more anxious to prove what he could do as a conquering Generalissimo in the next." *(209)* Cf. *London Illustrated News*, May 30, 1936, pp. 961–62. Other pictures by the Chancellor had been reproduced in issues of the same periodical on June 22 and August 31, 1935. A portfolio of color reproductions was published by the Verlag Heinrich Hoffman, Berlin, as *Adolf Hitler, Aquarelle*. The *Sun* (New York) on October 9, 1939, reproduced a water color by Hitler, as have other newspapers. *Life* (VII, No. 18 [October 30, 1939], 52–58) reproduced in color some other examples of the Chancellor's water colors, together with photographs of his work as a designer of architecture and interior decoration.

THE ROMANTIC IDEALISM OF *Mein Kampf*

(210) Adolf Hitler, *Mein Kampf*, complete and unabridged (New York: Reynal & Hitchcock, 1939), translation from the 1st German ed. of 1925 and 1927. *(211) Ibid.*, p. 20. *(212) Ibid.*, pp. 623–30. *(213) Ibid.*, pp. 44–50. *(214) Ibid.*, note on pp. 269–76. *(215) Ibid.*, pp. 750–63. *(216) Ibid.*, pp. 360, 488–89.

THE LEADER AS ARTIST

(217) Ibid., pp. 10–11. *(218) Ibid.*, pp. 13–14. *(219) Ibid.*, pp. 23–24. *(220) Ibid.*, pp. 26–27. *(221) Ibid.*, p. 29. *(222) Ibid.*, p. 45. *(223) Ibid.*, p. 360. *(224) Ibid.*, p. 705. *(225) Ibid.*, pp. 136–37. *(226) Ibid.*, pp. 230–31. *(227) Ibid.*, pp. 506–7, 720–21. *(228) Ibid.*, pp. 734–37; cf. p. 22 n.

(229) Ibid., pp. 23–24. (230) Ibid., pp. 26–27. (231) Ibid., pp. 163–64. (232) Ibid., pp. 28–29.
(233) Ibid., p. 22 n. (234) Ibid., pp. 352–55. (235) Ibid., pp. 358–59. (236) Ibid., pp. 361–64.
(237) Ibid., p. 693.

RACISM AND ART

(238) Ibid., pp. 404–5. (239) Ibid., p. 403. (240) Ibid., p. 402. (241) Ibid., pp. 389–92. (242)
Ibid., pp. 397, 608–10. (243) Ibid., pp. 947–50.

VI. CLASSICAL EXPLANATIONS OF ART

(244) The nearest parallel to Hitler in antiquity was Nero, who, when the executioners pursued him, committed suicide while exclaiming, "Qualis artifex pereo!" (Suetonius *De Vita Caesarum* vi. 49). The Latin *artifex* in this passage is today usually translated in accordance with the views of romantic idealism. It appears as *Künstler* in German (cf. Ernst Hohl, "Die römische Kaiserzeit," *Propyläen Weltgeschichte*, II: *Hellas und Rom* [Berlin, 1931], 392). It is given as "artist" in English (cf. Albert Guérard, *Art for Art's Sake* [Boston and New York, 1936], p. 9).

SOCRATES

(245) Diogenes Laertius ii. 18–19. The philosopher was sometimes confused with another sculptor named Socrates, to whom a group representing the Graces was attributed (cf. Overbeck, *Die antiken Schriftquellen* [Leipzig, 1868], Nos. 910–14). (246) Plato *Republic* ii. 373; Xenophon *Oeconomicus* vii. 15. (247) Xenophon *Memorabilia* iii. 10. 9. (248) *Oeconomicus* vi. 12. (249) *Ibid.* vi. 13; ii. 4. (250) *Ibid.* vi. 15–16. (251) *Memorabilia* iii. 8. 7. (252) Xenophon *Symposium* v. 3 ff. (253) *Memorabilia* iii. 10. 1; the story is repeated by Pliny, Cicero, and Dionysius Halicarnassus (cf. Overbeck, *op. cit.*, Nos. 1667–69). (254) *Memorabilia* iii. 10. 3. (255) *Ibid.* iii. 8. 10.

PLATO

(256) A. N. Whitehead, *Process and Reality* (New York, 1930), p. 63. (257) *Republic* x. 597 D, 605 B, 607 A. (258) *Phaedrus* 248 E; *Sophist* 219 B and 234 B. (259) Cf. *Laws* iii. 679 A; *Philebus* 56 C; *Republic* iii. 401 A. (260) *Sophist* 219 B. (261) *Ibid.*, 234 B. The translation, by H. N. Fowler, is from the "Loeb Library" edition. (262) *Sophist* 265 B–C. (263) *Ibid.* 266 C. (264) *Republic* x. 598 C. The translation, by Paul Shorey, is from the "Loeb Library" edition. (265) *Cratylus* 423 D. (266) *Republic* ii. 373 B. (267) *Gorgias* 465 A. The translation, by W. R. M. Lamb, is from the "Loeb Library" edition. (268) *Ibid.* 501 C. (269) *Phaedrus* 270 B. (270) *Philebus* 56 A. (271) *Republic* x. 602 B. (272) *Laws* x. 889 D. (273) *Republic* vi. 511 E; cf. *Epistle* vii. 342 A–344 B. (274) *Republic* vii. 533 A–C. (275) *Ibid.* 534 B. (276) *Philebus* 55 E. (277) *Ibid.* 56 B. cf. *Timaeus* 69 A. (278) *Republic* x. 603 A–B. (279) *Philebus* 51 C. (280) *Ibid.* 58 A and C. The translation, by W. R. M. Lamb, is from the "Loeb Library" edition. (281) *Ibid.* 59 C. (282) The Platonic Idea is capitalized to distinguish it from the modern idea, meaning "concept, thought, or notion." (283) *Republic* x. 597 E. (284) *Ibid.* 602 D. (285) *Ibid.* 599 A. (286) *Ibid.* 596 E. (287) *Ibid.* v. 476 C. (288) *Phaedrus* 277 E–278 A. (289) Athenaeus *Dipnosophistarum* xi. 505 B. (290) *Republic* vi. 500 C–501 E; cf. also *ibid.* 420 C; *Laws* vii. 793 C. (291) *Republic* x. 602 B; *Politicus* 288 C. (292) *Laws* ii. 654 E–656 A. (293) *Euthyphro* 6 C; *Republic* x. 605–6. (294) *Republic* iii. 395. (295) *Ibid.* 401 B. (296) *Epinomis* 974 E. (297) *Ibid.* 975 D. (298) *Laws* ii. 656 D. (299) *Protagoras* 311 C–D; *Ion* 533 B; *Hippias Major* 282 B; *Meno* 91 D; *Republic* vii. 540 C. (300) *Laws* vii. 810 A. (301) *Hippias Major* 295 C–297 D; *Gorgias* 474 D, 475 A. (302) *Republic* x. 595–608; *Laws* ii. 652–74. (303) *Philebus* 64 E, 66 A–B; *Timaeus* 87 C; *Politicus* 284 B; *Republic* vi. 486 D. (304) *Phaedo* 79 D; *Gorgias* 475; *Phaedrus* 250 D. (305) *Symposium* 211 A–B; *Republic* v. 479 A; *Phaedo* 100 C. (306) *Philebus* 15 D; *Timaeus* 34 C, 52 B. (307) *Theaetetus* 156 ff., 179 ff. (308) *Symposium* 207 D–E. (309) *Timaeus* 43 C–44 B. (310) *Ibid.*, 51 E–52 A. The translation is based on that by R. G. Bury in the "Loeb Classical Library." (311) *Phaedrus* 265 D–266 E. (312) *Phaedo* 100 D. (313) *Philebus* 15 ff. (314) *Parmenides* 130 D ff. (315) *Sophist* 252 E. (316) *Phaedrus* 247 C. (317) *Parmenides* 130 B–134 E. (318) *Ibid.*, 166 C. (319) *Parmenides* 132 C. (320) *Phaedrus* 275 D–E; *Protagoras* 329 A.

PLOTINUS

(321) *Enneads* III. iii. 6. (322) *Ibid.* VI. iii. 16. (323) *Ibid.* IV. iv. 23. (324) *Ibid.* IV. iii. 18. (325) *Ibid.* V. viii. 1; V. ix. 3. (326) *Ibid.* IV. iv. 31. (327) *Ibid.* II. ix. 18. (328) *Ibid.* 14. (329) *Ibid.* III. ii. 16. (330) *Ibid.* 17. (331) *Ibid.* 11. (332) *Ibid.* II. ix. 12. (333) *Ibid.* IV. iii. 10. (334) *Ibid.* III. viii. 7. (335) *Ibid.* V. viii. 1. (336) *Ibid.* 5. (337) The Absolute and things in the Intelligible World are often capitalized in English translation to distinguish them from their terrestrial counterparts. (338) *Enneads* VI. ii. 11. (339) *Ibid.* V. viii. 1. (340) Cf. *ibid.* V. ix. 3. (341) *Ibid.* i. 6. (342) *Ibid.* VI. ix. 11. (343) *Ibid.* vii. 35. (344) *Ibid.* IV. vii. 10. (345) *Ibid.* I. vi. 9. (346) Philosophical claims elsewhere are also supported by references to sculpture: *ibid.* V. viii. 4 (cf. *Phaedrus* 247 C); VI. vi. 6, i. 23; II. v. 1. (347) *Ibid.* III. viii. 4. (348) *Ibid.* ii. 11. (349) *Ibid.* VI. ii. 22. (350) *Ibid.* iii. 8. (351) *Ibid.* iv. 10; cf. *Republic* vi. 510 E. (352) *Enneads* V. viii. 5. (353) *Ibid.* V. ix. 11. (354) *Ibid.* I. vi. 3. (355) *Ibid.* II. ix. 18. (356) *Ibid.* V. iv. 1. (357) *Ibid.* VI. vii. 38. The designation of the Absolute as One is not to be found in Plato or Aristotle and may have been original with Plotinus. (358) *Ibid.* V. i. 4; vi. 1; ix. 5. (359) *Ibid.* III. viii. 9; V. i. 4. (360) *Ibid.* V. i. 8; V. viii. 13; II. ix. 2. (361) *Ibid.* V. ix. 9; V. vii. 1. (362) *Ibid.* V. v; cf. III. viii. 9 and ix. 1. (363) *Ibid.* III. iii. 2. (364) *Ibid.* V. v. 9; VI. ix. 5. (365) *Ibid.* III. ii. 2; IV. viii. 6; V. ii. 1. (366) *Ibid.* I. i. 8; V. i. 6; VI. vii. 5. (367) *Ibid.* I. i. 8; III. vi. 13; VI. iv. 10. (368) *Ibid.* III. viii; IV. iv. 44; V. iii. 5, 9, viii. 3. (369) *Ibid.* IV. viii. 7; V. i. 7, 8. (370) *Ibid.* II. iii. 17; III. viii. 4. (371) *Ibid.* III. v. 4; IV. viii. 3; VI. v. 9. (372) *Ibid.* II. iv; I. viii. 7; III. vi. 7; IV. iii. 9; VI. iii. 7. (373) *Ibid.* I. viii. (374) *Ibid.* II. ix. 2; IV. viii. 8; I. iv. 9; IV. iii. 30. (375) *Ibid.* I. i. 7; V. iii. 9; VI. vii. 7. (376) *Ibid.* I. iii. 4. (377) *Ibid.* V. iii. 4; VI. viii. 35; VI. iv. 4. (378) *Ibid.* I. vi; V. viii. (379) *Ibid.* I. vi. (380) *Ibid.* V. viii. (381) *Ibid.* I. vi. 1. Cf. *Hippias Major* 297 C–298 B; *Symposium* 211 A–B; Cicero *Tusculanarum Disputationum* iv. 31; Xenophon *Memorabilia* iii. 10. 1–5. (382) *Enneads* I. vi. 2; cf. *Phaedrus* 250; *Symposium* 209 B. (383) *Enneads* I. vi. 3. (384) *Ibid.* vi. 4; cf. *Phaedrus* 249 D. (385) *Enneads* I. vi. 5; cf. viii, and *Symposium* 208 E–209 B. (386) *Enneads* I. vi. 6; cf. *Phaedrus* 249 C. (387) *Enneads* I. vi. 7; cf. *Phaedrus* 252 B–D, 211 E; *Symposium* 209 D–E. Purification and initiation were also prominent in the mystery cults. It has been suggested that the temple with statues mentioned in the text was that of Isis in Rome. (388) *Enneads* I. vi. 8. (389) *Ibid.* I. vi. 9; cf. *Republic* 515 C–D, *Timaeus* 67 C. (390) Cf. *Phaedrus* 246 D–247 E; *Symposium* 210 B–C, 221 D. (391) *Enneads* v. viii. 1–2. (392) *Ibid.* v. viii. 3–4. (393) *Timaeus* 41 B–C and ff. (394) *Enneads* V. viii. 5–7. (395) *Ibid.* viii. 8. (396) *Ibid.* 9. On the power of the First, cf. also VI. viii. 20. (397) *Ibid.* V. viii. 10. (398) *Ibid.* 11. (399) *Ibid.* 12–13. (400) The influence of Plotinus on the romantic idealists was so great, although it was largely based on a misunderstanding, that Fritz Heinemann could assert: "Diese Vergöttlichung des Künstlers ist der Ursprung aller genialischen Ästhetik der Romantik" (*Plotin* [Leipzig, 1921], p. 211). Other studies of the influence of Plotinus from the romantic-idealist point of view include: M. Wundt, "Plotin und die Romantik," *Neue Jahrb. f. d. klass. Altertum*, Vol. XXXV (1915); Arthur Richter, *Neu-Platonische Studien* (Halle, 1867); P. F. Reiff, "Plotin und die deutsche Romantik," *Euphorion*, XIX (1912), 591 ff.; Karl P. Hasse, *Von Plotin bis Goethe* (Leipzig, 1909); Ernst Cassirer, *Die Platonische Renaissance in England und die Schule von Cambridge* (Leipzig, 1932). The great differences between Plato and Plotinus were finally perceived as a result of the work of Friedrich E. D. Schleiermacher (*Platons Werke* [Berlin, 1804–28]) and Eduard Zeller, who discussed Plotinus in *Die Philosophie der Griechen* (Tübingen, 1844–52), Part III, 2d half, pp. 666 ff.

ARISTOTLE

(401) Cf. W. W. Jaeger, *Studien zur Entstehungsgeschichte der Metaphysik des Aristoteles* (Berlin, 1912), which was preceded by R. Shute, *On the History of the Process by Which the Aristotelian Writings Arrived at Their Present Form* (Oxford, 1888), and Thomas Case, "Aristotle," *Encyclopaedia Britannica* (11th ed.). In what follows, it should be noted, the views expressed do not derive from those of Thomas Aquinas or his interpreters. This is said because today Aristotelian inspiration is often supposed to be limited to the scholastic movement; and elements derived from the same

source by such men as James, Dewey, Whitehead, and others are too often studied without recognition of their eventual origin. *(402) Poetics* i. 2. 1447 a. *(403) Politics* viii. 5. 8. 1340 a. *(404) Rhetoric* i. 11. 23. 1371 b. *(405) Poetics* iv. 6. 1448 b. *(406) Ibid.* iii. 4. 1448 b; cf. *Problems* xxx. 6. *(407)* Cf. *Poetics* i. 3. 1447 a; ii. 1. 1448 a. *(408) Categories* viii. 11 a 15; *Metaphysics* v. 15. 5. 1021 a and x. 3. 4. 1054 b. *(409) Ibid.* i. 1. 3–4. 980 b; *Poetics* iv. 4–5. 1448 b. *(410) Politicus* 258 E; *Laws* x. 892 B. *(411) Metaphysics* ii. 1. 5. 993 b. *(412) Nicomachean Ethics* vi. 1. 4–6. 1139 a. *(413) Physics* ii. 8. 199 a 20. *(414) Poetics* xvii. 1. 1455 a. The translation, by W. Hamilton Fyfe, is from the "Loeb Library" edition. *(415) Politics* viii. 5. 1340 a. *(416) On Memory and Recollection* i. 449 b–451 a. *(417) Rhetoric* i. 11. 11. 1370 b. *(418) On Dreams* i–ii. 458 b–460 b; *On the Soul* iii. 8. 431 b–432 a. *(419) Ibid.* i. 1. 403 b; *Physics* ii. 2. 194 a. *(420) Ibid.* iii. 1. 201 b. *(421) Politics* vii. 11. 1331 a. *(422) Ethics* vi. 7. 2. 1141 a. *(423) Metaphysics* v. 2. 1–5, 1013 a–b. *(424) Physics* ii. 3. 195 b. *(425) Ethics* ii. 6. 1106 a–1107 a. *(426) Poetics* vi. 15. 1450 a; cf. *Politics* viii. 5. 7. 1340 a. *(427) Poetics* vi. 20. 1450 b. *(428) Ibid.* xxv. 27. 1461 b. *(429) Ibid.* ii. 2. 1148 a. *(430) Politics* viii. 2. 3. 1337 b. *(431) Ibid.* 6. 1338 a. *(432) Ibid.* 3. 1. 1338 a. William Ellis freely translates this passage: "Thus they should be instructed in painting, not only to prevent their being mistaken in purchasing pictures, or in buying and selling of vases, but rather as it makes them judges of the beauties of the human form." *(433) Metaphysics* xiii. 3. 10. 1078 a. *(434) Ibid.* ii. 1078 b. *(435) Politics* vii. 4. 6. 1326 a. *(436) On Sense and Sensible Objects* iii. 439 a–440 b. *(437) On the Soul* ii. 6–7. 418 a–419 a. *(438) On Colors* 791 a–799 b. *(439) Politics* viii. 7. 7. 1340 a. *(440) Poetics* ix. 2. 1451 b. *(441) Ibid.* vi. 2. 1449 b; cf. Ingram Bywater, *Aristotle on the Art of Poetry* (Oxford, 1909), pp. 361–65, for a long list of different interpretations; cf. also Lane Cooper and Alfred Gudeman, *A Bibliography of the Poetics of Aristotle* ("Cornell Studies in English," Vol. XI [New Haven, 1928]). *(442)* Cf. Paul Natorp, *Platos Ideenlehre* (Leipzig, 1921), pp. 419–56. Similar tendencies are exhibited in the interpretations of Lotze, Auffarth, H. Cohen, N. Hartmann, and others. *(443) Metaphysics* i. 9. 1. 990 b; xiii. 4. 5–6. 1078 b. *(444) Ibid.* i. 9. 2–3. 990 b; 5–8. 990 b–991 a; xiii. 4. 7–8. 1079 a; 10–13. 1079 a–b. *(445) Ibid.* xiii. 4. 14–15. 1079 b. *(446) Ibid.* i. 9. 10–14. 991 a–b; xiii. 5. 2–6. 1079 b. *(447) Ibid.* i. 9. 16–30. 991 b–992 b; xiii. 6. 1–9. 23. 1080 a–1086 b. *(448) Ibid.* xiii. 9. 21–22. 1086 a–b. *(449)* Aristotle's doctrine of causes is to be found in *Metaphysics* i. 3. 1; v. 2. 1–9; viii. 4. 4–5; xi. 1. 4–7; xii. 3. 1–6; xii. 5. 4–5; and *Physics* ii. 3. 194 b 16–ii. 9. 200 b 9.

VII. CONTRIBUTIONS TO AN AMERICAN PHILOSOPHY OF ART

EXPERIENCE

(450) Metaphysics i. 1. 4–8. 981 a. *(451)* Cf. the translation of the *Metaphysics* in the "Loeb Library" (London, 1933), pp. 4–5.

THE SENSORY ASPECTS OF ART

(452) A. Philip McMahon, *The Art of Enjoying Art* (New York, 1938), pp. 111–71.

Index